HILARY OF POITIERS
ON THE TRINITY

PHILOSOPHIA PATRUM

INTERPRETATIONS OF PATRISTIC TEXTS

EDITED BY

J. H. WASZINK AND J. C. M. VAN WINDEN

VOLUME VI

LEIDEN

E. J. BRILL

1982

HILARY OF POITIERS ON THE TRINITY

De Trinitate 1, 1-19, 2, 3

BY

E. P. MEIJERING

IN CLOSE COOPERATION WITH J. C. M. VAN WINDEN

LEIDEN
E. J. BRILL
1982

Published with financial support from the Netherlands Organization
for the Advancement of Pure Research (Z.W.O.)

Also by E. P. Meijering:

Orthodoxy and Platonism in Athanasius. Synthesis or Antithesis? E. J. Brill, Leiden 1974².
God Being History. Studies in Patristic Philosophy. N.H.P.C. Amsterdam-Oxford 1975.
Tertullian contra Marcion. Gotteslehre in der Polemik (Adversus Marcionem I-II). E. J. Brill, Leiden 1977.
Theologische Urteile über die Dogmengeschichte. Ritschls Einfluss auf von Harnack. E. J. Brill, Leiden 1978.
Augustin über Schöpfung, Ewigkeit und Zeit. Das elfte Buch der Bekenntnisse. E. J. Brill, Leiden 1979.
Calvin wider die Neugierde. Ein Beitrag zum Vergleich zwischen reformatorischem und patristischem Denken. B. de Graaf, Nieuwkoop 1980.

Also by J. C. M. van Winden:

Calcidius on Matter. His Doctrine and Sources. A Chapter in the History of Platonism. E. J. Brill, Leiden 1965².
An Early Christian Philosopher. Justin Martyr's Dialogue with Trypho, Chapters One to Nine E. J. Brill, Leiden 1971.

Meijering, E. P. — Hilary of Poitiers on the trinity: De Trinitate 1, 1-19, 2, 3 / by E. P. Meijering; in close cooperation with J. C. M. van Winden. — Leiden: Brill. — (Philosophia patrum; vol. 6)

UDC 262 ·

ISBN   90 04 06734 5

PRINTED IN THE NETHERLANDS

IANO HENRICO WASZINK

MAGISTRO VENERANDO

D.D.D.

AUCTOR

CONTENTS

PREFACE

The core of the Arian controversy, "Who is Jesus Christ?" is a perennially important question. The reader of this book is not provided with a balanced answer to this question, but with an analysis of the answer one of the combatants in this controversy, Hilary of Poitiers, the 'Athanasius of the West', gives to it. The author believes Hilary's views to be theologically superior to those of his opponents, – but we are not so well informed about the Arian doctrine as we are about the orthodox one. It is fair to refer the reader to the splendid study by R. C. Gregg and D. E. Groh (which came out shortly before the present book went to the printers and could therefore hardly be taken into account), *Early Arianism. A View of Salvation*, Philadelphia 1981, in which the traditional evaluation of Arianism is challenged and in which it is stressed that the Arian theology centered around salvation, – just like orthodox theology.

I want to thank E. J. Brill's for editing the book and the *Netherlands Organization for the Advancement of pure Research* (*Z.W.O.*) for providing a subsidy.

I want to express my gratitude to Mrs T. C. C. M. Heesterman-Visser, Oegstgeest, for typewriting the manuscript, and Mrs S. Peletier-Bridgwater, Voorschoten, and my nephew Mr F. N. Marshall, London, for correcting my English.

I am most grateful to my colleague and friend J. C. M. van Winden for his very thorough correction of my original manuscript, especially of the translation. I had corrected Watson's translation, then Van Winden twice corrected mine, if the present translation proves to be sound it is primarily due to Van Winden, – but also the commentary owes much to his admirable scholarship.

The book has been dedicated to my highly venerated teacher Professor dr J. H. Waszink. More than twenty years ago he (and Professor Bakhuizen van den Brink) encouraged me to go into Patristics, and I have received stimulating help and advice from him ever since.

June 1981   E.P.M.
Oranjelaan 11
2341 CA *Oegstgeest* / The Netherlands

INTRODUCTION

At the beginning of the fourth book of the *De Trinitate* Hilary says that the first three books of this treatise contain the sufficient Scriptural doctrine of the Trinity, and that the books which will follow will contain a refutation of various Arian attacks on this doctrine, so that the knowledge of the truth will become even more certain, see *Trin* 4, 1: *Quamquam anterioribus libellis quos iam pridem conscripsimus absolute cognitum existimemus, fidem nos et confessionem Patris et Fili et Spiritus Sancti ex evangelicis adque apostolicis institutis obtinere .... tamen etiam his libellis quaedam necessario fuerunt compraehendenda, ut omnibus fallaciis eorum et impietatibus editis absolutior fieret cognitio veritatis.*

These remarks seem to justify a separate analysis of the contents of the first three books, an analysis in which the following books are used as a key of interpretation, since they are meant by Hilary as a further elaboration of various themes appearing in the first three books. According to Hilary these three books obviously form a unity.

But before analysing the first three books of the *De Trinitate* one has to comment on the question which has often been asked, whether the whole treatise *De Trinitate*, consisting of twelve books, was a unity right from the beginning or whether it consists of originally independent parts which have been put together by Hilary into a unity, in which case Hilary could only have succeeded in giving his treatise on the Trinity a semblance of unity.

In the chapters 20-36 of the first book of the *De Trinitate* Hilary gives an outline of what will be discussed in the books two to twelve. It is natural to ask whether this outline at the beginning is not in fact a summary written after the twelve books had been completed, and then put at the beginning. Is it conceivable that someone should have in mind, right at the beginning, a fairly detailed outline of such a vast piece of writing? Is it not more probable that the plan of the treatise was shaped in the actual process of writing? Furthermore Hilary repeatedly refers to his fourth book as the first one and to the fifth book as the second one (see *De Trin.* 6, 4 and 5, 3). Is this not a clear indication that the books four and following were originally meant as an independent treatise and that they were later combined with the first three books? In that case Hilary might have failed to correct certain cross-references. This view has been taken by several scholars, (see e.g. P. Galtier, *Saint Hilaire de Poitiers, Le premier docteur de l'église latine*, Paris 1960, pp 35 f, J. Doignon, *Hilaire de Poitiers avant l'exil* (Etudes augustiniennes), Paris 1971, pp 82 f. A detailed discussion of the various opinions is given by C. F. A. Borchardt, *Hilary of Poitiers' Role in the Arian Struggle*, The Hague 1966, pp 40 ff.) These scholars still disagree with each other regarding the question of to what extent the books one to three should be separated from the books four to twelve. Were the books one to three written during Hilary's exile and when he was acquainted with the theologians of the East (this is a view held by M. Simonetti, Note sulla struttura e la cronologia del *De Trinitate* di Ilario di Poitiers, *Studi Urbinati* (39, 1), 1965, pp 274 ff), or were they written before the exile, when Hilary had not yet studied the Greek theologians? (This view is held by J. Doignon, *op. cit.*, pp 82 f).

First of all we want to deal with the question of whether the *De Trinitate* was intended by Hilary right from the beginning as a treatise consisting of the twelve books which it now comprises. It seems fair to believe Hilary and to regard it as the unity in which he presents it, – unless one can produce decisive evidence to the contrary. In his detailed paper M. Simonetti suggests that books one to three were originally intended as an independent treatise, that Hilary started book four as the beginning of a completely new treatise (hence the references to book four and five as to book one and two in *De Trin.* 6, 4 and 5, 3), but that somewhere between the end of book six and chapter ten of book nine (which contains the first clear reference to a passage in one of the first three books of the *De Trinitate* in its present shape) he changed his mind and decided to merge books one to three and the following books into the one treatise. The reference to the first three books in *De Trin.* 4, 1 is according to Simonetti part of this merging operation, in which *De Trin.* 4, 1-2 and 1, 20-36 were added in order to make the twelve books look like parts of one design. – Several objections can be made against this view: *De Trin.* 9, 10 is not the first reference to a passage in one of the first three books. The seventh book is in its beginning correctly referred to as such (*De Trin.* 7, 1; Simonetti explains this fact by saying that the introduction to book 7 was also added by Hilary when he merged all the books into one treatise (*op. cit.*, p 294)). Simonetti does not explain the fact that in the beginning of the fifth book (*De Trin.* 5, 1) Hilary speaks of the refutation of the heretics in the earlier *books* (plural), which is obviously a reference to the books one to four. Of course this, too, could be explained as part of the merging; in that case all introductions to the various books could be regarded as later additions. In 7, 28 there is a reference to the statement made in 1, 19 and 4, 2 about the insufficiency of human comparisons in order to describe divine matters. Simonetti is forced to deny that this is a reference to either 1, 19 or 4, 2 and to take it as a reference to 6, 9; but this seems highly unlikely: Hilary says that this statement was made *in exordio sermonis nostri*. Simonetti explains this as meaning "the beginning of this section of our treatise'', but it is much more natural to translate *sermo* not as 'section of our treatise' but as 'treatise', as it means in *e.g. De Trin.* 8, 2; 6, 32; 9, 29; 1, 26; 5, 3; 5, 35. The reference must be either to 1, 19 or 4, 2; in both cases the supposed merging took place well before *De Trin.* 9, 10. It seems the more likely that it is a reference to 4, 2; since 1, 19 is in the middle of book one (if one followed the suggestion made by Simonetti and many others that 1, 20-36 were added later on, it is even towards the end of book one), it would be strange to call 1, 19 ''the beginning of our treatise''. Furthermore, in 4, 2 Hilary refers to 1, 19 not as ''the beginning of our treatise'' but as ''in the first book'', which is a perfectly correct statement. So *De Trin.* 7, 28 must be regarded as a first reference to *De Trin.* 4, 2. If 4, 1-2 are a later addition to the fourth book as part of the merging of the books, then this merging must have taken place before 7, 28, and Hilary should after that moment never again have referred to book four as the beginning of his treatise, since he would have wanted to erase all traces of an originally independent treatise beginning with what is now called book four. But he does not do so: in *De Trin.* 8, 2 he gives a summary of what has been dealt with so far in his reply to the heretics, a summary which comprises the contents of books 4 to 7: *Quorum vesanis mendaciis renitentes usque eo iam sermonem responsionis nostrae tetendimus ut eum Deum et Deum* (book four), *et verum Deum in vero Deo demonstrassemus ex lege* (book five); *tum deinde perfectam ac veram unigeniti Dei nativitatem ex evangelicis atque apostolicis doctrinis ostenderemus* (book six); *postremo ut verum Deum Dei filium et indifferentis a Patre naturae, eodem praedicationis nostri cursu doceremus.* – All these facts, it seems to us, can only be explained if we suppose that Hilary intended the books beginning with the fourth book as a *renewed beginning* within the whole treatise which he had in mind, as he states in 4, 1. The reader has been informed about this new beginning and knows that any reference to ''at the beginning'' or to ''book one or two'' may either refer to what now is actually book one or two, or to what is now book four of five. If Hilary had merged books one to three and some of the books coming after book three into one treatise, thereby trying to camouflage that they were originally intended as separate works, he did it very clumsily indeed. The first thing one does in such a case is to make sure one has got one's numbers right, but Hilary then not only did not get his numbers right, but even contradicted himself regarding the numbers of his books in one and the same sentence: in *De Trin.* 6, 4 he refers to what is now book four as the first book, but correctly refers to what is now book six as the sixth book (cf. C. F. A. Borchardt, *op. cit.* p 46).

We even believe that the outline of the whole work consisting of twelve books as given in *De Trin.* 1, 20-36 is the preconceived scheme and not a summary at the end. In itself it could be possible that this fairly detailed outline was added after completion of the twelfth book, even if he intended right from the beginning to write a work of twelve books. But there is one important place in this outline which makes us believe that it was indeed written before the beginning of book two.

In *De Trin.* 1, 27 Hilary says that in the seventh book he shows that the Son is God in name, generation, nature, power and witness and that he will show from Scripture that each of these implies the other ones: *Deum esse eum qui Dei Filius non negaretur his modis docentes: nomine nativitate natura potestate professione: ne aliud esset quem nuncuparetur, neque nuncupatio non nativitatis esset, neque nativitas naturam amisisset, neque natura non retinuisset potestatem, neque potestas non etiam conscia sibi veritatis professione notesceret. Causas ergo omnes singulorum generum ita ex evangelicis excerptas subiecimus, ut nec professio tacuerit potestatem, nec potestas non exseruerit naturam, nec natura non suae nativitatis sit, nec nativitas non sui nominis.* In *De Trin.* 7, 9 he starts by saying that the godhead of Christ is known by His name, generation, nature, power, and witness: *Deum igitur Dominum nostrum Jesum Christum his modis novimus: nomine nativitate natura potestate professione.* In 7, 16 he says, as he had done in 1, 27, that it was his original intention to deal with all these aspects separately: *Propositionis quidem ordo id exigebat, ut singula quaeque genera singularum quarumcumque causarum pertractarentur: ut quia Deum esse Dominum Jesum Christum Dei Filium nomine nativitate natura potestate professione didicissemus, demonstratio nostra gradus singulos dispositionis propositae percurreret.* But then he goes on to say that the nature of the generation of the Son does not tolerate such a treatment, since it alone implies name, nature, power and witness. Therefore he is forced to change his original scheme: *Sed nativitatis id natura non patitur, quae in se et nomen et naturam et potestatem et professionem sola complectitur ... Hanc igitur tractantes incidimus in eam necessitatem, ut superius commemorata ad ordinem tractatus proprii differre non liceat* (cf. the conclusion in 7, 21: *Habet igitur hoc sacramenti sola nativitas, ut complectatur in se et nomen et naturam et potestatem et professionem, quia universa nativitas non potest non in ea esse natura unde nascatur.*) So in 1, 27 a scheme is announced of what will be said in the seventh book, a scheme which will be corrected in the course of writing the seventh book. It is hardly conceivable that somebody should change his mind on the contents of a book and then provide in the introduction the uncorrected version, if this introduction is written after the completion of the whole work and is meant to give the whole work a semblance of unity. At the utmost it could be argued that Hilary provided on purpose the original scheme in the introduction in order to give the impression that the introduction was written right in the beginning, but then it is inconceivable that somebody who so shrewdly conceals his real method of working should be so careless in giving the numbers of the books of which his treatise consists (see *supra*, 1 f).

The repeated past tense in those chapters of the introduction given in 1, 20-36 are not to us an indication that this introduction was written after the completion of the work, as M. Simonetti believes (*op. cit.*, p 277 and the exact references in note 11). Again such a carelessness would be inexplicable if the introduction were meant as a means to give the work a semblance of unity; in that case one would certainly expect Hilary to use the future tense consistently, and not, as he actually does, every now and then (see for the future tense 1, 20, 34, 35. The general rule in this outline is that the past and the present tense are used.)

It seems likely that the old suggestion, already given by Jerome, that Hilary intended to imitate Quintilian's twelve books on Rhetoric by writing twelve books on the Trinity (see Jerome, *Epist.* 70, 5: *Hilarius, meorum temporum confessor et episcopus, duodecim Quintiliani libros et stilo imitatus est et numero*) is correct. As has been shown by H. Kling, *De Hilario Pectaviensi artis rhetoricae ipsiusque, ut fertur, Institutionis oratoriae Quintilianae studioso*, Heidelberg-Freiburg 1909, and J. Doignon, *op. cit.*, *passim*, the influence of Quintilian on Hilary is indeed to be detected practically everywhere. It can, of course, be argued that Hilary decided, after merging his pieces of writing into one treatise, to give this treatise the shape of Quintilian's *Institutio oratoria*. But there are a few small indications that this could have been his purpose right from the beginning. In *De Trin.* 1, 37 (which is not part of the survey of the contents of the twelve books, but which belongs to the prayer with which the first book ends) he expresses his wish that the breath of God's spirit may fill the sails of his faith and confession and may send him forward on his voyage of preaching: ... *orandum est, ut extensa tibi fidei nostrae confessionisque vela flatu Spiritus tui impleas, nosque in cursum praedicationis initae propellas.* A similar metaphor is used by Quintilian at the very beginning of his work, *viz.*, in his letter to his publisher Trypho: ... *permittamus vela ventis et oram solventibus bene precemur.* (This similarity has been overlooked by H. Kling, *op. cit.* p 18, who does, however, refer to other instances in Hilary and Quintilian where the image of a sea-voyage is used.) The difference is, of course, that Hilary wants the sails of his faith to be filled with the winds of the Spirit, whilst Quintilian merely says that his voyage is about to begin. Hilary, so to speak, gives a Christianized version of this metaphor. In itself this is not an unusual metaphor (see G. Assfahl, *Vergleich und Metaphor bei Quintilian*, Stuttgart 1932, pp 66 ff, especially p 68 where more examples are given), so it would be rash to suppose dependence only on the basis of this similarity. Just like Quintilian Hilary returns repeatedly to this comparison (see *infra* 84, *De Trin.* 2, 8); both Quintilian and Hilary return to it at the beginning of the twelfth book (see *Inst.* 12, Prooem. 2-3, *De Trin.* 12, 1-2) (cf. H. Kling, *op. cit.*, p 18), be it with this difference that Quintilian says that he still has a long way to go, whilst Hilary is confident that the safe harbour is in sight. This could perhaps be explained by the fact that Hilary wants to show that he who puts his trust in the wind which is the Holy Spirit is superior to the navigators who depend on changing winds, see *De Trin.* 12, 2: *Non incertis autem neque otiosis nautarum modo nitimur spebus: quos interdum votis magis quam fiducia navigantes, vagi instabilesque venti aut deserunt aut depellunt. Caeterum nobis adest inseparabilis fidei Spiritus dono unigeniti permanens, et nos indemutabili cursu ad tranquilla deducens.* To Quintilian, too, the end is in sight, but he feels surrounded by the sky and the ocean, and he can no longer even expect guidance from Cicero in describing the ideal orator.

So, right from the beginning Hilary used the metaphor of the sea voyage for his writing, just like Quintilian, and just like Quintilian he uses it repeatedly, especially at the beginning of the twelfth book.

There are two more similarities which could be mere coincidence, but which should not be left unnoticed. At the beginning of his fourth book Quintilian says that he now has a new motive for diligence (*Inst.* 4, Prooem. 1: *Nova insuper mihi diligentiae causa*). He says that poets, when they have reached some important passage, repeat their vows and utter fresh prayers for assistance; he himself omitted to invoke the help of the gods at the beginning of the whole work, so he does it at the beginning of the fourth book. (*Inst.* 4, Prooem. 4-5: *Quodsi nemo miratur poetas maximos fecisse, ut non solum initiis operum suorum Musas invocarent, set provecti quoque longius cum ad aliquem graviorem venissent locum, repeterent vota et velut nova precatione uterentur, mihi quoque profecto poterit ignosci, si, quod initio, quo primum hanc materiam inchoavi, non feceram, nunc omnes in auxilium deos ipsumque in primis, quo neque praesentius aliud nec studiis magis propitium numen est, invocem.* If we suppose that it was Hilary's intention right from the beginning to write a work consisting of twelve books, then the renewed beginning in the fourth book could be an imitation of Quintilian as well: after the three books which positively explain the doctrine of the Trinity, in book four the refutation of the Arian attacks on this doctrine begins. It is even quite understandable that somebody should pause for a while after having written the first section of his work (cf. *De Trin.* 4, 1 where Hilary refers to the first three books *quos iam pridem conscripsimus*).

It is interesting to see that both in Hilaray's *De Trinitate* and in Quintilian's *Institutio oratoria* the ninth book is the longest one.

The outline which Hilary gives in *De Trin.* 1, 20-36 is what Quintilian calls a *partitio* which follows the *exordium* (given by Hilary in *De Trin.* 1, 1-14), the *narratio* (statement of facts, given by Hilary in *De Trin.* 1,

15-19, *viz.*, the heretic attacks on Christian faith and a brief description of this faith); this is the order advised by Quintilian in *Inst.* 4. The reason why such a *partitio* should be provided is, according to Quintilian, lucidity and grace in speech. This partition has the function of milestones which relieve our fatigue upon a journey by reading the distances, see *Inst.* 4, 5, 22 ... *partitio ita opportune adhibita plurimum orationi lucis et gratiae confert ... non aliter quam facientibus iter multum detrahunt fatigationis notata inscriptis lapidibus spatia.* Similarly Hilary motivates his outline by saying that with the help of it the reader as a traveller may reach the heights via what has been levelled to a gentle slope, *De Trin.* 1, 20: ... *nos quoque quaedam gradiendi initia ordinantes arduum hoc intellegentiae iter clivo quasi molliore lenivimus ... ut prope sine scandentium sensu euntium proficeret conscensus* (for other similar passages in Quintilian see H. Kling, *op. cit.*, p 19).

But there remains one important difference between Quintilian and Hilary. According to Quintilian such an outline must be brief and should not be burdened with a single superfluous word, *Inst.* 4, 5, 26 ... *brevis nec ullo supervacuo onerata verbo.* This applies to the outline Quintilian himself gives of the contents of his twelve books in *Inst.* 1, Prooem. 21 f, but it certainly does not apply to the lengthy outline given by Hilary in *De Trin.* 1, 20-36. Now Hilary sometimes regards as "brief" what we would not regard as such at all (see *infra*, 143 ff, *De Trin.* 3, 9). But it can reasonably be asked: is it conceivable that somebody has such a detailed plan of such a vast work in mind before he starts writing? We are inclined to answer this question in the affirmative in the case of Hilary. If we take the books four to twelve independently they still are an impressively vast work, they form in fact about eighty-five percent of the work in its present shape. As early as in the fourth book he refers to what will actually be discussed in the twelfth one: in 4, 22 he says that a longer discussion of *Proverbs* 8 will follow later (and this will be the case in the twelfth book, *De Trin.* 12, 35 ff); in *De Trin.* 6, 16 he says that later on he will discuss the meaning of the expression *ex utero* (and this he will do in *De Trin.* 12, 8 ff). In themselves these are not cogent proofs that as early as the fourth or the sixth book (in case of an originally independent work beginning with what is now the fourth book: as early as the first or the third book) he knew what he was going to say in the twelfth, *c.q.* the ninth, book. These could either be additional remarks made after the two works had been merged into one (but in that case one might expect an exact reference), or they may not imply that Hilary knew that he would deal with these matters in the twelfth book and merely indicate that he reserved these expositions without knowing exactly when he would discuss them. – Furthermore, Hilary may be verbose in the presentation of the outline in *De Trin.* 1, 20-36, the points he actually makes are fairly limited and can be summarized briefly: Book II explains the baptizing in the name of the Father, Son and Holy Ghost (1, 21). Book III explains John 14:10 "I am in the Father and the Father is in Me" (1, 22). Books IV-VI refute the Arian doctrine as expressed in the letter of Arius which emphasizes the unity of God and therefore denies the true divinity of Jesus Christ, with texts from the Old Testament (books IV and V, see 1, 23-24; this proof from the Old Testament may be announced in *De Trin.* 1, 17, see *infra*, 57 f) and the New Testament (book VI, this book also detects the Arian fraudulence of smearing the orthodox with heretical views, see 1, 25). Book VII shows how the heretics, Arians, Sabellians and Photinus fight each other and therefore – without realizing it – fight the battle of the church against all of them, and it deals with the name, nature, generation, power and witness of the Son (1, 26-27). Book VIII refutes the Arians' assertion (based on texts like *Acts* 4:32, I *Cor.* 3:8, *John* 17:20-21) that the unity of Father and Son is merely a unity of will (1, 28). Book IX refutes the Arians' attack on the divinity of Christ which makes use of texts like *Luke* 18:19, *John* 17:3, *John* 14:28, *Mark* 13:32 (1, 29-30). Book X refutes the Arians' exegesis of *Matth.* 26:38-39, *Matth.* 27:46 in connection with the passibility of Christ as man, which according to Hilary does not contradict His divinity (1, 31-32). Book XI refutes the Arians' exegesis of *John* 20:17, I *Cor.* 15:17-28, texts which according to them exclude the true divinity of Christ (1, 33). Book XII refutes Arian slogans like "There was a time when He was not" and the Arians' exegesis of *Proverbs* 8:22; furthermore it provides a doctrine of the Holy Spirit (1, 34-36). It is well possible that Hilary had such a fairly lucid outline in mind right from the beginning and that, instead of presenting this very briefly to his readers (as Quintilian does), he did so with his usual verbosity (which he himself, however, may have regarded as brevity, see infra, 143 ff).

One has to prove that the De Trinitate cannot originally have consisted of the present twelve books, and that Hilary wrongly gives the impression that he intended from the beginning to write a work on the Trinity consisting of twelve books. One need not prove the opposite, it is enough to answer objections against Hilary's presentation and make suggestions as to why this presentation could be correct. The strongest argument against Hilary's presentation is the fact that a few times he gets his numbers wrong and refers to the fourth and the fifth book as the first and the second one (see *supra*, 1), but this can, it seems to us, be explained by the fact that in the fourth book he makes a renewed beginning. The strongest argument in favour of Hilary's presentation is the fact that in outlining the contents of the seventh book he gives the "uncorrected version" which he corrected in the course of writing the seventh book (see *supra*, 4 f). The noted similarities with Quintilian may not in themselves suggest more than that after he decided to merge the two independent pieces of writings into one work he imitated Quintilian, the image of the sea-voyage which appears in *De Trin.* 1, 37, so *before* the possible inclusion of *De Trin.* 1, 20-36, is not conclusive proof, since this is a *topos* in Latin literature (see *supra*, 5).

We would like to end this discussion of the structure and composition of the *De Trinitate* with a more general observation. As Doignon has shown, Hilary was already influenced by Quintilian in his earliest writings; is it then not highly likely that when he decided to write a work on the Trinity it was his intention right from the beginning to imitate Quintilian and to write a work of twelve books consisting of an *exordium* (*De Trin.* 1, 1-14), a statement of facts (*De Trin.* 1, 15-19), a *partitio* (*De Trin.* 1, 20-36), a positive proof of his doctrine of the Trinity (*De Trin.* 2-3) and a refutation of the heretic attacks on this doctrine (*De Trin.* 4-12, 51) and a peroration (12, 52-57) (for this scheme see *e.g.* Quintilian, *Inst.* 3, 9, 1)? (This is a generally accepted rhetorical scheme, see H. Lausberg, *Handbuch der literarischen Rhetorik*, München 1960, pp 146 ff).

Another important question is whether books one to three were written before the exile or in it, *i.e.* before Hilary had read the Greek Fathers, or after he had read them. (If the question is put this way it implies that Hilary was not acquainted with the Greek Fathers before he went into exile in *Asia Minor*.) This question is independent of the question of whether he intended to write a work consisting of twelve books. If this was his intention right from the beginning it is still possible that his work was interrupted after book three and that he resumed his writing in exile.

Was he familiar with the Greek Fathers when he wrote books one, two and three? Hilary does not give any names in the whole of the *De Trinitate*, so we have to look for possible quotations or reminiscences. Here we do not get further than *probabilities*, since reminiscences of *e.g.* writings of Athanasius need not imply direct dependence, as they may merely reflect generally held views. If there were significant points on which Hilary changed his mind after the completion of the third book, *i.e.* if there were statements in the books 4-12 which contradict statements made in books 1-3, and if the statements made in books 4-12 could be proved to be borrowings from Greek Fathers, then it would be clear that books 1-3 were written before Hilary was acquainted with Greek Fathers. But no such evidence can be produced, whilst there are quite a number of reminiscences of Athanasius in books 1-3 which make Hilary's acquaintance with him at that stage of his writing possible.

Were books 1-3 written before the exile or not? This is very difficult to determine. In 1, 1 he says that leisure in poverty is like exile from life. In these opening chapters Hilary elaborates on the difference between man and the animals or between spiritual and carnal life. Later on he accuses the Arians a few times of attitudes which belong to carnal life (see *infra*, 18, 24). It could be that the reference to a symbolic exile from life right in the beginning of book one is meant to indicate that, whilst he is literally in exile, regarding his knowledge of the truth he is not, while his opponents are. This would be in line with what he says in *De Trin.* 10, 4: although truth has gone in exile from many who follow their own teachers, it will not go into exile from the saints; see also *De Syn.* 78 where he says that he prefers exile to impiety and would rather be always in exile if only the truth began to be preached: *coegerunt enim nos ad voluntatem exsulandi, dum impietatis imponunt necessitatem. Sed exsulemus semper, dummodo incipiat verum praedicari.* (This seem to be a Ciceronian motive, see Cicero, *Tusc.* 5, 37, 107 ff, cf. A. Giesecke, *De philosophorum veterum quae ad exilium spectant sententiis*, Leipzig 1891, p 103). So in the beginning of book one Hilary may suggest that physically he is in exile, but spiritually it is not he who is in exile, but the Arians. So we are inclined to agree with M. Simonetti that the whole of *De Trinitate* was written in exile with knowledge of the Greek Fathers, especially Athanasius. Where we differ from Simonetti is regarding the question of whether the *De Trinitate* was meant to consist of twelve books right from the beginning, we do not differ from him in that it was written in exile. We agree with P. Smulders' original view (see *La doctrine trinitaire de S. Hilaire de Poitiers* (Analecta Gregoriana, vol. XXXII) Rome 1944, p 41) that Hilary wrote the twelve books when he was in exile and did it according to the scheme announced in the first book, and we believe that it was not necessary that Smulders corrected himself, as he does in his edition of the *De Trinitate*, p 2*.

We want to stress that our method of using books 4-12 as one of the keys of interpretation of books 1-3 is independent from the question of whether the *De Trinitate* was meant to consist of twelve books right from the beginning. If Simonetti is right in saying that the whole of the *De Trinitate* was written in exile (although Hilary changed his mind on the actual structure of the book) our method still seems legitimate. Even if the first three books were written before the exile our method would still be legitimate, unless it could be proved that Hilary in the course of time changed his mind on important thoughts expressed in the first three books.

We shall try to explain the contents of *De Trin.* 1-3 against the background of other writings of Hilary and especially of *De Trin.* 4-12; furthermore, following Doignon, we shall use the Latin Fathers and Irenaeus as background, and, following Simonetti, we shall use the writings of Athanasius.

There will be introductions to the various parts of the first three books of the *De Trinitate*. The various chapters will first be summarized briefly and then be translated and explained. The translation is to a fairly large extent the one given by E. W. Watson in *St. Hilary of Poitiers. Select Works. E. W. Watson, L. Pullan and others, Edited by W. Sanday* (A Select Library of Nicene and Post-Nicene Fathers of the Christian Church, Volume IX), New York 1899. The translation has, however, been altered wherever correction or improvement seemed necessary or desirable. Watson's translation was based on the text of the Benedictine edition in the PL, we have made use of the most recent text, *viz.*, the one given by P. Smulders, *Sancti Hilarii Pictaviensis episcopi De Trinitate, Praefatio, Libri I-VII*, Turnholti MCMLXXIX (Corpus Christianorum (Series Latina LXII). Quotations will be given after this edition with the exception of certain aspects of orthography.

The reason why the outline given in *De Trin.* 1, 20-36 and the final prayer in 1, 37-38 have not been commented upon is that it seemed more suitable to treat these chapters together with the books 4-12 as a background to *De Trin.* 1, 1-19, 2 and 3.

BOOK I

CONTENTS

I. INTRODUCTION: THE SEARCH FOR AND THE FINDING OF THE TRUTH
(1-14)

According to Quintilian an *exordium* is aimed at preparing the reader's or listener's mind (see Quintilian, *Inst.* 4, 1, 5; see J. Doignon, *op. cit.*, p 100). The speaker must tell a little about himself (Quintilian, *Inst.* 4, 1, 7: ... *pauciora de se ipso dicit et parcius*). The listener must be made to be well-disposed, attentive and ready to receive instruction (Quintilian, *Inst.* 4, 1, 5: ... *si benevolum, attentum, docilem fecerimus* (sc. *auditorem*). The whole section *Inst.* 4, 1 is an instruction how to win the goodwill of the judge).

If we keep in mind what the purpose of such an instruction is, we may cast some light on the much debated (see J. Doignon, *op. cit.*, pp 73 ff) question regarding the extent to which this introduction is autobiographical. There must be some autobiographical material in it, but the readers must also recognize themselves in what is said, since this is the best way of making them *benevoli* (cf. Quintilian, *Inst.* 4, 1, 52: ... *dicturus intueatur ... qua vulgi fama dicendum sit, quid iudicem sentire credibile sit, antequam incipimus*). Now this introduction contains themes which hardly play any role in the *De Trinitate*: the difference between man and animal, the attack on polytheism, the fear of death and how it is conquered, these are themes of popular philosophy. (There is, however, one theme which is important in the Prologue and in the rest of the *De Trinitate*: the infinity of God, see 1, 6; 1, 12; 1, 15; 2, 6; 2, 24-26; 2, 31; 3, 4; 3, 24-26, cf. *infra*, 183 f.) It is, however, very unlikely that it was Hilary's intention to win the favour of Pagan readers, they could hardly be expected to be interested in the controversies in the Christian church about the doctrine of the Trinity. This work must have been intended primarily for Christian readers and especially for those Christians who, just like Hilary, were trained in popular philosophy, became dissatisfied with Pagan ethics and polytheism and consequently were converted to Christianity. They could be expected to be interested in the story of Hilary's conversion. In order to appeal to as many readers as possible this story had to contain, apart from autobiographical, also stereotype material. An entirely fictitious story is hardly convincing; a completely personal story, certainly if it is presented in such a condensed way, is hardly convincing either. It is entirely credible that the conversion to Christianity of an intellectual trained in popular philosophy, especially in Cicero, took place along the lines indicated by Hilary.

The search for the truth, the ability to search for the truth, distinguishes according to Cicero man from the animals. This inevitably leads to the conclusion that man's true happiness must differ from the animals' pleasure and cannot consist of leisure and abundance. Pagan philosophers, especially Cicero, have rightly seen that man is born for more, and that it is his duty to perform glorious acts and to pursue virtues. But even this does not lead to real happiness, which can only be found if man knows his Creator who not only grants life but also immortality and thereby liberates man from the fear of death.

Once the quest for God is created in man polytheism becomes repulsive and unreasonable. Through divine guidance man becomes acquainted with Scripture and here he learns about the one eternal and unchanging God. This God is of an unmeasurable infinity. He reveals himself in the Old Testament (a revelation which largely confirms natural, philosophical knowledge of God) and even more clearly in the New Testament. Here man learns about "God from God", the core of the doctrine of the Trinity, and about the mystery of the incarnation which grants, in a way transcending natural human understanding, men to become sons of God and so receive deification. He who has reached the stage of this knowledge of the truth is safe and can proclaim the truth to others as well.

The structure of this Introduction is fairly simple. Man's conduct of life is reviewed according to the scheme of the *homo carnalis* who seeks happiness in carnal pleasure, of the *homo animalis* who seeks happiness by living according to moral precepts which appeal to common sense, and of the *homo spiritalis* who seeks happiness by knowing the true God. The finding of knowledge of God is described in a similar way: first popular polytheism is rejected, then the concept of God given in the Old Testament which is in accordance with natural knowledge of God as expressed by the philosophers is described, and finally the knowledge of God as given in the New Testament, which transcends the previous stage, is stated (cf. for this way of reaching the divine truth Hilary's comment on the 61st Psalm, *In Ps.* LXI 2, where a similar way is described as a *communis hominum affectus*, this is a further indication that Hilary tells us in the Prologue not only a personal story, but also a typical story of conversion). The reason why he does not talk here in the Prologue about the *homo carnalis, homo animalis* and *homo spiritalis*, as he does in his commentary on the 14th Psalm (see *infra*, 18 ff), is presumably that here in the prologue he stresses the difference between man (*homo*) and the animals (*animalia*), so the expression *homo animalis* (who is on a higher level than the *homo carnalis*) would be confusing. But Hilary's way of arguing is the same as in his commentary on the 14th Psalm.

CHAPTER 1

Searching after true happiness man finds that leisure and abundance do not provide it, since if it did man would not differ from the animals.

Translation and Commentary:

> **(1)** "When I was seeking an employment which belongs to human life and is religious, which, because it is either prompted by nature or suggested by the researches of the wise, might provide me with something worthy of this divine gift of understanding which has been granted to us many things occurred to me which in general esteem seemed to render life both useful and desirable."

Hilary is looking for an employment which both belongs to man and is religious. These very first words indicate that he wants to stress the difference between man and the animals. As Cicero says, the seeking of the truth distinguishes man from the animals, see *De off.* 1, 4, 13: *In primisque hominis est propria veri inquisitio atque investigatio*; 1, 6, 18: *primus ille* (sc. *locus), qui in veri cognitione consistit, maxime naturam attingit humanam. Omnes enim trahimur et ducimur ad cognitionis et scientiae cupiditatem* (for other reminiscences of Ciceronian language see J. Doignon, *op. cit.* p 105, n. 1). The employment he seeks must be religious, – according to Hilary religion is one of the distinctive marks between man and the animals, see *infra*, 23 ff on *De Trin.* 1, 3. Another distinctive mark is intellect which is a divine gift to man; again this is a commonplace in popular philosophy, expressed by, amongst others, Cicero, see *e.g. De nat. deor.* 2, 59, 147: *Iam vero animum ipsum mentemque hominis, rationem, consilium, prudentiam qui non divina cura perfecta esse perspicit, is his ipsis rebus mihi videtur carere*, for parallels in Pagan literature see A. S. Peases's edition of the *De natura deorum* II, Harvard University Press 1958, p 932; Christian writers adopted this view, see *e.g.* Tertullian, *De Paen.* 1, 2: *Ceterum a ratione eius tantum absunt quantum ab ipso rationis auctore. Quippe res dei ratio.* Lactance, *De ira dei* 7, 2 ff; *De op. dei* 2, 1 ff; Athanasius, *De Inc.* 11 (men are *logikoi*, because they are created in the image of the *Logos*); Hilary, *In Ps.* CX-VIII, X, 1: *Commune iudicium est, inter omnia terrena Dei opera nihil homine utilius, nihil esse speciosius ... Et hoc unum in terris animal rationale, intelligens ...*, cf. *In Ps.* LII 7. The activity he is looking for is either prompted by nature or suggested by the research of the wise. It is impossible to detect a difference between these two, as far as the actual content is concerned. The pleasure given by leisure and abundance which is discussed in this chapter may be prompted by nature, but also philosophers (the Epicureans) recommend it. The virtues which are discussed in *De Trin.* 1, 2-3 are the virtues advocated by philosophers (see *infra*, 19 ff), but Hilary also says that men are prompted by nature to pursue them (see *De Trin.*

1, 2, *infra*, 19). So the *a natura manans* may refer to natural thoughts of any rational creature, the *a prudentum studiis profectum* to what one has learned from others, nevertheless both have the same content. The *opinio communis*, which regards many things as able to produce a useful and desirable life, has indeed, as Doignon (*op. cit.*, p 119 n. 1) says, nothing to do with the Stoic concept of κοινὴ ἔννοια, but should be translated as "general esteem", "common sense"; similar expressions used by Hilary for this same concept are: *opinio sensus communis* (*De Trin.* 1, 34), *sensus communis intellegentiae* (*De Trin.* 4, 16; 8, 4), *sensus humanae opinionis* (*De Trin.* 5, 6), *communis sensus* (*De Trin.* 6, 25; 11, 30, *De Syn.* 75), *sensus communis opinionis* (*De Trin.* 6, 29), *opinio humani sensus* (*De Trin.* 7, 16; 12, 18), *communis humani generis assensus* (*De Trin.* 9, 44), *sensus communis iudicii* (*De Trin.* 9, 59), *humanae intellegentiae sensus* (*De Trin.* 10, 36; 12, 5), *commune iudicium* (*De Trin.* 12, 11).

> "And especially that which not only now but also always in the past is regarded amongst mortal men as the most desirable, *viz.*, leisure combined with wealth (came before my mind)."

As H. Kling, Hilarius von Poitiers und Sallust, *Philologus* (69) 1910, pp 567-569, has shown, Hilary here evokes the language and thoughts of Sallust, see *Cat.* 36, 4 ... *domi otium atque divitiae, quae prima mortales putant, affluerent*; Sallust himself does not share this esteem of leisure and wealth, since it creates factions, see *Jug.* 41, 1: *ceterum mos partium et factionum ... ortus est otio atque abundantia earum rerum quae prima ducunt*, cf. *Cat.* 10, 2 ... *eis otium, divitiae, optanda alias, oneri miseraeque fuere.* – Hilary now gives the reason why leisure and wealth must go together:

> "For the one without the other seemed rather a source of evil than an opportunity for good, for leisure in poverty is felt to be almost an exile from life itself."

All agree that abundance and leisure must go together in order to provide pleasure. Hilary now wants to show that one without the other is indeed something evil. The first possibility is that man has leisure in poverty instead of in abundance. This is stated as a general rule: Leisure in poverty is a kind of exile from life. But it could be that behind this general statement there is also a hidden sly dig at the Arians: As appears from another section of Hilary's writings he knew people who lived in leisure, but poverty, *viz.*, the heretics and the philosophers, whom he attacks in his commentary on *Psalm* 64, in that they try to commend their perverse doctrine with the righteousness of meaningless labour by suffering cold, practising sexual abstinence and eating dry bread, see *In Ps.* LXIV 3: *Plures enim sunt in demersissimo erroris profundo locati, qui doctrinae suae perversitatem quadam inanis laboris probitate commendent. Cernimus namque nudis philosophos corporibus algere: ipso etiam coniugiorum usu magistri abstinent: haeretici sicco panis cibo vivunt. Sed qui tandem otiosi huius propositi profectus est? Totum hoc inane atque ridiculum est, et cum ipsis superstitionis causis miserabile. Deo ergo vovenda sunt contemptus corporis, castitatis custodia, jejunii tolerantia* (cf. *In Ps.* XIV 8). The true *otium* is according to Hilary to reflect on the divine truth, see *De Trin.* 1, 8; 1, 14; *infra*, 40, 52. Hilary may want to suggest with the remark that leisure in poverty (which he detects in the heretics) is an exile from life, that whilst he himself is literally in exile, the Arians are symbolically in exile regarding the true way of life (cf. *supra*, 10, and *infra*, 24, regarding more sly digs at the Arians in this prologue to the *De Trinitate*). – The second possibility is to live in abundance and lack of leisure:

> "And wealth possessed amid anxiety causes more calamity in the degree to which one suffers with a greater indignity the loss of the things which are the most desired and sought for use."

So to suffer the loss of what one has most desired and sought produces an anxiety in indignity; as J. Doignon has shown, this *inquietudo cum indignitate* is the opposite of the famous Ciceronian *otium cum dignitate*, see J. Doignon, *op. cit.*, p 106 n. 5. This second possibility could well be referred to by Hilary with the intention of showing the impossibility of happiness in abundance and leisure. Animals, having no foresight (see *infra*, 23), may take pleasure in these two, man who does have foresight must always anticipate the possibility that he may lose again the wealth he has acquired.

> "And yet, though these two embrace the highest and best of the luxuries of life, they seem not far removed from the normal pleasures of the beasts, for they, roaming towards places which are woody and above all rich in herbage, enjoy at once being safe from toil and being satisfied by food. For if this be regarded as the best and most perfect aim of human life, to be in quietness and abundance, then this very conduct must be common to us and the whole unreasoning animal world, each according to the feeling of its race, namely that all of them, because of that bounteous provision and leisure which nature bestows, have full scope for enjoyment without anxiety for possession."

As appears from a statement made elsewhere by Hilary, such a life in leisure and abundance is carnal life (life of the *homo carnalis*) in which man does not differ from the animals, see *In Ps.* XIV 7: *Apostolus enim et carnalem hominem posuit, et animalem, et spiritalem: carnalem, beluae modo divina et humana negligentem, cuius vita corporis famula sit, negotiosa cibo, somno, libidine.* (These three stages of the *homo carnalis*, *homo animalis* and *homo spiritalis* appear in what will follow in the next two chapters). Similarly Lactance attacks what the Epicureans regard as the highest good by saying that in enjoying pleasure man does not differ from the animals, see *e.g. Epit.* 28, 6: *Epicurus animi adservit voluptatem ... sed hoc bonum etiam muta contingit, quae cum pabulis saturata sunt, in gaudium et lasciviam resolvuntur,* cf. *De op.* 8, 2: *illa* (sc. *animalia*) *vero depressit* (sc. *deus*) *ad terram ut quia nulla his immortalitatis expectatio est, toto corpore in humum proiecta ventri pabuloque servirent.* Man and the various animals may have different sorts of leisure and abundance, since they all have different feelings, but in principle they are on the same level if man strives only after these two goods. Hilary concedes that nature does provide these two goods, but nature itself also impels men to transcend these pleasures. This will be discussed in the next two chapters.

Chapter 2

Most men have seen that human life ought to be more than animal life. Human life is progress towards eternity, a progress in which man should practise virtue and seek glory.

Translation and Commentary:

> **(2)** "And I believe that the majority of men have spurned for themselves and censured in others this acquiescence in a foolish, animal life, for no other reason than that nature itself has taught them to regard it as unworthy of man, to believe themselves to be born only in order to serve their stomach and their sloth and that they were not brought into this life in order to pursue glorious deed or good employment or that this life was not granted in order to make some kind of progress in eternity."

The view held by the *homo carnalis* on life was rejected in the previous chapter. The view of the *homo animalis* represents a higher stage, and the difference between these two stages is discussed in this chapter. In his commentary on the Psalms Hilary says that as *homines animales* Christians have ideas in common with the Pagans. The most important thing a *homo animalis* wants is to avoid sin and to acquire the fame of goodness, see *In Ps.* XIV 7: *illa, licet magna atque praeclara sint, solent tamen cum gentibus esse communia, ut vitium caveant, ut famam bonitatis acquirant. Sed haec animalium, non spiritalium virtus est.* So as a Christian Hilary can make use of the arguments which a Pagan as a *homo animalis* produces against the conduct of life of a *homo carnalis*, and this is what he does in these chapters. To be born in order to serve the stomach and sloth is a notion which is rejected by Sallust in very similar words: those who lead such a life are *velut pecora, quae natura prona atque ventri oboedientia finxit,* they are *dediti ventri atque somno* (*Cat.* 1, 1, see H. Kling, *op. cit.*, pp 568 f). The majority of men have seen that man is born to pursue glorious deed and good employment; again, Hilary here follows Sallust, *Cat.* 2, 9: *Verum enimvero is demum mihi vivere at-*

que frui anima videtur, qui aliquo negotio intentus praeclari facinoris aut artis bonae famam quaerit, see H. Kling, *op. cit.*, p 569. Kling is not right in saying that Hilary attacks this view, he regards it as a step forward compared with the conduct of life of the *homo carnalis*, but he will show (see *infra*, 37 ff) that it is still below the conduct of life of the *homo spiritalis*. Hilary's attitude towards glory is ambivalent: man must glory in the Lord and not in himself, since all he possesses he has received from the Lord, see *In Ps.* CXXIII 2: *Quis enim relictus est nobis gloriandi locus, recordantibus omnia ex Deo esse*, cf. *In Ps.* LI 5, *In Matth.* 3, 5; 4, 2. Glory is an important concept with Cicero, Tertullian and Lactance in connection with mortality: actions of virtue, says Cicero, will be followed by glory, see *Tusc.* 1, 38.91: *Qua re licet etiam mortalem esse animum iudicantem aeterna moliri, non gloriae cupiditate, quam sensurus non sit sed virtutis quam necessario gloria, etiamsi tu id non agas, consequatur.* Many of our actions are motivated by the fact that we are concerned about our reputation in the future after our death, see *Tusc.* 1, 14, 31 ff, – see on this matter A. D. Leeman, *Gloria. Cicero's waardering van de roem en haar achtergrond in de hellenistische wijsbegeerte en de Romeinse samenleving*, (Diss. Leiden), Rotterdam 1949, pp 71 ff. – Tertullian passes a negative judgment on the philosopher as a *gloriae animal* in *De anima* 1, 2 (for further instances of Christian criticism of the thirst for glory of the philosophers, see J. H. Waszink's edition of *De anima*, p 87; on this subject more in general, A. J. Vermeulen, *The Semantic Development of Gloria in Early-Christian Latin*, Nijmegen 1956, pp 39 ff and his paper *gloria* in the *R.A.C.* (82) pp 198 ff). But he also uses this thirst for glory after death as a proof of man's immortality, see *De test. an.* 4, 9-10: *Nam omnibus fere ingenita est famae post mortem cupido ... Quis non hodie memoriae post mortem frequentandae ita studet ut vel litteraturae operibus vel simplici laude morum vel ipsorum, sepulcrorum ambitione nomen suum servet? Unde animae hodie affectare aliquid quod velit post mortem et tantopere praeparare quae sit usura post obitum? Nihil utique de postero curaret, si nihil de postero sciret*, see on this passage (which shows similarity with Cicero, *Tusc.* 1, 14, 31 ff) J. H. Waszink, *Tertullian über die Seele*, Artemis Zürich-München 1980, pp 310 f, and A. D. Leeman, *op. cit.*, pp 79 f. – Lactance stresses that temporal honours do not render anybody happy, but only innocence and justice, *De ira dei* 24, 8: *non faciunt beatum ... caduci honores quibus inlaqueatus animus humanus et corpori mancipatus aeterna morte damnatur, sed sola innocentia, sola iustitia; Epit.* 29, 8: *... honores non appetet* (sc. *homo*), *qui sunt breves et caduci; Divin. Inst.* 3, 11, 12: *id* (sc. *bonum*) *quid esse dicemus? ... num gloriam? num honorem? num memoriam nominis? at haec omnia non sunt in ipsa virtute, sed in aliorum existimatione atque arbitrio posita*, cf 3, 8, 3, 8 ff. Hilary certainly shares Lactance's view that man's own glory, which manifests itself in

man's deed, is no escape from mortality; on the true glory of man according to Hilary see *infra*, 25 f on *De Trin*. 1, 3.

Life is a progress which continues in eternity: this is stated repeatedly
by Hilary, see e.g. *De Trin*. 1, 14; *In Ps*. LIX 14. The constant growth of
man is used by Hilary as a reasonable argument for immortality:
Because of his constant growth man can expect promotion to a higher
state of being, see *De Trin*. 9, 4: *Ipsum quoque participem rationis hominem
contuere. Semper proficit augmento, numquam vero deminutione contrahitur; nec sese
caret, quod excrevit in sese ... Naturae ergo nostrae necessitas in augmentum semper
mundi lege provecta, non imprudenter profectum naturae potioris exspectat*, cf. the
very similar argument given by Seneca, *Epist*. CII, 23: *Quemadmodum
decem mensibus tenet nos maternus uterus et praeparat non sibi sed illi loco in quem
videmur emitti iam idonei spiritum trahere et in aperto durare, sic per hoc spatium
quod ab infantia patet in senectutem in alium maturescimus partum*. Irenaeus
describes corporal life as a constant growth and not as a diminution in
Adv. Haer. 2, 15, 2. – On the increase of knowledge in eternity, see
Irenaeus, *Adv. Haer*. 2, 41, 3.

> ''– A life indeed which then one would confidently assert ought not to be
> regarded as a gift of God, since, racked by pain and laden with trouble, it
> consumes itself within its bounds from the blank mind of infancy to the
> wanderings of age.''

Whilst Hilary had conceded in the previous chapter that nature can provide some sort of leisure with abundance, he now refers to the misery of
life, which is obvious if man cannot pursue virtues and cannot regard life
as an eternal progress. If human life were no more than animal life, then
it would not mean growth but constant decease below the level of rational
thinking. Man's life would begin in ignorance (*pueritiae ignoratio*) and end
in it (*senectutis deliramenta*); in between there would be pain and trouble,
the leisure and abundance which may be available to man do not help
him, since in enjoying them man lives on the level of the ignorant
animals. Such a life cannot be regarded as a gift of God.

After this sentence *in parenthesi* Hilary resumes the argument that the
majority of men have risen above the level of animal life:

> ''And that therefore they have raised themselves through teaching and prac-
> tice to certain virtues of patience, temperance and placability, because they
> believed that only right action and thought mean right living.''

Hilary is here still talking about the view on life of the majority of men.
As Doignon, *op. cit.*, p 109, has shown these are virtues which also appear
in the writings of Cicero and Sallust, see Cicero *De off*. 1, 34, 122; 1, 25,
88; Sallust, *Cat*. 2, 5 (see also Lactance, *Epit*. 28, 9, who speaks of the

malorum laborumque tolerantia of the Stoics). Although these are virtues which, according to Hilary, the Christian has in common with the Pagans who have risen to the level of *homines animales*, he does say that *continentia* ('temperance') is difficult, *In Ps.* LIV 6: *Difficillimum autem hominis infirmitati est, intra se ipsum perturbationes mentis commotionesque cohibere, ut non etiam usque ad ipsam vultus demutationem, tacito licet motu, significatio anxietatis vel indignationis erumpat,* cf. Cicero, *De off.* 1, 29, 102: *efficiendum autem est, ut appetitus rationi oboediant eamque neque praecurrant nec propter pigritiam aut ignaviam deserant sintque tranquilli atque omni animi perturbatione careant; ex quo ducebit omnis constantia omnisque moderatio … Licet ora ipsa cernere iratorum aut eorum, qui aut libidine aut aliqua aut metu commoti sunt aut voluptate nimia gestiunt; quorum omnium voltus, voces, motus statusque mutantur.* Patience must, according to Hilary, by practised in circumstances of misfortune, see *In Ps.* LXI 1, 5; CXVIII 14, 7, especially CXXVIII 1, where *patientia* is defined as *tolerantia praesentium passionum,* in *De Trin.* 1, 14 he says that such a forbearance leads to the reward of immortality. – Right action and thought produce the right way of living, see on the couple of *bene agere* and *bene intellegere infra,* 24 f, on *De Trin.* 1, 3.

> "And that life should not be regarded as being given by the immortal God only to end in death, for one could not understand how a good Giver would have bestowed the most pleasant sense of life in order to let it turn into the most gloomy fear of dying."

The majority of men know that since life is an eternal progress it has not been granted to man in order to end in death. Hilary produces repeatedly as a reasonable argument for man's immortality the fact that it is incompatible with God's goodness only to have given a mortal life, see *In Ps.* CXVIII 14, 1: *Neque enim quisquam tam demens aut inops sensu est, ut in id cum nullus esset natum se esse existimet, ut rursum postquam natus est nullus esset; cum sine dubio meminerit ex bonitate Dei profectum esse quod natus est, nec id in bonitatem eius malitiae cadat, ut in nobis hoc suum quo nascimur munus interimat* (from this passage it appears that *boni largitoris* here in *De Trin.* 1, 2 should not be translated by "the Giver of good", as Watson does, but by "a good Giver"), see further *In Ps.* LIX 14 and *De Trin.* 1, 9; 1, 12, see *infra,* 40 f, 47. – The fear of death is called *tristissimus*: according to Hilary nothing is graver for human nature than to be aware of danger, for what is unknown or sudden implies a miserable feeling of safety but no fear for the future, see *De Trin.* 7, 3 *Nihil humanae naturae gravius est periculi conscientia, – nam ea quae aut ignorata aut repentina sunt, habent quidem miserabilem securitatem, sed non habent metum futuri*; man, of course, is well aware of his mortality. For man's natural fear of death cf. Tertullian, *De test. an.* 4, 8, 9 and Athanasius, *De Inc.* 28: ἔστι μὲν γὰρ κατὰ φύσιν ὁ ἄνθρωπος δειλιῶν τὸν θάνατον.

CHAPTER 3

Man needs more than a morally correct conduct of life, he must know God, the Giver of his intellect.

Translation and Commentary:

> **(3)** "And yet, though I could not regard their view as absurd and useless, that man should keep his conscience free from all blame and should either foresee sagaciously or deliberately avoid or endure patiently all troubles of life, still I could not regard these men as guides competent to lead me to the good and happy life."

Here we are on the level of the *homo animalis*, of whom Hilary says in *In Ps.* XIV 7: *Animalis autem, qui a iudicio sensus humani quid decus honestumque sit sentiat, atque ab omnibus vitiis animo suo auctore se referat, suo proprio sensu utilia et honesta diiudicans ... Sed praesens in his tantum et inter homines homini erit usus.* For similar statements made by Cicero, which Hilary may have in mind, here in *De Trin.* 1, 3, see J. Doignon, *op. cit.*, p 110 n. 1. In his commentary on the Psalms he says that a Pagan can avoid sins by striving after innocence, see *In Ps.* I 6: *Possunt enim haec et in saeculari viro reperiri ... ut a peccatis se per studium modestae innocentiae refrenet.* In *De Trin.* 5, 21 he says that an innocent life could help to gratify one's conscience, but does not lead to knowledge of God: *Adsit licet saecularis doctrinae elaborata institutio, adsit vitae innocentia, haec quidem proficient ad conscientiae gratulationem, non tamen cognitionem Dei consequentur.* (This is what Hilary has here, in *De Trin.* 1, 3, in mind as well, see *infra*, 26). – *Providere prudenter* is typical of man and distinguishes him from the animal; this was already hinted at in *De Trin.* 1, 2 where life *in ignorance* between youth and old age was characterized as being afflicted with pain and trouble, in such a life it is impossible to do what the philosophers advise, *viz. molestias providere prudenter.* On this difference between man and the animals see further *De Trin.* 9, 59: *Humanae naturae quod agere definiunt, quantum in se est, praesciunt*; of the *ferae beluaeque* he says: *extra rationem consilii providentis animata, ipsum quod agunt nesciunt*, cf. Cicero, *De off.* 1, 4, 11: *Sed inter hominem et beluam hoc maxime interest quod haec ... ad id solum quod adest quodque praesens est, se accomodat, paulum admodum sentiens praeteritum et futurum. Homo autem, quod rationis est particeps ... facile totius vitae cursum videt ad eamque degendam praeparat res necessarias*; Athanasius, *Contra gentes* 31, τὰ μὲν γὰρ ἄλογα μόνα τὰ παρόντα βλέπει, καὶ πρὸς μόνα τὰ ἐν ὀφθαλμοῖς ὁρμᾷ, κἂν μετὰ ταῦτα τὴν βλάβην ἔχῃ, ὁ δὲ ἄνθρωπος οὐ πρὸς τὰ βλεπόμενα ὁρμᾷ, ἀλλὰ τῷ λογισμῷ τὰ διὰ τῶν ὀφθαλμῶν ὁρώμενα κρίνει. On *ferre patienter* see *supra*, 21 f, *De Trin.* 1, 2. These doctrines cannot lead to a happy life, since they are on the level of the life of the *homo animalis*, where there is no difference between Pagans and Christians. It is now Hilary's intention to mark the difference between this doctrine and the specifically Christian one, or to mark the difference between the *homo animalis* and the *homo spiritalis* (cf. *supra*, 15).

> "They only fixed doctrinal precepts which were common and convenient to human reason: not to understand these precepts was animal-like, yet to have understood them and not to practise them seemed to be beyond the madness of beastly barbarism."

The animals cannot understand the virtues of the *homo animalis*, men can understand them, if they do not practise them, then they are as *homines carnales* below the level of the animals, since the animals cannot help being what they are; the *homines carnales* ought to know better (*sensus humanus* here has the meaning of 'reasoning power, understanding', as it often has with Hilary, see R. J. Kinnavey, *The Vocabulary of St. Hilary of Poitiers*, Washington D.C. 1935, p 277). Similarly, Hilary accuses the Arians of either having no knowledge or neglecting what they know, and of their therefore being, in fact, *homines carnales*, see *De Trin.* 4, 26: *Quae perfidiae caecitas est, quae increduli cordis obtunsio est, quae inreligiositatis temeritas, aut ignorare haec aut non ignorata neglegere. De Trin.* 5, 26: *Primum haec impietatis stultitia fuit, ut quae superius dicta sunt aut non intellegerentur, aut intellecta cum essent, tacerentur.* – It is interesting to see that elsewhere Hilary puts common doctrinal precepts on a level with the law of the Old Testament, see *De Trin.* 9, 16: ... *tamquam communium praeceptorum et in lege scriptorum magistrum interrogat Dominum*; this is in line with his view that the revelation given in the Old Testament is largely in line with the natural, philosophical concept of God of the *homo animalis* (see *infra*, 30 ff).

> "But my mind not only hastened to do the things which not to have done was absolutely wrong and painful, but to know this God and Father of such a great gift."

In the very first sentence of the *De Trinitate* he had indicated his desire for an employment of the gift of intellect which belongs to human life and is religious, *viz.*, the knowledge of God. What has been said so far merely paved the way to attain this. Now his mind is anxious to reach the end of the road. The word 'to hasten' (*festinare*) indicates that he is on a right way, *viz.*, to revelation, see *De Trin.* 11, 24 (explaining Phil. 3:16: *verum in quo festinavimus in ipso ingrediemur*), *De Trin.* 12, 45 in explaining *John* 14:6: *Ego sum via*, he says: *Via est dux euntium, festinantium cursus.* In obedience to the Father Jesus hastens towards his death, see *De Trin.* 9, 55; 10, 30, 33, 49. Hilary may want to suggest that his hastening towards knowledge of God takes place under divine guidance. Another possible motive behind this haste could be that truth must be found quickly, since life is short (see on this *infra*, 152, *De Trin.* 3, 13). This is expressed by Lactance, *Div. Inst.* 3, 16, 8: *cito inveniri debet* (sc. *sapientia*), *ut cito sucipi possit, ne quid pereat ex vita, cuius finis incertus est.* – An innocent life is not enough without true knowledge. In *De Trin.* 8, 1 he says when describing the *sacerdos* that innocent life and knowledge of the Christian doctrine must go together, one without the other is not enough: ... *quia non statim boni atque utilis sacerdotis est, aut tantummodo innocenter agere, aut tantummodo scienter praedicare: cum et innocens sibi tantum proficiat, nisi doctus sit, et doctus sine doctrinae sit auctoritate, nisi innocens sit.* Similarly Quintilian says of the orator, *Inst.* Praef. ad I 18 ... *Sit* ... *nec moribus modo perfectus* ... *sed etiam scientia* ..., cf. Lactance. *Div. Inst.* 3, 12, 29: *Haec enim duo sunt, quae simul efficiant illud quod quaeritur: scientia id praestat, ut quomodo et quo perveniendum sit noverimus, virtus, ut perveniamus. Alterum sine altero nihil valet.* As a rational being man must know God, cf. *De Trin.* 6, 15 (on this passage see *infra*, 77) and *De Trin.* 2, 35: ... *animus humanus* ... *habebit* ... *naturam Deum intellegendi.* It is in religion where the most important difference between man as a rational being and the irrational animals lies, see *e.g. De Trin.* 8, 30: ... *ne pecudum modo per ignorationem Dei, vitae nostrae ignoremus auctorem.* This idea is also expressed by Cicero, see *e.g. De leg.* 1, 8, 24: *nullum est animal praeter hominem quod habeat notitiam aliquam dei,* and it is echoed in many writings of the Christians, see *e.g.* Novatian, *De Trin.* 1, 5, Theophilus, *Ad Aut.* 2, 17, Irenaeus, *Adv. Haer.* 3, 39, Lactance, *De ira dei* 7 (quoting Cicero), Athanasius, *De Inc.* 11, 13. According to Hilary the knowledge of God is the only adequate use of the divine gift of intellect he was seeking, see *De Trin.* 1, 1, *supra*, 16 ff.

> "For to Him it owed its whole self, it felt that by serving Him it had to reach its honour; on Him all its hopes should be fixed, in His goodness it could, amid such great troubles of this anxious life, come to rest as in a completely safe and familiar harbour."

It is stressed that the mind owes its totality to God, cf. *In Matth.* 23, 2: ... *extra querelam iniuriae est Caesari redhibere quod Caesaris est, Deo autem quae eius sunt propria reddere nos oportere, corpus, animam, voluntatem,* J. Doignon, *Hilaire de Poitiers sur Matthieu* II (S.C. 258), Paris 1979, p 155 n. 10, refers as background to Tertullian, *De idol.* 15, 3: *Reddite* ... *quae sunt Dei Deo, id est* ... *imaginem Dei Deo quae in homine est,* cf. *De corona* 12, 5 ... *cum te deo debes, etiam in communibus, credo, potiori.* – The true honour of man lies in serving God: this honour differs fundamentally from the *studia praeclari facinoris* mentioned in *De Trin.* 1, 2, see *supra*, 20 f; cf. Irenaeus, *Adv. Haer.* 4, 25, 1: *Haec enim gloria hominis, perseverare ac permanere in Dei servitute*; 4, 28: *Deerat autem homini gloria Dei, quem nullo modo poterat percipere, nisi per eam obsequentiam, quae est erga Deum*; Tertullian, *Adv. Marc.* 2, 4, 5 ... *ut solus homo gloriaretur, quod solus dignus fuisset qui legem a Deo muneret.* – All his hopes are fixed on God, since God grants immortality to mortal man, see *supra*, 22, *De Trin.* 1, 2. – It is a *topos* in classical literature to compare life with a sea-voyage and to compare (life after) death with a safe harbour, see C. Bonner, Desired Haven, *Harvard Theol. Review* (34) 1941, pp 49 ff. To Hilary and the Christians the Christian knowledge of the divine truth, in this life, is a safe harbour, see *e.g.* Irenaeus, *Adv. Haer., Praef.* ad IV, 1; Cyprian, *Ad Don.* 14, *De mort.* 3, *De bono pat.* 16; Tertullian, *De anima* 2, 1 (see J. H. Waszink's edition p 99); Lactance, *Epit.* 47: *Una igitur spes hominibus vitae est, unus portus salutis, unum refugium libertatis, si abiectis quibus tenebantur erroribus aperiant oculos mentis suae deumque cognoscant, in quo solo domicilium veritatis est, Div. Inst.* 1, 1, 11. (On Hilary's use of the image of the sea-voyage see *supra*, 5 f and *infra*, 84, *De Trin.* 2, 8.)

> "Thus it was inflamed with a most passionate desire to comprehend or to know Him."

Here he expresses the desire to be on the level of the *homo spiritalis* of whom he says in *In Ps.* XIV 7: *Spiritalis autem est, cui superiora illa ad Dominum studia sint, et hoc quod agit per scientiam Dei agat, intellegens et cognoscens quae sit voluntas eius.* But the desire to know God leads to the question: Who is the true God?

CHAPTER 4

Attack on Pagan idolatry and polytheism.

Translation and Commentary:

(**4**)   Hilary's description of the way he receives knowledge of God resembles his description of the conducts of life. First of all he rejects polytheism in the same uncompromising way in which he rejected the conduct of life of the *homo carnalis*:

> "For many of them introduced numerous households of uncertain gods, and believing that masculine and feminine sex is active in the divine creatures they asserted births and lineages of gods from gods."

The 'uncertain gods' (*dei incerti*) are, as J. Doignon suggests, *op. cit.*, p 111 n. 3, presumably not the category of the *dei incerti* mentioned in Tertullian, *Ad nat.* 2, 9, 3, but gods of an uncertain origin, see Minucius Felix, *Oct.* 8, 1. Opposition against sex amongst the gods is expressed by saying that immortal gods know no beginning or end, see Lactance *Epit.* 6: *immortalibus vero quid opus est aut sexu aut successione, quos nec voluptas nec interitus attingit*, cf. *Div. Inst.* 1, 8, 5. Hilary stresses that the infinite God has no beginning or end, see *infra*, 32, cf. Tertullian, *Adv. Marc.* 1, 3, 2; see R. Braun, *Deus christianorum. Recherches sur le vocabulaire doctrinal de Tertullien*, Paris 1962, pp 45 ff; Irenaeus, *Adv. Haer.* 2, 56, 1; 3, 8, 3.

> "Others proclaimed greater and smaller gods, differing in power."

J. Doignon, *op. cit.*, p 111 n. 3, quotes as parallels Lactance, *Div. Inst.* 1, 3, 8, and Tertullian, *Ad Nat.* 2, 12, 2. Against these gods who vary in power, Hilary will proclaim the one omnipotent God, see *infra*, 32 f.

> "Some denied the existence of any God and confined their reverence to that nature which according to them came into some kind of being through chance-led motions and collisions. The majority, however, said, because of public opinion, that there is a God, but proclaimed Him heedless and indifferent to human affairs."

Here Hilary seems to present as two separate views what is held by the Epicureans. Doignon (*op. cit.*, p 112 n. 2) suggests that this prolongs the list of errors and is caused by different statements made by Lactance, who says in *De ira* 4, 6-7 that Epicure denies the existence of God and in *De ira* 17, 1-2 denies God's providence. That this could be, as Doignon suggests, a deliberate misrepresentation, may appear from the fact that in his commentary on the Psalms Hilary speaks about those who deny creation (explaining it by chance-led collisions) and providence by denying the existence of God as about the same people, see *In Ps.* I 2: *Et impios quidem eos esse natura ipsa iudicii communis ostendit ... qui nullum esse mundi creatorem irreligiosa opinione praesumunt, qui mundum in hunc habitum ornatumque fortuitis motibus constitisse commemorant, qui ne quod iudicium creatori suo ob vitam recte criminosove gestam relinquant, volunt ex naturae necessitate se nasci, et ex eadem rursum necessitate dissolvi; In Ps.* CXIX 3: *Hi sunt qui abnegantes Deum, nullum humanis rebus asserunt reliquum esse in religione Dei profectum ... adimentes Deo curam, providentiam, arbitrium, potestatem.* (For further examples of attacks by Hilary on the Epicureans see H. O. Saffrey, Saint Hilaire et la philosophie, *Hilaire et son temps, Actes du Colloque de Poitiers 29 septembre-3 octobre 1968*, Etudes augustiniennes, Paris 1969, pp 255 ff.) Here the deniers of providence are called *abnegantes Deum*, which means atheists, and there is no difference between deniers of creation and deniers of providence. – Another possibility is that Hilary first attacks those who are atomists and atheists and realizes that they form a minority (*nonnulli*) compared with those (*plerique*) who do not deny the existence of gods, but do deny any providential and creative activities of the gods. The latter group could then not only be the Epicureans, but also Aristotle and his followers. Aristotle is attacked by Platonists and Christians because of his doctrine of providence which is confined to the celestial spheres above the moon. The Platonist Atticus attacks him by saying that there is virtually no difference between Epicure's denial of any providence and Aristotle's denial of God's care for earthly affairs (see J. Baudry, *Atticos, Fragments de son oeuvre avec introduction et notes*, Paris 1931 3, 7 f, = Eusebius (*Praep. Ev.* XV, 799 d f), and suggests that Aristotle could not escape the accusation made against Epicure that it was because

of fear that he did not want to pass for an atheist that he expressed belief
in the existence of Gods (Baudry, *Fragm.* 3, 12 f, = Eusebius, *Praep. Ev.*
XV, 800 c f). If Hilary does have Aristotle in mind, he would suggest the
same by saying that there are people who deny that God cares for human
affairs although they assert his existence according to public opinion.
Other Christian apologists attack Aristotle as well for his restriction of
providence, see *e.g.* Tatian, *Oratio ad Graecos* 2, Athenagoras, *Legatio* 25,
Origen, *Contra Celsum* 1, 21, 9 (see further instances quoted by A. J.
Festugière, *L'idéal réligieux des Grecs et l'évangile*, 1932, pp 240 ff and J. C.
M. van Winden, *An Early Christian Philosopher. Justin Martyr's Dialogue with
Trypho*, I-IX, Leiden 1971, p 37).

> "Again, some worshipped in the elements on earth and in heaven the actual
> bodily and visible forms of creatures."

J. Doignon, *op. cit.*, p 112 n. 3, refers to Lactance, *Div. Inst.* 2, 5, 4:
*quidam hebetis obtunsique cordis elementa, quae et facta sunt et carent sensu, tam-
quam deos adorant*, cf. Hilary, *In Ps.* LII, 14; LXIII, 5: ... *nunc aquis, nunc
terrae, nunc atomis, nunc caelo Dei nomen indulgens* (sc. *philosophia*), LXV 7,
CXLII 3, CXLVIII 3; Aristides, *Apol.* 4. The "elements in heaven" are,
of course, the stars. This is a polemical remark against astrology.

> "And finally some made their gods dwell within images of men or beasts,
> tame or wild, of birds or of snakes and confined the Lord of the universe and
> Father of infinity within these narrow prisons of metal or stone or wood."

This attack on idolatry is a common one both amongst Pagan
philosophers and Christian writers, see *e.g.* Athanasius, *Contra Gentes* 13 ff
and the explicative note of P. Th. Camelot in *Athanase d'Alexandrie, Contre
les Paiens* (2e édition revue et corrigée) (S.C. 18 bis), Paris 1977, p 92 f, n.
2; see further B. Gärtner, *The Areopagus Speech and Natural Revelation*, Uppsala 1955, pp 219 ff. What is attacked is in the first place that men and
even animals are used as images of God, and in the second place that
God is confined to a corporeal form. It is interesting to see that when
Hilary calls Christ the Image of God he wants to avoid the idea that God
is confined to a human image. He says explicitly that an image confines
God to a corporeal form. Christ is not the bodily image of the infinite
God, but in His actions the Father can be seen, *De Trin.* 8, 48 f. Lifeless
pictures cannot be equal to the living beings they represent, therefore
Christ is the living picture of the living Father.

> "And it was no longer appropriate to regard those as people who express the
> truth, who, tracking out ridiculous, foul and impious theories, contradicted
> each other in the very opinions of their completely senseless ideas."

The major objection made here is that the proclaimers of idolatry contradict each other, furthermore their theories are in themselves complete-

ly rejectable. It is customary amongst Christian writers and Pagan
philosophers to attack theories or stories about gods on the ground that
these are morally rejectable, see *e. g.* Athanasius, *Contra Gentes* 12 and the
explicative note of P. Th. Camelot, *op. cit.*, pp 88 f, n. 1. On the fact that
the proclaimers of idolatry contradict each other, see Cicero, *De nat. deor.*
1, 1, 2: *nam et de figuris deorum et de locis atque sedibus et de actione vitae multa
dicuntur, deque his summa philosophorum dissensione certatur;* 1, 6, 14;
Athanasius, *Contra Gentes* 23, 24; *De Inc.* 46 (for further examples from
Pagan and Christian writers see P. Th. Camelot, *Athanase d'Alexandrie,
Contre les Païens et sur l'Incarnation du Verbe* (S.C.), Paris 1946, p 55, n. 2).

> "But amidst all these assertions my agitated soul strove along a useful and
> necessary road after knowledge of God, for it could not believe that neglect
> of things created by Himself was worthy of God and (it) could not under-
> stand how sexes of gods and lines of begetters and begotten were ap-
> propriate to a mighty and incorruptible nature."

Along his road to knowledge of the true God (on the Ciceronian
background of the *via utilis et necessaria* see J. Doignon, *op. cit.*, p 115, n. 1)
it has become clear to him that the denial of God's providence is
unacceptable, since it is unworthy of God not to extend providence over
what He has created; cf. for this argument *supra*, 22, the argument for
immortality. In the second place he knows that sexual distinctions and
births and deaths are incompatible with the power and incorruption of
the divine nature. This latter remark will now be elaborated in his proof
of the unity and eternity of God.

> "Furthermore, it was sure that that which was divine and eternal must be
> one and without distinction, for that which is the cause of its own existence
> cannot have left anything outside itself superior to itself. Hence om-
> nipotence and eternity are the possession of One only, for omnipotence is
> incapable of degrees of strength or weakness, and eternity (is incapable of)
> priority or succession. And in God we must only worship eternity and
> power."

This is a condensed argument for the unity of God, which should be explained in the following way: The unity of the Divine is proved by the
fact that it causes its own existence. If the Divine is its own cause, then its
power is superior to all other things which are caused by it. The Divine
does not leave anything outside itself which is superior to it, since if it did
it would not be the most powerful itself, but one (that) would itself be
caused by that (other) superior being. So divine omnipotence implies unity of the divine, since in omnipotence there are no degrees of strength, so
there can be no gods who differ in strength (power) (as is the case in
Pagan polytheism, see *supra*, 26 f); equally divine eternity implies unity of
the divine, since in eternity there is no earlier or later, this excludes births

and deaths of gods (as are postulated in Pagan polytheism, see *supra*, 29). The one God knows no distinction in sexes; this unity of God also excludes the possibility that Father and Son are of distinct natures, see *e.g.* *De Trin.* 7, 13: *quia unius atque indifferentis naturae unum Deus nomen est*, cf. R. J. Kinnavey, *op. cit.*, p 177. God cannot have left anything outside Himself superior to Himself: God as the all-embracing (see *infra*, 33 ff) leaves nothing outside Himself, this is a commonplace amongst Christians when they prove the unity of God (cf. for the following: R. M. Grant, *The Early Christian Doctrine of God*, The Univ. Press of Virginia, 1966, pp 107 ff): see Irenaeus, *Adv. Haer.* 2, 1, 1; 2, 7, 2; 4, 33, 2; Tertullian, *Adv. Marc.* 1, 11, 2-3; Athanasius, *Contra Gentes* 6; Novatian, *De Trin.* 4, 25. In particular, what causes its own existence, *i.e.* what is eternal, lets nothing appear outside itself which is stronger than itself. Similarly Tertullian argues that God's eternity, the fact that God has no beginning and no end, causes God to be *summum magnum*; if God is *summum magnum* nothing can be compared to Him, so he must be one, see *Adv. Marc.* 1, 3, 2-4 (cf. R. Braun, *op. cit.*, pp 43 f). God's omnipotence, says Hilary, excludes weaker and stronger, so there can be no weaker or stronger gods, cf. *supra*, 27, and Lactance, *Div. Inst.* 1, 3, *De ira* 11, 2 ff. God's eternity excludes earlier and later, this commonplace in the speculations about eternity (see *e.g.* Irenaeus, *Adv. Haer.* 2, 16, 4; Origen, *De Princ.* 2, 2, 1; Athanasius, *Contra Arianos* 2, 33; *Ep. ad ep. Aeg. et Lib.* 17, Plutarch, *De E apud Delphos* 20, 393 A) excludes that gods are born or die, cf. *supra*, 29, In God only eternity and power must be worshipped, cf. Tertullian, *Adv. Marc.* 1, 6, 2-3: *quia deus non erit dicendus, quia nec credendus, nisi summum magnum. Cum ergo summum magnum cogatur agnoscere quem deum non negat, non potest admitti ut summo magno aliquam adscribat diminutionem, qua subiciatur alii summo magno. Desinit enim, si subiciatur.*

CHAPTER 5

The revelation of the one God given in the books of the Old Testament.

Translation and Commentary:

(5)   In his description of the moral conducts of life, he discusses the *homo animalis* after the *homo carnalis*. The *homo animalis* is superior to the *homo carnalis*, but since he only knows precepts which appeal to common sense he is inferior to the *homo spiritalis*, who knows the will of God. Similarly Hilary now discusses the concept of God which is superior to Pagan polytheism, *viz.*, the concept of God as revealed in the Old Testament which is in accordance with the natural knowledge of God as ex-

pressed by certain philosophers (but which still is inferior to the revelation given in the New Testament, see *infra*, 42 ff). On this natural knowledge of God see *e.g. In Ps*. 1, 6: *Possunt enim haec et in saeculari viro reperiri: ut unum Deum esse creatorem mundi opinetur ...*

> "When my mind was dwelling on this multitude of thoughts and on other similar thoughts, I chanced upon those books which according to the religion of the Hebrews were written by Moses and the prophets."

J. Doignon, *op. cit.*, p 121, referring to Quintilian, *Inst.* 9, 3, 73 and Cicero, *Top.* 1, 1, suggests that this is, in fact, meant as a divine chance. That this is indeed the case is made probable by statements of Hilary himself: *Incidere* does have this meaning in a few places in Hilary: In *De Trin.* 10, 2 he quotes 2 *Tim.* 4, 3 where it is forecast that the time will come when people will no longer endure the sane doctrine, and in *De Trin.* 10, 3 he comments: *Incidimus plane in hoc prophetiae apostolicae molestissimum tempus*, cf. *Contra Aux.* 5. But, even more important, in *De Trin.* 6, 19 he says that God led him, as a rational being, to knowledge of God through the holy books of Moses and the prophets: *Sed cum me in vitam animatum rationis quoque intellegentem praestitisses, ad cognitionem me tui sacris, ut arbitror, per servos tuos Moysen et profetas voluminibus erudisti*. It is hardly conceivable that Hilary believed that God decided to instruct him through the books of Moses and the prophets after he had run into them by chance.

> "In them were contained, in a testimony of the Creator Himself about Himself the following words: 'I am that I am' and again: 'You shall say this to the sons of Israel: He that is has sent me unto you.' "

In his reference to the Old Testament Hilary begins with the revelation given to Moses. From other sections of his writings it becomes clear that on the one hand he says that God's revelation to the world began with Moses, see *De Trin.* 5, 36: *Veritatis ratio postulat ab eo initium intellegentiae istius sumi, per quem manifestari saeculo Deus coeptus est, Moyse namque ...* On the other hand the revelation given through Moses does not differ from what the *sensus communis* thinks about God's being, see *De Trin.* 12, 24: *Quod igitur et per Moysen de Deo significatum, et per communem sensum nihil aliud nobis intellegendum permittitur* (sc. *Deo proprium est, semper esse*). Here Hilary is in line with Tertullian, who says that in his natural knowledge of God man knows no other God than the God who revealed Himself in the writings of Moses, see *Adv. Marc.* 1, 10, 2: *Denique maior popularitas generis humani, ne nominis quidem Moysi compotes, nedum instrumenti, deum Moysi tamen norunt. Exodus* 3:14 was one of the Biblical texts which was used by the Fathers in an attempt to define God's substance, cf. G. C. Stead, *Divine Substance*, Oxford 1977, p 167. On Hilary's views on the value of the revelation given in the Old Testament see *infra*, 42 ff, *De Trin*. 1, 10 and 160 f; *De Trin*. 3, 17.

> "I indeed admired such unrestricted denoting of God, because it expressed in terms best adapted to human understanding the unattainable knowledge of the divine nature."

Hilary can say that the revelation given through Moses and common sense are in harmony, because this revelation is adapted to human understanding. – This denoting of God expresses a *cognitio incomprehensibilis*, which means that the divine nature transcends human understanding, so *Exodus* 3:14 confirms natural negative theology, cf. Athanasius, *De Decr*. 22: Ὅταν γοῦν λέγῃ, Ἐγώ εἰμι ὁ ὤν, ... οὐδὲν ἕτερον ἢ αὐτὴν τὴν ἀκατάληπτον αὐτοῦ οὐσίαν σημαινομένην νοοῦμεν, and *De Syn*. 35.

> "For nothing else could be understood to be more characteristic of God than being, because being itself cannot be predicated of what once comes to an end or once began."

'Being' here has the meaning of 'eternal being'. Hilary states repeatedly that 'being' is a correct definition of God, see *e.g. De Trin*. 7, 11 where it is said that being is not an accidental title for God, but an eternal reality, lasting cause and inherent character of God's nature: *Esse non est accidens nomen, sed subsistens veritas et manens causa et naturalis generis proprietas*. This means that God's being is self-caused, and therefore eternal, cf. *De Trin*. 12, 25: *et in eo quod est, significatur aeternitas; per id quoque, cui quod est proprium est, proprium est et aeternum*, cf. also the definition of *essentia* in *De Syn*. 12: *Proprie autem essentia idcirco est dicta quia semper est*. God's eternal being has no beginning and no end, see on this statement *supra*, 29 f, and *De Trin*. 1, 6; 3, 13; 5, 13; *In Ps*. II 13.

> "And that which joins continuity of being with the possession of incorruptible felicity could not in the past, nor can in the future, be at any time non-existent, because whatsoever is Divine is neither subject to destruction nor to beginning. And therefore, since God's eternity is in nothing lacking from itself, it was worthy of God that He only showed this, that He is, as the declaration of His incorruptible eternity."

God's eternal being which is never lacking of Himself is combined with God's incorruptible felicity; this is stated more clearly in Hilary's commentary on the second Psalm: In His felicity God is perfect, God is immutable in His felicity. The mutable creatures have different emotions and therefore become different from what they were. God cannot change since God as the Being lacks an origin, see *In Ps*. II 13: *Nihil enim in aeternam illam et perfectam naturam novum incidit ... sumusque per haec aliud aliquando quam fuimus, cum eam quae praesens sit, mentis affectionem subrepens per inconstantiam infirmitatemque nostram motus appetitionis alterius inquietet, et ex eo quod fuimus, in id quod sumus conversio nos repentina demutet. Deus autem beatus atque perfectus profectu non eget, cui nihil deest: demutatione non novus est qui origine caret. Ipse est, qui quod est non aliunde est, et ipse sibi omnia est ...* That divine felicity excludes mutability and emotions is an important Epicurean concept, see *e.g.* Lucrece, *De rer. nat.* 5, 168-173; Cicero, *De nat. deor.* 1, 17, 45; Lactance, *De ira dei* 15, 6; further examples in H. Usener, *Epicurea*, Leipzig 1887, pp 241 ff. Christian theologians shared this view, but denied that it must lead to the consequence that there is no divine providence (see M. Pohlenz, *Vom Zorne Gottes*, Göttingen 1909); for Hilary's views on anthropomorphism see further *infra*, 129 f, *De Trin.* 3, 2. Perfect felicity must be eternal, cf. Augustin, *De civ.* 11, 11 and the further places quoted by A. Solignac in *Oeuvres de Saint Augustin* (14), *Les Confessions*, p 569. – This concept of God which Hilary provides in explaining *Exodus* 3:14, *viz.*, that God as really being is always identical, is in accordance with *e.g.* the middle-Platonic and later Platonic doctrine of God which was adopted by many Christians, see *e.g.* Numenius, *fragm.* 17 and 11 (ed. Leemans), Atticus, *fragm.* 9, 5; 5, 6; 8, 2 (ed. Baudry); Porphyry, *Sent.* 39, Justin, *Dial.* 3, 5, Irenaeus, *Adv. Haer.* 2, 37, 3; 2, 56, 1; 4, 21, 2; 4, 62; Athanasius, *Contra Arian.* 1, 18; 1, 35; see further J. C. M. van Winden, *op. cit.*, pp 59 ff.

CHAPTER 6

Man is unable to define God's infinity.

Translation and Commentary:

> **(6)** ''And for this indication of God's infinity the word of Him who says ''I am that I am'' seemed enough, but we also needed to apprehend the operation of His majesty and power.''

The important notion of God's infinity is here introduced for the first time. The way towards it was prepared in the previous chapter (hence the words *hanc ... significationem*) by saying that the Divine is subject neither to destruction nor to a beginning, which means that it has no beginning and no end. It will be argued that as such God cannot be grasped by human knowledge. God's being is infinite, God's power, manifesting itself in the fact that God embraces and pervades the whole world, is infinite as well (as appears from what will be said in this chapter). – God's being becomes manifest in God's power (see *infra*, 116 f; *De Trin.* 2, 29); God's infinite being manifests itself in God's power to embrace the whole universe, cf. *In Ps.* LXIII 9: *... audient ... Deum ... indefinitae ut essentiae ita et virtutis; ipsum a nemine, sed ex eo omnia, moderantem ea ipsa omnia continentem.* In his commentary on the psalms he says that God's infinite nature cannot be known completely, his infinite power can be *admired* by us, *In Ps.*

CXLIV 2: *Possumus enim eum maxime quantum in nobis est admirari; cognosci autem a nobis quantus ipse est non potest.* Similarly he may intend to say here in *De Trin.* 1, 6 that *Exodus* 3:14 says enough about God's infinite being and that the reader must now be led to admiration of His infinite power.

> "For while being is peculiar to Him who, abiding eternally, had no begin-
> ning at any moment, we hear again this worthy word of the eternal and in-
> corruptible God about Himself: "Who holdeth the heaven in His palm and
> the earth in His hand" (*Is.* 40:12), and again "The heaven is my throne
> and the earth is the footstool of my feet. What house will ye build Me or
> what shall be the place of my rest? Did not my hand create this? "(*Is.* 66,
> 1-2). The whole heaven is held in the palm of God and the whole earth is
> grasped in His hand."

God has no limit (beginning or end) in time (see *supra*, 29 f), equally He has no limit (beginning or end) in space, but embraces everything. The latter statement is a commonplace in early Christian and in Pagan philosophy as well; see apart from the examples given *supra*, 29 f, *De Trin.* 1, 4, also Novatian, *De Trin.* 2, 10; 3, 18; 17, 98; Tertullian, *Adv. Marc.* 2, 25, 2 (cf. J. Doignon, *op. cit.*, pp 124 ff); Hippolytus *Ref.* 1, 19, 6 (with reference to Plato, *Leges* 715 e); Athanasius, *De Inc.* 8, *Contra Arian.* 1, 23; 3, 22; Philo, *De somniis* 1, 63 ff; Plutarch, *Plat. Quaest.* 3, 2. In what follows now Hilary will try to specify this generally-held view:

> "Now the word of God, although it helps us to the opinion of a religious
> understanding, reveals a deeper meaning to the meditating student than to
> the momentary hearer."

This idea, that the words spoken by God in the Bible reveal a deeper meaning when man not only hears them but tries to penetrate into them, is stated more clearly elsewhere. In referring to 2 *Cor.* 12:2, 4 Hilary says that Paul knows that there are things that cannot be understood im-mediately, the infirmity of man needs time to review before the true and perfect tribunal of the mind that which is poured into the ears. Com-prehension follows the spoken words more slowly than hearing, this understanding is revealed by God, see *De Trin.* 11, 23: ... *non ignorans* (sc. *apostolus*) *tamen quaedam non statim posse atque audiuntur intellegi, quia infir-mitas nostra serius in verum atque absolutum mentis iudicium ea, quae in aures transfunderentur, acciperet, longiore ad cunctandum mora sensui potius quam auditui derelicta ... Deo tamen intellegentiae cupidis intellegentiam revelante*; cf. also *In Ps. CXXIV 1: Faciunt nobis plerique obscuritatem, volentes Scripturas pro-pheticas solo aurium iudicio aestimare, et non aliud in his intellegere, quam quod sub singulis rerum quarumque vocabulis audiatur*, and 2, *In Ps.* CXXXIV 1; H. Kling, *op. cit.*, p 20, refers as background to Quintilian, *Inst.* 10, 5, 8 where it is said that we should not run through the writings of the great writers in a careless way, but should handle each separate phrase and give it close examination: *Non enim scripta lectione secura transcurrimus, sed tractamus singula et necessario introspicimus.* This indeed resembles *De Trin.* 1, 6: ... *plus tamen significationis introspectus sensu continet quam exceptus auditu.* On Hilary's way of exegesis see *infra*, 60, 118.

> "For the heaven which is held in His palm is also God's throne, and the earth which is grasped in His hand is also the footstool of His feet, (this was written) lest one could, because of the throne and the footstool, understand this as the extension of a corporeal figure, according to the posture of somebody who sits, for that which is His throne and footstool is also held in palm and hand by that mighty Infinity. (It was written) that in all these originated creatures God might be known within them and outside them, surpassing and indwelling, surrounding all and interfused through all, since the grasp of His palm and hand reveals the might of His external control, and since throne and footstool show that things exterior to Him are subjected to Him, since He is interior, because whilst sitting inside of that which is outside Himself, He again contains it inside Himself as from outside. And in this way He contains in His totality everything inside and outside Himself, and neither is He in His infinity absent from anything nor is anything not inside Him who is infinite."

So careful introspection into the meaning of the Biblical texts quoted above shows that God embraces things not only from outside, but also from inside. Furthermore the fact that God is outside and inside the whole world makes it clear that God is not embraced by space. God Himself embraces space and pervades space. Opposition against God's sitting on His throne in an anthropomorph way is expressed in similar terms by Irenaeus, *Adv. Haer.* 4, 4, 3: *Nec enim sciunt quid sit Deus, sed putant eum more hominis sedere, et contineri, non autem continere.* – Hilary states repeatedly that God is outside and inside all things, see *e.g. De Trin.* 3, 2; 8, 24; *In Ps.* CXXXVIII 16; more in general on the infinity of God in space see *De Trin.* 2, 6, 31; *In Ps.* CXVIII XIX 8; CXXII 2; CXXXI 5, 23; CXXVIII 18. On God's infinity in time see *supra*, 29 f. – God is in His totality outside and inside all things, see on this *infra*, 79 f, *De Trin.* 2, 6.

> "So in these most devout thoughts about God my soul, engrossed in the pursuit of truth, took its delight."

The knowledge of the truth creates joy; on this *topos* in Christian and Pagan writers, see *e.g.* J. C. M. van Winden, *op. cit.*, pp 58 ff; R. Holte, *Béatitude et Sagesse. Saint Augustin et le problème de la fin de l'homme dans la philosophie ancienne*, Paris-Worcester, Mass., 1962.

> "For it thought that nothing else was worthy of God than to be beyond the intelligence of things in such a way that to the degree in which the infinite mind stretches itself towards the bound of even a presumed opinion, that to the same degree the infinity of boundless eternity exceeds all infinity of a nature which tries to reach it."

(Cf. for the following: J. M. McDermott, Hilary of Poitiers: The Infinite Nature of God, *Vigiliae Christianae* (27) 1973, pp 172 ff, who *inter alia* rightly points out, against E. Mühlenberg, *Die Unendlichkeit Gottes bei Gregor von Nyssa. Gregors Kritik am Gottesbegriff der klassischen Metaphysik*, Göttingen 1966, that Gregory was not the first Christian theologian to make a systematic use of God's infinity, but that Hilary did so before him.) The meaning of this sentence is: Human mind can far surpass the limits of its existence, but it cannot set any bound to God's infinity, *i.e.* it cannot define God. This is stated repeatedly by Hilary, see *e.g. De Trin.* 1, 13: ... *ut ... omnem terrenae mentis amplexum potestas aeternae infinitatis excedat*; 2, 6: *Curre sensu si quid ei putas ultimum: esse eum semper invenies, quia cum semper intendas, semper est quod intendas*; 9, 72: ... *natura moderata est infirmis, naturae infinitae et potentis sacramentum intellegentiae opinione non occupet*; 12, 24: ... *id quod infinitum in Deo est, semper se infiniti sensus nostri recursui subtrahat; In Ps.* CXLIV 6: *Finem magnificentia ipsius nescit: et aliquam ementiendi se opinionem immensa magnitudo non patitur*; for the Christian background of these statements see J. Doignon, *op. cit.*, pp 127 ff. The doctrine that God is infinite does not appear clearly in the Greek-speaking world before Philo, Plotinus was the first Greek philosopher to try to work out the idea of God's infinity with any precision (usually the predicate 'infinite' was a negative one given to matter) and the Greek fathers were influenced by him; see on this most important subject, apart from E. Mühlenberg, *op. cit.*, A. H. Armstrong, Plotinus' Doctrine of the Infinite and its Significance for Christian Thought, *Plotinian and Christian Studies*, Variorum Reprints, London 1979, chapter V. It could be that Hilary here also resumes what he had said in *De Trin.* 1, 2 about life as an eternal progress (see *supra*, 21). God's infinity, so to speak, invites man to think about God without ever reaching a definition of God.

> "I had come by my reverent reflection to understand this, but also found it confirmed by the following words of the prophet: 'Whither shall I go from Thy Spirit? Or wither shall I flee from Thy face? If I ascend up into heaven, Thou art there; if I go down into hell, Thou art there also, if I have taken my wings before dawn and made my dwelling in the uttermost parts of the sea (Thou art there). For thither Thy hand shall guide me and Thy right hand shall hold me' (*Psalm* 138:7-10)."

So his introspection into the meaning of *Is.* 40:12 and 66:1-2 is confirmed by Scripture. This statement must be seen in connection with Hilary's view that the revelation given in the Old Testament confirms the natural knowledge of God which transcends polytheism. In his meditation on the meaning of the Old Testament he can make use of his natural knowledge of God and this is again confirmed by Scripture. – It is not unusual to refer to *Psalm* 138:7 ff as a proof of God's infinity, see Novatian, *De Trin.*

6, 31 and Hilary, *De Trin.* 4, 8 where it is said that the Arians use this text in order to show that God the Father is *capiens omnia*.

> "There is no space without God and no space which is not in God. He is in heaven, in hell, beyond the seas. He is inside all things and exceeds them outside. So, holding and being held, He Himself is not confined to anything, and there is nothing in which He is not."

These sentences give a summary of the whole argument in this chapter: Being inside and outside all things, God is not confined to one thing, in which case He would not be infinite, nor can God be conceived as existing with parts of His being in the various parts of creation; – God is in His totality everywhere, see *infra*, 179 f, *De Trin.* 2, 6 (cf. the similar argument of Augustin, *Conf.* 7, 1, 2, where the idea that parts of God are in parts of creation is rejected). This is also important in Hilary's doctrine of the Trinity, see *infra*, 90 ff.

CHAPTER 7

The inexplicability of God's nature. Man often cannot find words to express the beauty of the created world, he has even more difficulty describing God's beauty.

Translation and Commentary:

> **(7)** "So although my mind took joy from conceiving this excellent and inexplicable intelligence, because it venerated this infinity of boundless eternity in its Father and Creator, yet with a still more eager desire it sought that splendid appearance of its infinite and eternal Lord, in order to have the idea that the boundless immensity (of God) is in some splendour of a beautiful intelligence."

In his mind he has surpassed the abominable images of polytheistic idolatry. But he is still tempted to believe that somehow he can conceive a superb image of God in that special gift of God which is his mind, with which he can transcend the temporal and spatial limitations of the "here and now". This will prove to be impossible, since it would still confine the infinite God to a splendid appearance (*species*), cf. *De Trin.* 3, 2: *Aeternitas Patris ... locos tempora speciem ... excedit*, and 8, 48.

> "When my mind was here a prisoner of the error due to its weakness, it caught through the words of a prophet this way of expressing most beautiful thoughts about God: 'By the magnitude of His works and the beauty of His creatures the Creator of generations is duly discerned' (*Wisd. Sal.* 13:5)."

He is tempted to conceive the infinite God in some superb appearance. But the Old Testament shows another way: the beauty of the world is an indication of the inexplicable beauty of the Creator of the world. Unlike a statement made in the previous chapter (see *supra*, 33 f), here the Old Testament contradicts natural knowledge of God. In contrast with the Old Testament, natural knowledge of God is in constant danger of falling back into idolatry. However, the interpretation given by Hilary to this verse from the Old Testament is in accordance with, *inter alia*, an important tenet in Platonic philosophy:

> "The Creator of great things belongs Himself to the greatest things, and the Creator of the most beautiful things belongs Himself to the most beautiful things. And since the work transcends thought itself, it is certainly necessary that the Maker surpasses all thought."

The Creator is more than what is created, cf. Cicero, *De nat. deor.* 2, 33, 86: *ea quae efferant aliquid ex sese perfectiores habere naturas quam ea quae his efferantur*; Porphyry, *Sent.* 13 (cf. W. Theiler, *Porphyrius und Augustin*, *Forschungen zum Neuplatonismus*, Berlin 1966, p 174; E. R. Dodds, *Proclus, The Elements of Theology*, Oxford 1963², p 194), amongst Christian writers see e.g. Irenaeus, *Adv. Haer.* 4, 62; 2, 37, 3; 2, 56, 1; 3, 8, 3; Tertullian, *Adv. Marc.* 1, 13, 2; 2, 9, 7; *Adv. Herm.* 18, 5; Athanasius, *Contra Gentes* 1, 47. On the basis of this tenet Hilary can prove that if the beauty of the world is inexplicable, the beauty of the Creator of this world is even more inexplicable. This is already a brief summary of what will be said in the rest of this chapter.

> "Thus heaven, air, earth, seas, yea the whole universe is fair, which, because of its beauty, as also the Greeks teach, rightly seems to be called *kosmos, i.e.* world-order."

J. Doignon, *op. cit.*, p 130 n. 1, refers as background to Tertullian, *Apol.* 17, 1: ... *Deus unus est qui totam molem istam ... de nihilo expressit in ornamentum maiestatis suae, unde et Graeci nomen mundo 'kosmon' accommodaverunt*, see further *Adv. Herm.* 40, 2: *cum ornamenti nomine sit penes Graecos mundus* ...; *Adv. Marc.* 1, 13, 3: (... *mundi* ...) *cui et apud Graecos ornamenti et cultus, non sordium, nomen est.* Tertullian *inter alia* wants to show with this that the Greeks, unlike the Marcionites, do not despise this world.

> "But if our thought can estimate this beauty of the universe by a natural instinct in such a way (as also happens in the species of certain birds and tame beasts) that, whilst speech is below thought, nevertheless thought does not express with words the very thing it understands, which nevertheless – all speech being the product of thought – thought, understanding it, says to itself, is it then not necessary that the Lord of this beauty itself is understood to be the most beautiful of this total beauty? So whilst the splendid appearance of His eternal beauty evades the understanding of all intelligence, nevertheless the understanding of intelligence does not forsake the idea man has about this beauty. And God must be confessed to be the most beautiful in such a way that God is neither confined by the grasp of human understanding nor is outside the idea man has about Him."

Just like certain animals man can have an idea of the beauty of the world without being able to express it with words. The inability to express it is caused by the fact that speech is inferior to thought. Then certainly man can have an idea of the beauty of the Creator of the world without being able to define it. It is impossible to describe God's beauty, but man can have a certain idea about it. Just as the human mind could try to follow God's infinity without ever reaching the bounds of His infinity, man can think God's beauty without confining His beauty – either in thoughts or in words – to a certain, however beautiful, appearance. God's beauty is not defined by an understanding man has about it, but this beauty is hinted at by this idea. – J. Doignon, *op. cit.*, p 130 n. 3, refers to an interesting parallel in Cicero, *De fin.* 2, 33, 110, where it is said that certain animals have indications of piety and knowledge. – Hilary states repeatedly that speech is beyond thought (*ratio*), see *De Trin.* 5, 7, where he develops the scale of truth – thought – meaning – words: *Verba sensum enuntiant. Sensus rationis est motus. Rationis motum veritas incitat. Ex verbis igitur sensum sequamur et ex sensu rationem intellegamus et ex ratione veritatem adpraehendamus*, cf. 5, 8; 11, 44; 2, 7; 2, 15; *De Syn.* 5; 65; *In Matth.* 14, 12. J. Doignon, *St. Hilaire de Poitiers sur Matthieu* II, p 25 n. 14 refers as background to Quintilian, *Inst.* 9, 1, 16 and 19: ... *natura prius est concipere animo res quam enuntiare*, and *Saint Hilaire avant l'exile*, p 131, to Tertullian, *Adv. Prax.* 5, 5-6, see further *e.g.* Novatian, *De Trin.* 8, 40: *quem* (sc. *deum*) *mens omnis humana sentit, etiamsi non exprimit*; Athanasius, *Contra Arianos* 2, 35: καὶ ὁ μὲν τῶν ἀνθρώπων λόγος ... μόνον ἐστὶ σημαντικὸς τῆς τοῦ λαλοῦντος διανοίας. – On the more general theme that the beauty of the world is an indication of the beauty and goodness of the Creator see *infra*, 178 ff, *De Trin.* 3, 25.

The core of the argument given in this chapter is that whilst it is impossible to conceive in one's mind any, however, splendid, appearance of God (since such an appearance would always confine God) it is possible to have a pious opinion about God's beauty which transcends even the ineffable beauty of creation. It could be that behind this argument lies apart from the Biblical text quoted by Hilary also 2 *Cor.* 5:7: "Faith is our guide, we do not see Him".

CHAPTER 8

To reflect on God's infinity and incomprehensibility is the right activity of the human mind.

Translation and Commentary:

   (8) "Thus my mind, filled with the pursuit of this pious opinion and doctrine, rested on its own as in a quiet watch-tower upon this glorious conclu-

sion, understanding that nothing else had been left to it by its nature with which it could render a greater service or tribute to its Creator, than that it understood Him to be so great as on the one hand He cannot be understood and on the other hand He can be believed, for on the one hand the faith of a religion which it needs admits an intelligence and on the other hand the infinity of God's eternal power transcends this intelligence.''

Now he has found the *officium* he was looking for at the beginning of his spiritual journey, see *supra*, 16, *De Trin.* 1, 1 and *infra*, 52 f, *De Trin.* 1, 14. The possibility to know God has been left to him by his nature; this remark resumes what he said in *De Trin.* 1, 1 that he was looking for an *officium vel a natura manans*. – The 'pious opinion' (*pia opinio*) seems to be the natural knowledge of God, the 'doctrine' the instruction about God given by the Old Testament. In the reflection about the truth he has found he needs both faith and reason, but faith transcends reason, since one can believe in God's infinity but one cannot understand it. Hilary speaks repeatedly about the relationship of faith and reason (cf. for the following: C. F. A. Borchardt, *op. cit.*, pp 45 ff and J. E. Emmenegger, *The Functions of Faith and Reason in the Theology of Saint Hilary of Poitiers*, Washington D.C., 1947, esp. pp 68 ff): Man cannot understand that he has been created out of nothing by God and that God will prevent him from returning to nothing, see *De Trin.* 1, 12. Faith ranks above intelligence, reason, therefore God should in the first place be adored, see *De Trin.* 9, 72: *sensu vero non persequendus est, sed adorandus* (sc. *Deus*), but reason may and must follow faith, in the sense that faith makes use of reason, see *De Trin.* 1, 12: ... *ut ... non idcirco non crederet, quia non intellegeret, sed idcirco se meminisset intellegere posse, si crederet*; 2, 7: *Credendus est, intellegendus est, adorandus est* (sc. *Deus*) (here the order is important!); De Trin. 11, 23: *Intellegentiae vero a Deo donum fidei munus est, per quam infirmitas sensus gratiam revelationis meretur*. See further Hilary's views on *curiosity* (*infra*, 78 ff, *De Trin.* 2, 5) and on *authority* (*infra*, 127 f, *De Trin.* 3, 1).

CHAPTER 9

The hope of an incorruptible blessedness after death as a reward for devout knowledge of God and a correct conduct of life.

Translation and Commentary:

(9) ''But beneath all these reflections there was still a natural thought so that the hope of an incorruptible blessedness nourished the profession of piety, a blessedness which the saint opinion of God and good conduct of life could earn as the reward of a triumphant warrior.''

The right conduct of life was discussed in *De Trin.* 1, 1-3, the right knowledge of God in *De Trin.* 1, 4-8. These two problems are closely related and so is a third problem which was touched upon in *De Trin.* 1, 2

and 3: Can man overcome death? This question is now resumed. It is
common amongst Christians to describe their conversion as receiving an
answer to these questions, see *e.g.* Justin, *Dial.* 1, 4-5, where the denial of
providence and a careless life are discussed, and *Dial.* 8, 2 where it says
that the words of Christ have a certain menace to discourage people to
turn away from the right road, see J. C. M. van Winden, *op. cit.*, pp 30
ff, 119 and finally *Dial.* 3-6 where Platonism is examined with regard to
the knowledge of God and the immortality of the soul; cf. also Augustin
who comments on the questions he kept asking himself, *Conf.* 7, 5, 7:
Talia volvebam pectore misero, ingravidato curis mordacissimis de timore mortis et
non inventa veritate. – On eternal blessedness after death as a reward for a
soldier (implying that life is a *militia*) see further *De Trin.* 1, 14 (*infra*,
52 f); 11, 43: *... certissimum militiae nostrae stipendium est incorrupta aeternitas*;
Lactance, *Inst.* 7, 27, 16: *Intendamus ergo iustitiae ... infatigabilem militiam*
deo militemus ... ut victores ac devicto adversario triumphantes praemium virtutis
quod ipse promisit a domino consequamur. Hilary calls the hope of an eternal
blessedness which nourishes the profession of piety, a *sensus naturalis*. This
resumes the argument given in *De Trin.* 1, 2 that men are prompted by
nature itself to regard life as an eternal progress, and in *De Trin.* 1, 1 that
he is looking for an *officium* which *vel natura manans*, see *supra*, 16 f, 21.

> "For there would be no reward of the correct view about God, if all percep-
> tion were destroyed and annihilated by death and a kind of fall of a waning
> nature."

This is a common argument in favour of providence (extending beyond
man's death), see *e.g.* Justin, *Dial.* 1, 4-5; J. C. M. van Winden, *op. cit.*,
pp 30 ff.

> "Further reason itself pleaded that this is not worthy of God that He should
> have taken man into this life which is gifted with reason and wisdom under
> the law of waning life and eternal death: so that he was created out of non-
> existence only for this reason that, once created, he may not exist, whilst this
> was understood to be the only reason of our creation, that what was not
> should begin to be, not that what had begun to be should not be."

For Hilary's arguments in favour of immortality see *supra*, 22, *De Trin.* 1,
2. It could be that his statement that it was unworthy of God to have
created man with reason and wisdom and then let him die, has as its
background the argument in favour of immortality which says that
thanks to his reason man can transcend the 'here and now' and therefore
himself must transcend the 'here and now' of this life, cf. Lactance, *Inst.*
7, 9, 12: *apparet animam non interire neque dissolvi, sed manere in sempiternum,*
quia deum, qui sempiternus est, et quaerit et diligit (see H. W. A. van Rooijen-
Dijkman, *De vita beata, Het zevende boek van de Divinae Institutiones van Lac-*
tantius, Analyse en bronnenonderzoek, Leiden 1967, pp 74 ff), Athanasius,

Contra Gentes 32: Πῶς, τοῦ σώματος θνητοῦ κατὰ φύσιν ὄντος, λογίζεται ἄνθρωπος τὰ περὶ ἀθανασίας ... ἢ πῶς, προσκαίρου τοῦ σώματος ὄντος, τὰ αἰώνια φαντάζεται ἄνθρωπος; Clement Al., *Strom.* 6, 8, 68 (see L. Leone, *Sancti Athanasii Archiepiscopi Alexandriae Contra Gentes, Introduzione – Testo Critico – Traduzione*, Napels 1965, p 65.) – For the statement that it is *unworthy* of God first to create man and then let him die, Athanasius provides a striking parallel, *De Inc.* 6: οὐκ ἄξιον γὰρ ἦν τῆς ἀγαθότητος τοῦ θεοῦ τὰ ὑπ᾽ αὐτοῦ γενόμενα διαφθείρεσθαι ... οὐκοῦν ἔδει τοὺς ἀνθρώπους μὴ ἀφιέναι φέρεσθαι τῇ φθορᾷ διὰ τὸ ἀπρεπὲς καὶ ἀνάξιον εἶναι τοῦτο τῆς τοῦ θεοῦ ἀγαθότητος: – The parallels J. Doignon, *op. cit.*, p 137, produces from Tertullian do not say very much, since they refer to God's wrath (*De anima* 16, 5) and to the idea that it is unworthy of a god not to have created anything (*Adv. Marc.* 1, 11, 6); – there is a closer parallel in *Adv. Marc.* 2, 27, 1: ... *quia nihil tam dignum deo quam salus hominis*, this is said in connection with the incarnation, but it is put in such general terms that it can be applied to any act of God, and the act of granting immortality will certainly have been regarded by both Tertullian and Hilary as part of *hominis salus* (cf. also *Adv. Marc.* 2, 26, 2: ... *nihil deo indignum est quod efficit deo credere.*) J. C. M. van Winden draws our attention to a most interesting parallel in Gregory of Nyssa, who says that if God creates man with all the qualities of wisdom and likeness of God and then lets man die, God can be compared with playing children: they diligently make things and then quickly destroy them, see *In Sanctum Pascha* (*Gregorii Nysseni Opera* IX, 253, 22 ff).

CHAPTER 10

The revelation given in the New Testament, especially in the Prologue of the Gospel according to St. John, surpasses the one given in the Old Testament and natural knowledge of God.

Translation and Commentary:

(10) "My soul, however, became tired, partly because of fear for itself, partly for its body. And while it contained its firm conviction about the pious confession of God, and also had come to harbour a deep anxiety about itself and the bodily dwelling which must, it thought, share its destruction, then after the knowledge of the Law and the Prophets it also learned the following truths taught by the Gospels and the Apostles."

Despite the rational arguments given for immortality the fear of death has not subsided. Obviously a more perfect revelation is needed. Acquaintance with the Old Testament has provided him with a pious view of God, *viz.*, that God is in His nature and power infinite. But he has not yet found a solution for his fear of death. This fear of death will be overcome by belief in the revelation given in the New Testament. In this context Hilary only gives a quotation from *John* 1, but in 1, 13 he will quote from one of the letters of Paul. Since he regards the New Testament as a doctrinal unity, allowing him to interpret the verse written by one author with a verse written by another author (see *De Trin.* 10, 42: *Praestant autem sibi mutuam Evangelia plenitudem: dum alia ex aliis, quia omnia unius Spiritus praedicatio sit, intelleguntur.*), *evangelicae adque apostolicae instituta* should be translated with 'the truths taught by the gospels and apostles'. Hilary focuses first of all on the Prologue of the gospel according to St. John.

> "In the beginning was the Word, and the Word was with God, and the Word was God. This was in the beginning with God. All things were made through Him, and without Him not anything was made. That which was made in Him is life, and the life was the light of men, and the light shines in darkness, and the darkness apprehended it not. There was a man sent from God, whose name was John. He came for witness, that he might bear witness of the light. He was not the light, but he was in order to bear witness of the light. That was the true light, which lightens every man that comes into this world, and the world was made through Him, and the world knew Him not. He came into His own things, and they that were His own received Him not. But to as many as received Him, He gave the power to become sons of God, who were born not of blood nor of the will of man nor of the will of the flesh, but of God. And the Word became flesh and dwelt amongst us, and we beheld His glory, glory as of the Only-begotten from the Father, full of grace and truth."

The way Hilary interprets this section from the fourth Gospel and the way he stresses the differences between what is said here and what is sensed in natural knowledge of God, is indicative of his views on the relation between Pagan philosophy and Christian theology. In this respect there is a clear difference between Hilary and Augustin. As is well known, Augustin tells us in the *De Civitate Dei* that a Platonist said that the first verses of the fourth gospel ought to be written on conspicuous places in all churches (indicating that what was said there was in accordance with Platonism), 10, 29, 2: *Quod initium sancti Evangelii, cui nomen est, Secundum Joannem, quidem Platonicus ... aureis litteris conscribendum, et per omnes Ecclesias in locis eminentissimis proponendum esse dicebat.* The Platonist Amelius says, according to Eusebius, *Praep. Ev.* 11, 19, 1, that the Christian doctrine of the eternal Logos, its incarnation and ascension to heaven is derived from Greek philosophy (see on this subject P. Courcelle, *Recherches sur les Confessions de Saint Augustin*, Paris 1968[2], pp 168-174). Augustin acknowledges that the Platonists do know about an eternal Logos which was in the beginning with God, but do not (want to) know about its incarnation in humility, because they themselves know no humility, see *Conf.* 7, 9, 13 ff. We shall see that according to Hilary there is a much wider gap between the philosophical knowledge of God (which to Hilary is not the Neo-Platonic one, since he does not seem to be familiar with this philosophy, his source of philosophical knowledge being Cicero) and the doctrine of the New Testament.

> "Here my soul makes an advance beyond the understanding of natural reason and it is taught more than it was able to think so far about God. For it learns that its Creator is God from God. It hears that the Word was God and was in the beginning with God. It understands that the light of the world was abiding in the world and not known by the world. It understands that He also came into His own things and that they who were His own did not receive Him, but that they who did receive Him due to their faith advanced to be sons of God, being born not of the embrace of the flesh nor of the conception of the blood nor of bodily satisfaction, but of God; finally that the Word has become flesh and dwelt amongst us and that His glory was seen, which as from the Only-begotten from the Father, is perfect with grace and truth."

This is a mere paraphrase of the text from *John* 1 quoted above and an indication of what will now be discussed: What light will the belief in the eternal Logos and its incarnation cast on the problems discussed so far: the right knowledge of God, the right conduct of life and man's mortality?

CHAPTER 11

The knowledge of the Father and the Son. Faith leads men to become sons of God. This faith is made possible through the incarnation.

Translation and Commentary:

> **(11)** "Here already my trembling and frightened soul found more hope than it expected. And first it was introduced to the knowledge of God the Father. And what it first thought with its natural reason about the eternity, infinity and splendid appearance of its Creator it now here learned to belong to God the Only-begotten as well."

The thoughts about God's eternity, infinity and splendid appearance are said to be the results of natural knowledge, but in chapters 5-7 these were also expressed with quotations from the Old Testament, see *supra*, 30 ff. Here again appears Hilary's belief that the Old Testament and natural knowledge of God (which has surpassed polytheistic idolatry) are on the same level, whilst the New Testament surpasses both, since it also teaches God the Son. On the revelation given in Christ and the Old Testament see further *infra*, 160 f, *De Trin.* 3, 17.

> "It did not unloose its faith into a plurality of gods, for it heard that He is God of God, nor did it fall into the error of attributing a difference of nature to this God of God, for it learned that this God of God is full of grace and truth, nor did it regard this God of God as later in time (than the Father), because it learned that He was as God in the beginning with God."

This is a brief summary of his views on the relationship between Father and Son, the various aspects of which will be discussed later; on the rejection of a plurality of gods see *infra*, 95 ff; on the rejection of a difference of nature between Father and Son see *infra*, 69 f; on the rejection of the idea that the Son is later in time than the Father (implying a temporal growth in God) see *infra*, 102.

> "And next it learned that faith in this saving knowledge is very rare, but that its reward is very great, for those who were His own did not receive it and those who did receive it have been promoted to sons of God, not by a birth of flesh but of faith. It learned that to be sons of God is not a necessity but a possibility, for whilst the Divine gift is offered to all it is not bestowed by heredity but received as a reward of free choice."

On the very few who become sons of God see *infra*, 149, *De Trin.* 3, 11; on the difference between free will and nature see *infra*, 134 f, *De Trin.* 3, 4. Being a son of God is a reward, this is stressed repeatedly by Hilary, see *In Matth.* 2, 3: *Non enim successio carnis quaeritur, sed fidei hereditas. Dignitas igitur originis in operum consistit exemplis et prosapiae gloria fidei imitatione retinetur; De Trin.* 2, 35 (see *infra*, 123 f); 8, 12: *Honorem ergo acceptum a Patre Filius omnibus qui in se credituri sunt dedit, non utique voluntatem: quae si data esset, non haberet fides praemium, cum fidem nobis necessitas affixae voluntatis inferet*; 12, 13: *Fuimus enim aliquando filii iracundiae, sed filii Deo per spiritum adoptionis effecti, et dici id meremur potius quam nascimur; In Ps.* II 16: ... *cum libertatem nobis voluntatis ad bonitatem promerendam reliquisset, quia meritum naturae necessitas non haberet* ... Whilst firmly rejecting the idea that the sonship of God is given by nature and against this stressing that it is a reward for free choice, he also says that the deification of man, which is a consequence of the sonship, is a gift received through the sacrament of baptism and the eucharist, Christ verily dwells in our nature and there is not merely a unity of will between Christ and us, see *De Trin.* 8, 7-17, especially 8, 8: *Quod unum sunt in tanta gentium, conditionum, sexuum diversitate, numquid ex assensu voluntatis est, aut ex sacramenti unitate, quia his et baptisma sit unum, et unum Christum induti omnes sunt? Quid ergo hic animorum concordia faciet, cum per id unum sint, quod uno Christo per naturam unius baptismi induantur*; 8, 13: ... *interrogo utrumne per naturae veritatem hodie Christus in nobis sit, an per concordiam voluntatis? Si enim vere Verbum caro factum est, et vere nos Verbum carnem cibo dominico sumimus, quomodo non naturaliter manere in nobis existimandus est* ...? 8, 17: *Haec idcirco a nobis commemorata sunt, quia voluntatis tantum inter Patrem et Filium unitatem haeretici mentientes, unitatis nostrae ad Deum utebuntur exemplo, tamquam nobis ad Filium, et per Filium ad Patrem, obsequio tantum ac voluntate religionis unitis, nulla per sacramentum carnis et sanguinis naturalis communionis proprietas indulgeretur.* Whether man wants to receive the sacrament is an act of free will, the gift of the sacrament surpasses free will. Harnack's description of the "physische Erlösungslehre" of the Greek fathers, *viz.*, that this is like an ellipse with moral life and the gift of divinization through the incarnation and the sacraments as its two poles, applies to Hilary as well, see *Lehrbuch der Dogmengeschichte* II, Berlin 1909[4], p 57, cf. p 167 (on Hilary's doctrine of the divinization of man see further *infra*, 49 f, *De Trin*. 1, 13).

> "And lest just this fact that everybody has the possibility of becoming a son of God should stagger the weakness of our trembling faith – for most we desire, but least expect, that which because of its very difficulty we find very hard to hope for –, God the Word became flesh, in order that through the incarnation of the Word God flesh might make progress towards God the Word."

The incarnation of the Word is an adaptation to human weakness, which can hardly believe that men have the possibility of becoming sons of God, cf. *De Trin*. 3, 9 (*infra*, 142); Athanasius, *De Inc*. 8, Irenaeus, *Adv. Haer*. 4, 62, 63. On the progress towards towards God see *infra*, 46 f, *De Trin*. 1, 12.

> "And lest the incarnate Word was either anything other than God the Word or not flesh of our body, He dwelt amongst us, in order that whilst He 'dwelt' He remained nothing else but God, and that whilst 'dwelling amongst us' in His incarnation He became nothing else but of our flesh: by deigning to assume the flesh He is not destitute of His own attributes, because as the Only-begotten of the Father, full of grace and truth, He is both perfect in His own attributes and truly in ours."

Two things are stressed: in the incarnation Christ remained truly God and in the incarnation a truly human body was assumed. That Christ in the incarnation remained God is stated time and again by Hilary, see *e.g. In Ps*. II 11, CXXXVIII 2, *De Trin*. 3, 3, 16; 5, 17, 18; 9, 38; 10, 7, 66; 11, 16. On the verity of Christ's human body, see *infra*, 165 ff, *De Trin*. 3, 20.

CHAPTER 12

Imbued with this faith man believes the acts of God, though he cannot understand them.

Translation and Commentary:

> (12) "So my mind gladly accepted this instruction in the divine mystery, making progress towards God through the flesh, called to a new birth through faith and entrusted with the power to win heavenly regeneration."

The mind makes progress towards God through the flesh; this was briefly stated in *De Trin*. 1, 11 and will be said of the whole life in *De Trin*. 1, 14; as background one may refer to Irenaeus who says that there is a constant growth towards God, in the knowledge of God, see *Adv. Haer.* 4, 63, 2: *homine vero paulatim proficiente, et perveniente ad perfectum, id est, proximum infecto fieri*; 4, 34, 7; 4, 19, 2; 4, 21, 2; 2, 41, 3; cf. also Tertullian, *Adv. Marc.* 2, 4, 1 (see G. Quispel, *De Bronnen van Tertullianus' Adversus Marcionem*, Leiden 1943, p 39). – A regeneration is necessary for faith in the acts of God, cf. *De Trin.* 1, 18 (*infra*, 59), 5, 35. This regeneration makes us sons of God and is a regeneration to eternal life, see *De Trin.* 1, 13 (*infra*, 49 f) and 8, 7: *Omnes enim renati erant ad innocentiam, ad immortalitatem, ad cognitionem Dei, ad spei fidem.* This meaning is present here in *De Trin.* 1, 12 as well: he has been given the power to win the heavenly regeneration, which *inter alia* is the hope of immortality:

> "Being conscious of the providential care of its Father and Creator it estimated that it could not be annihilated by Him who had brought it out of nothing into this very being."

Hilary reproduces the argument, which he had given earlier, for immortality, see *supra*, 22, *De Trin.* 1, 2 and *supra*, 41 f, *De Trin.* 1, 9. It is interesting that he adds no new one in this context, where he discusses the highest stage of revelation, *viz.*, the incarnation of the Word God. He could have found an argument for immortality, derived from the incarnation, in Irenaeus, who says that if human flesh could not be saved (in the resurrection), the Word would not have become flesh, see *Adv. Haer.* 5, 14, 1: *Si enim non haberet caro salvari, nequaquam Verbum Dei caro factum esset*, cf. Tertullian, *De res. mort.* 2, 6: *obducti dehinc de deo carnis auctore et de Christo carnis redemptore, iam et de resurrectione carnis revincentur, congruenter scilicet et deo carnis auctori et Christo carnis redemptori.*

> "And it estimated all this as above the perception of human intelligence, for reason, on the level of common opinion, is incapable of conceiving the heavenly plan and thinks that only what it perceives in itself or what it can produce out of its own power exists in nature."

Hilary had already stated that the infinity of God's nature and power exceeds human understanding (see *supra*, 37 ff). Now he stresses that God's saving acts in the incarnation of Christ are beyond human understanding as well. Human mind is at fault if it measures God's power with its own laws; – on this important thought in Hilary's theology see *infra*, 176 ff, 181 f, *De Trin.* 3, 24 and 3, 26.

> "But my mind measured the mighty workings of God wrought in the scale of the splendour of His eternal power, not by its own understanding, but by its boundless faith. So that the fact that it could not understand that God was in the beginning with God and that the Word became flesh and dwelt amongst us, was not a reason not to believe, but was a reason for it to bear in mind that it could understand if it believed."

Human mind and understanding cannot grasp God's infinity (see *supra*, 37 ff), only faith can believe it, if it transcends the limitations of mind and understanding. On the relation between faith and understanding see *supra*, 40, *De Trin*. 1, 9 and *infra*, 83, 91, 163. On the eternal generation of God the Son as an indication of God's omnipotence see *infra*, 138 f, *De Trin*. 3, 6.

CHAPTER 13

Faith, not impeded by useless philosophical questions, can enjoy the fruits of the incarnation, *viz.*, the remission of sins and the gift of immortality.

Translation and Commentary:

> (13) "And lest my mind be held back by some erroneous straying of secular wisdom, it was in addition instructed by the following words of the apostle towards the perfectly unconditioned faith of this pious confession: 'Beware lest any man spoil you through philosophy and vain deceit, after the tradition of men, centered on the elements of the world, and not after Christ, for in Him dwells all the fulness of the Godhead bodily; in whom you were also circumcised with a circumcision not made with hands in putting off the body of the flesh, but with the circumcision of Christ, buried with Him in baptism, wherein also you have risen again through the faith in the working of God, who raised Him from the dead. And you, when you were in sins and in the uncircumcision of your flesh, He has quickened with Him, having forgiven all your sins, blotting out the bond which was against us by its ordinances, which was contrary to us; and He has taken it out of the way, nailing it to the cross; having put off the flesh, and He made a show of powers openly, triumphing over them through confidence in Himself (*Col* 2:8-15)'."

On Hilary's attitude towards Pagan philosophy (in which context *Col.* 2:8 ff plays an important role) see *infra*, 91 ff, *De Trin*. 2, 12 and 74 ff, *De Trin*. 2, 5 (on curiosity).

> "Steadfast faith rejects the sophistical and useless enquiries of philosophy, and truth refuses, by falling before the treachery of human fooleries, to deliver itself as a prey to falsehood. It does not confine God to the limits of the common understanding, nor judge after the elements of the world concerning Christ, since in Him dwells the fulness of the godhead bodily; so that, since in Him there is an infinity of eternal power, the power of His eternal infinity transcends every embracing by an earthly mind."

On the useless enquiries (*quaestiones*) see *infra*, 92, De Trin. 2, 12; on the statement that God cannot be confined to the limits of common sense see *infra*, 176 ff, *De Trin*. 3, 24. – Christ cannot be judged after the elements of the world. Elsewhere Hilary gives the reason why this is impossible: the elements of this world have been created out of nothing, whilst Christ has no temporal beginning; they are either lifeless or have made progress towards life, whilst Christ is life; they have been made by God, whilst Christ is God, see *De Trin.* 8, 53: *Elementa enim mundi ex nihilo substiterunt. Sed Christus non de substantibus manet, nec coepit ad originem, sed originem ab origine sumpsit aeternam. Elementa enim mundi aut inanima sunt, aut ad animam profecerunt. Sed Christus vita est, ex Deo vivente in viventem Deum natus. Elementa mundi a Deo sunt instituta, non Deus sunt. Christus ex Deo Deus hoc totum est ipse quod Deus est.* This must be seen in connection with the tenet (see *supra*, 38, *De Trin.* 1, 7) that the cause transcends that which is caused. – On the divine infinity which transcends human mind see *supra*, 33 ff, *De Trin.* 1, 6.

> "Drawing us towards His divine nature He no longer binds us to a bodily observation of His precepts, and he does not teach us any longer through the Law, which is a mere shadow (of what will come), the rites of circumcising the flesh, but He wants that our mind, circumcised of all vices, should by the cleansing of the sins purify all natural necessity of the body."

Participation in the divine nature, which is granted through the incarnation, transcends the observation of the precepts given in the Old Testament. On the function of the Law as the shadow of what will come, cf. *In Ps* XCI 1: *Post legis tempora et cognitionem veritatis, convenit corpus ipsum potius quam umbram corporis contueri. Lex enim eorum, quae in Domino nostro Jesu Christo implenda erant, speciem complectitur. Non ipsa veritas, sed in ea meditatio veritatis, utilis fide potius quam effectu, imitatione quam genere.* See further *infra*, 160 f, *De Trin.* 3, 17 on the difference between the Old and the New Testament. The difference between carnal and spiritual circumcision is in *De Trin.* 9, 9 expressed in the following way: *Circumcidimur itaque, non circumcisione carnali, sed circumcisione Christi, id est, in novum hominem renati.*

> "We had to be buried with His death in baptism, in order to return to eternal life, since rebirth to life was death to (former) life, and dying to our sins we were reborn to immortality, because He abandoned His immortality in order to die for us, so that we might be raised from death together with Him to immortality."

There is a *return* to eternal life, so man was originally created as an immortal being. Because of sin eternal life was lost, so rebirth to immortality must be a dying to sinful life. This return or rebirth to immortality is possible because man's Creator abandoned His immortality in order to die for man, so that man might be raised with Him to immortality, which was Christ's original state and which was the original destination of man. This is in fact deification of man through the incarnation. Deification, to Hilary as to the Greek fathers, implies two things: in the first place the gift of immortality, see *e.g. De Trin.* 3, 13 (*infra*, 152 f); 4, 42: ... *corruptionem carnis humanae gloria corporis sui perimens*; 10, 63: ... *Christum non sibi*

mori, sed vitae nostrae, ut per immortalis Dei mortem, mortalium vita renovetur, cf.
further 10, 71; 11, 35, 36; in the second place it implies remission of sins:

> "For He took upon Him the flesh of sin, that by assuming our flesh He
> might forgive sins, because He shares flesh with us by wearing it, not by
> sinning in it. He blotted out, through death, the sentence of death, that by a
> new creation of our race in Himself He might sweep away the penalty ap-
> pointed by the former decree. He permitted Himself to be nailed to the
> cross, in order that by the curse of the cross He might abolish all the curses
> of earthly damnation by nailing them to the cross."

On the theme of remission of sins cf. *De Trin.* 9, 9-10; 10, 47. On the so-
called "physische Erlösung" which implies pardon of sins and the gift of
immortality cf. *supra*, see R. M. Hübner, *Die Einheit des Leibes Christi bei
Gregor von Nyssa. Untersuchungen zum Ursprung der 'physischen' Erlösungslehre*,
Leiden 1974 (this book is weak so far as it is meant as a criticism of Harnack's views, cf. E. P. Meijering, *Theologische Urteile über die
Dogmengeschichte. Ritschls Einfluss auf von Harnack*, Leiden 1978, pp 74 f,
but excellent in its analysis of the thoughts of Gregory and other Greek
fathers). Christ shared our bodily existence without sinning, this theme is
elaborated in the tenth book (cf. P. Smulders, Eusèbe d'Emèse comme
source du *De Trinitate* d'Hilaire de Poitiers, *Hilaire et son temps*, p 211). In
the incarnation Jesus Christ wrought His own body through the virgin
birth and therefore did not come into existence through sin (which
manifests itself in sexual intercourse, see H. von Campenhausen, Die
Jungfrauengeburt in der alten Kirche, *Urchristliches und Altkirchliches*,
Tübingen 1979, pp 52 ff, who shows that this view is already to be found
in Origen and is typical of Ambrose and Augustin, see further *infra*, 109 ff);
this causes his sinlessness, 10, 25: *Habuit enim corpus, sed originis suae proprium, neque ex vitiis humanae conceptionis existens, sed in formam corporis nostri
virtutis suae potestate subsistens: gerens quidem nos per formam servi, sed a peccatis
et a vitiis humani corporis liber*; in the incarnation the Word remains what it
is and therefore it is sinless, see 10, 26 (and *infra*, 164), cf. 10, 47: *Portans
enim peccata nostra, peccati nostri scilicet corpus assumens, tamen ipse non peccat*.

> "Finally He suffered in man in order to put the powers to shame, because
> He, God, going to die according to Scripture, He also triumphed over these
> powers because of the trust in Himself as gaining victory; because, Himself
> immortal and unable to be overcome by death, He died for eternal life of
> those who are mortal."

As man Christ suffered, but being God and immortal Christ could not be
overcome by death, but conquered death and put to shame the powers of
sin. In His suffering Christ's existence in a human body is apparent, in
His resurrection His divinity, see *De Trin.* 9, 10-11, especially 9, 11:
Naturam Dei in virtute resurrectionis intellege: dispensationem hominis in morte

cognosce. Et cum sint utraque suis gesta naturis, unum tamen Christum Jesum eum memento esse qui utrumque est; 10, 48: *secundum hominem pro nobis infirma omnia pati, sed secundum Deum in his omnibus trumphare* (see on the subject of Christ's passibility further C. F. A. Borchardt, *op. cit.*, pp 17 ff); cf. Irenaeus, *Adv. Haer.* 3, 20, 3: *Sicut enim homo erat ut temptaretur, sic et Verbum ut glorificaretur, requiescente quidem Verbo ut posset temptari et inhonorari et crucifigi et mori, absorpto autem homine in eo quod vincit et sustinet et resurgit et adsumitur.* The same idea already occurs in the *Homily on the Passion* of Melito of Sardes, 47 f: καὶ ὡς ἄνθρωπος ταφεὶς ἀνέστη ἐκ νεκρῶν ὡς θεός, φύσει θεὸς ὢν καὶ ἄνθρωπος. – Hilary stresses that the cross of Christ and His death is not a natural necessity caused by human weakness, but that it is Christ's triumph, see *De Trin.* 10, 48: *quis, rogo, furor est, repudiata doctrinae apostolicae fide immutare sensum religionis, et totum hoc ad contumeliam imbecillis rapere naturae, quod et voluntas est et sacramentum, quod et potestas est et fiducia et triumfus? Triumfus plane est quaeri ad crucem etc*; cf. further *De Trin.* 9, 10-11, *In Ps* LIII 12 (where he says of this belief that Christ did not die because of a natural necessity: *Quod ... frequenter, imo semper praedicamus*), *In Ps* LXVII 2, 23; Athanasius, *De Inc.* 22, 29, 30.

Here Hilary's explanations of the verses quoted from *Col* 2:8-15 end.

> "These acts of God, wrought in a manner beyond the comprehension of human nature, do no longer fall into the natural understanding of our minds, for the work of an infinite Eternity requires, in order to be grasped, an infinite judgement."

On the infinite nature of God which transcends all human understanding see *supra*, 33 ff and *infra*, 78 ff. Unlike Augustin Hilary believes that secular philosophy cannot know that there is an eternal Word of God (see *supra*, 42 ff), but just like Augustin he stresses that the act of the incarnation is beyond rational knowledge.

> "So that when God becomes man, when the Immortal One dies, when the Eternal One is buried, this does not belong to the order of rational understanding but is an exceptional power, in the same way in the opposite case it does not belong to the order of intellect but of power that out of man He is God, out of death immortal, out of grave eternal. So we are raised by God together with Christ through His death. But, since in Christ there is the fulness of the Godhead, we have both an indication of God the Father who raises us in Him who died and (an indication) that Christ should only be confessed as God in the fulness of the Godhead."

As the act of the incarnation is beyond man's rational understanding, so is the act of Christ's glorification in the resurrection. This latter act is a guarantee for man's resurrection. But then it is necessary to confess Christ as the true God. This is what the Arians refuse to do (see *infra*, 69 f), so their doctrine can be no answer to the question: How can death be overcome? If our assumption is correct that there are sly digs on the Arians in the Prologue to the *De Trinitate*, then he has by now suggested that they do not have the right answers to the three principal questions: a) "What is the right conduct of life" (see *supra*, 17 f); b) "What is the right knowledge of God" see *supra*, 24) and c) "How can death be overcome?"

CHAPTER 14

Life is a preparation for eternity.

Translation and Commentary:

> **(14)** "In this calm consciousness of its safety my soul gladly and hopefully had taken its rest, and it so little feared the intervention of death belonging to this life, that it regarded it even as leading towards eternal life."

These reflections are the right use of the *otium* man can find in life (see *supra*, 16 ff, *De Trin.* 1, 1, and *supra*, 39 f, *De Trin.* 1, 8, cf. *De Trin.* 1, 37: *Ego quidem hoc vel praecipuum vitae meae officium debere me tibi, Pater omnipotens Deus, conscius sum, ut te omnis sermo meus et sensus loquatur.*) As appears from *In Ps.* I, 6 Hilary is well aware that Pagans know about this *otium* as well: *Possunt enim haec et in saeculari viro reperiri: ... ut honorum dignitatibus privatae et tranquillae vitae otium anteponat* (see on this text further *supra*, 23, *De Trin.* 1, 5); on the *otium* which should be used for private meditation see further *In Ps.* LXII 1), and this *otium* can only be found if the fear of death is overcome. The fear of death is overcome by the thought that it is unworthy of God first to create man and then to annihilate him in death (see *supra*, 42), and through faith in Christ's resurrection which is a guarantee for our resurrection. – The way in which Hilary describes the absence of fear of death is, as J. Doignon, *op. cit.*, p 151 states, typically Stoic; see, apart from the quotation from Cicero, *Tusc.* 2, 1, 2, also the famous statement by Seneca, *Ep.* 65, 24 that death is *aut finis aut transitus.* To Hilary it is, of course, only a *transitus*.

> "And it not only did not regard the life of this body as a burden of affliction or illness so that it believed it to be what the alphabet is to the children, medicine to the sick, swimming to shipwrecked sailors, education to the young men, military service to the future commanders, *viz.*, the forbearance of temporal things which leads to the reward of blessed immortality."

Temporal life is, of course, only then a preparation for eternal life, if man has the right knowledge of God. The non-believers do not have this knowledge and they are therefore like shipwrecked sailors who cannot be served by the incarnation of the Word, see *In Ps.* LI 13. On life as a progress towards eternity see further *supra*, 21, 41. The philosophers, too,

advocate a *tolerantia* or *patientia praesentium* (see *supra*, 21 f, 23, *De Trin.* 1,
2-3). Hilary obviously wants to say that man can only reach this virtue if
he firmly believes in eternal life after death.

> "My soul even proclaimed – because of the duty of the episcopate which
> had been laid upon me – to others what it believed for itself, extending its
> office to work on the salvation of all men."

On his duty as a bishop see *De Trin.* 6, 2: ... *officii necessitatem qua hoc
ecclesiae episcopus praedicationis evangelicae debeo ministerium* (cf. Irenaeus, *Adv.
Haer.*, Praef. ad V: ... *quoniam et in administratione sermonis positi sumus*);
a bishop must be a man of knowledge and moral innocence, see *De Trin.*
8, 1 (*supra*, 25).

Here his way towards true knowledge of God has come to an end. He
has reviewed the moral and intellectual life of the *homo carnalis* and the
homo animalis, he has shown that the former life is rejectable and the latter
inadequate, and he has found the moral and intellectual life of the *homo
spiritalis*. This life is made perfectly clear in the New Testament
preaching about the eternal Word of God and its incarnation. He has
found the destiny of his life by meditating about this truth and by
preaching it as a bishop to others.

All could now be fine and peaceful – if only it were not for the heretics
who spoil everything.

II. THE HERETICS' ATTACK ON THE ORTHODOX
DOCTRINE
(15-19)

The heretics disturb the peaceful quietness. Refusing to submit
themselves to God's revelation, they dare to establish their own doctrines. Hilary primarily thinks of the Sabellians and the Arians. Against
them he states the true and eternal divinity of Christ. In order to understand the divine truth man must be reborn, and in expounding the divine
truth man must be aware of the inadequacy of human images for the
Divine.

CHAPTER 15

The characterization of the heretics.

Translation and Commentary:

> **(15)** "When I was thus engaged, there emerged spirits of an impious
> rashness, desperate in themselves and raging against all, men who

measured God's mighty nature with the infirmity of their own nature. They
did not strive to ascend to an infinite idea of infinite things, but to confine
what cannot be confined to the limits of their understanding, and to be
themselves masters of religion, whilst the work of religion is a service of obedience: men unaware of what they are, negligent of what is Divine, correc-
tors of the divine precepts.''

The heretics are desperate in themselves and raging against others, this is
said repeatedly by Hilary in similar words (cf. for the following: I. Opelt,
Hilarius von Poitiers als Polemiker, *Vigiliae Christianae* (27), 1973, pp 215
ff), see *De Trin.* 1, 33: ... *desperatissimos homines* ...; 5, 10: *O desperatae mentis furor perdite!*: 8, 2: *homines mente perversi et professione fallaces, et spe inanes,
et sermone viperei* ...; 8, 3: *istis haeretico furore amentibus sollicitudinis maximae
est ... ut ... ultra spem vitae nostrae vitae suae desperatione potiores sint*; 8, 37:
Nisi forte eo usque ultimae desperationis furor audebit erumpere; 9, 2: *stulto atque
imperito furore adversus divinitatis naturam loquuntur*, cf. 5, 38; 6, 15; 6, 17,
47; 7, 6. This could be in line with Quintilian, *Inst.* 7, 2, 35 ff, who
recommends a proof derived from causes or motives, such as anger,
hatred, fear, greed or hope; the accuser must make it plausible that these
motives may lead a man to commit any crime: *Proxima est ex causis probatio
in quibus haec maxime spectantur, ira, odium, metus, cupiditas, spes ... quorum si
quid in reum conveniet, accusatoris est efficere ut ad quidquid faciendum causae valere
videantur* (cf. also the dark colours with which Tertullian pictures the
heretics in *Adv. Prax.* 1, *Adv. Herm.* 1, and especially *Adv. Marc.* 1). The
temerity (*temeritas*) of the heretics appears in their audacity to contradict
or neglect the revelation given in Scripture, see *De Trin.* 4, 26: ... *quae inreligiositatis temeritas, aut ignorare haec aut non ignorata neglegere!* 5, 10: *O stulta
caecae inpietatis temeritas! Audis Deum et Deum ... Quid tu subicis verum et non
verum?* etc; 7, 16: ... *ne temeritas contradicendi sub libertate diversae in hominibus
intellegentiae audeat professionibus divini de se testimonii contraire.* Irenaeus and
Tertullian also attack the heretics for altering the tradition of the apostles,
see *e.g.* Irenaeus, *Adv. Haer.* 1, 25, 2: ... *et solus* (sc. *Marcion*) *manifeste ausus
est circumcidere Scripturas*; 3, 1, 1: *nec enim fas est dicere quoniam ante
praedicaverunt* (sc. *apostoli*) *quam perfectam haberent agnitionem; sicut quidam au-
dent dicere, gloriantes emendatores se esse apostolorum* (cf. 3, 11, 12; 3, 14, 4; 4,
53, 1); Tertullian, *Adv. Marc.* 1, 19, 5; 2, 17, 1; 4, 4, 5: *nisi quod humanae
temeritatis, non divinae auctoritatis, negotium est haeresis, quae sic semper emendat
evangelia dum vitiat.* – The heretics fail to understand the infinity of God,
which asks for an infinite faith, and therefore confine God to the measure
of their understanding, just like polytheistic idolaters, see *supra*, 30 ff.
They want to be themselves masters of religion (instead of letting God be
the Master of religion), this is what Hilary does not want to be, see *De
Trin.* 12, 52: *Neque in id umquam stultitiae atque impietatis erumpam, ut om-*

nipotentiae tuae sacramentorumque arbiter, hunc infirmitatis meae sensum ultra infinitatis tuae religiosam opinionem ... erigam. The work of religion is the service of obedience and it is here that man reaches his true honour, see *supra*, 25, *De Trin.* 1, 3. The heretics are unaware of themselves, *i.e.* unaware of their human weakness, see on this *infra*, 61 f, *De Trin.* 1, 19; they are negligent of the Divine, this accusation is repeated in *De Trin.* 4, 26 and 6, 8 (cf. *supra*, 24); they claim to improve on divine precepts, cf. *De Trin.* 6, 8; 6, 17: *O gravissimum humanae stultitiae atque insolentiae dedecus, professionis suae de se Deum non modo arguere non credendo, sed emendando damnare*; 10, 65; 12, 3.

Hereby the heretics have been introduced as men with wicked motives and horrifying arrogance. Now a brief description of their doctrines will be given.

CHAPTER 16

The doctrines of Sabellius and Arius.

Translation and Commentary:

> **(16)** "Not to touch upon the other most stupid strivings of the heretics – concerning which, however, when the course of our argument gives occasion, we shall not be silent – some of them corrupt the mystery of the faith of the Gospel in such a way that they deny – under the pious cloak of professing only one God – the birth of God the Only-begotten, so that there is an extension into man rather than a descent, and that He, who during the time that He took our flesh was the Son of Man, had not been previously nor is the Son of God; lest in Him there be a birth of God, but an identicality of Begetter and Begotten, so that the unbroken continuity in the incarnation might preserve the incorruptible faith in the one God, as they believe, since the Father extends Himself into the Virgin and is born as His own Son."

The doctrine which is rejected here is the Sabellian one as appears from *De Trin.* 2, 4: *ut Sabellius Patrem extendit in Filium*; 2, 23: *Patrem et Filium, si audet, Sabellius eundem praedicet; De Syn.* 45: *Quidam enim ausi sunt innascibilem Deum usque ad sanctam virginem substantiae dilatatione protendere*; cf. *De Trin.* 10, 50. The Sabellians deny the eternal generation of Christ as a separate entity, because this would endanger the unity of God. The incarnation is not the descent of the eternal Only-begotten God, but an extension of the Father. So Jesus Christ in His appearance as man is not identical with the eternal pre-existent and risen Only-begotten God, but is identical with the Father who extended Himself into the virgin. The Arians accuse the orthodox of holding a Sabellian view, see on this and on Hilary's counterattack *infra*, 71, *De Trin.* 2, 4.

> "But others – because (as Scripture says) there is no salvation without Christ who in the beginning was God the Word with God – deny His birth

> and declare that He was merely created, in order that birth may not allow His true divinity, but that creation may teach His false godhead.''

These "others" are heretics as well, since they deny His divinity. As appears from *De Trin*. 2, 4 (*aliqui huius nunc temporis praedicatores, qui ... Deo in Fili creatione subveniant*), the Arians are meant here. The Arians deny Christ's eternal generation as well, but they do so for a different reason: they do not want Christ to be truly God, and they realize that if He were eternally generated, He would be truly God. So they declare Him to be a creature. In this brief description of their doctrine by Hilary rendering and interpretation go together: the Arians deny that the Son is truly God (see *infra*, 69 f), but it is Hilary's interpretation that they want to teach His *false* godhead, the Arians never say this. In *De Trin*. 1, 17 Hilary shows that he knows they do not teach this, because there he rejects the identicality of Father and Son (the Sabellian position) and something like a compromise between a true and a false god (the Arian position). – In *De Trin*. 5, 6-7 Hilary says in explaining *Genesis* 1:26 that it is impossible to put together what is true and what is false, therefore the plural *faciamus* cannot be applied to a true and a false God: *Et quidem sensu humanae opinionis commune iudicium est, nequaquam veris falsa sociari ... Quae cum ita sint, interrogo inter verum et falsum Deum quomodo hoc dictum intellegatur: Faciamus hominem ...* In saying that Christ, if He is not the true God, is a false God, Hilary uses the rhetorical argument from opposites, cf. on this argument G. C. Stead, Rhetorical Method in Athanasius, *Vigiliae Christianae* (30), 1976, p 126.

> "Because this false doctrine (about God), whilst it lies about the faith of one God in divine reality, does not exclude this faith in the sacrament. But subjecting His true birth to the name and the belief of a creature they separate Him from the one true God, so that as a creature called into being He may not claim for Himself that perfection of divinity which had not been given to Him by a true birth.''

It is obvious that the Arians who do not confess Christ as the truly divine Son of God are meant here. But especially the antithesis *in genere-in sacramento* is unclear, so that this sentence must be regarded, if not as a *crux*, then certainly as highly cryptic.

CHAPTER 17

The true doctrine of the Father and the Son.

Translation and Commentary:

> **(17)** "My soul was inflamed to answer the furor of these men, calling to mind that for it it was particularly beneficial the belief not merely in God, but in God the Father, to have put its hope not merely in Christ, but in Christ the Son of God, and not in a creature, but in God the Creator, born of God.''

On the furor of the heretics see *supra*, 53 f, *De Trin*. 1, 15. One must not only believe in God, but in God the Father, see on this *supra*, 44 f, *De Trin*. 1, 11 and *infra*, 161 f, *De Trin*. 3, 17; one must not only believe in Christ, but in Christ as the Son of God. To confess Jesus as Christ is merely a tribute of honour (as the Arians give Him by calling Him a creature surpassing all other creatures), but to call Him Christ, the Son of God, is the acknowledgement of the divine mystery, see *De Trin*. 6, 36: *Neque enim Petro tantum ex confesso honore laus reddita est, sed ex agnitione mysterii, quia non Christum solum, sed Christum Dei Filium esse confessus est. Nam utique ad confessionem honoris suffecerat dixisse: "Tu Christus es." Sed inane fuerat Christum ab eo confessum fuisse, nisi Dei Filium confiteretur*. On Christ as the Creator and not as a creature see *infra*, 99 ff.

> "So our first priority is by the clear assertions of prophets and evangelists to refute the insanity and ignorance of men who use the in itself pious and profitable confession of the unity of God as a cloak for their denial either that in Christ God was born or that He is truly God, so that the creation of a mighty creature leaves the mystery of the faith within the bounds of a belief in only one God, because in their view the birth of God would lead the religion of the confessors outside the bounds of the belief in one God."

On the insanity (*vaesania*) of the heretics cf. *De Trin*. 6, 1. – Hilary wants to refute the heretics with the clear assertions of prophets and evangelists. It is interesting to see that in the books 1-3 (apart from the outline of the whole work in 1, 20-36) hardly any references to the Old Testament are to be found (only in *De Trin*. 2, 10 a reference to *Is*. 53, 8, a text which is quoted in *Acts* 8, 33, *De Trin*. 2, 13 a reference to *Genesis* 1, 1 in explaining *John* 1, 1, *De Trin*. 2, 27 a possible reference to *Is*. 7, 14 – the usual Scriptural proof for the virgin birth –, *De Trin*. 3, 8 a reference to *Is*. 29, 14 – a text which is quoted in I *Cor* 1, 19 a passage which Hilary quotes subsequently – and a few allusions in *De Trin*. 3, 17 (*infra*, 161 f) –, but there are numerous references to the New Testament. Extensive quotations are, however, given from the Old Testament in books 4-5. The remark made here that he wants to refute the heretics with texts from the prophets and evangelists could well be a further indication (see *supra*, 2 ff) that it was Hilary's intention right from the beginning to write a work consisting of twelve books. – Those who deny that Christ is God born are presumably the Sabellians, who say that God the Father extended Himself into the man Jesus (see *supra*, 55), those who deny that Christ is truly God are the Arians (see *supra*, 55 f). Both Arians and Sabellians do so under the cloak of wanting to safeguard the untity of God (see *supra*, 55, *De Trin*. 1, 16).

> "But we, divinely taught to confess neither two gods nor a solitary God, will adduce this evidence from the preaching of the evangelists and the prophets

in confessing God the Father and God the Son that they are both in our faith a unity, not one person; we confess them neither as identical nor do we confess a something else between a true and a false god, because when God is born from God, the birth permits neither identicalness nor difference.''

On the rejection both of two gods and of a solitary God see *infra*, 95 ff. Hilary says repeatedly that Father and Son are *unum* (a unity), not *unus* (one person), this is the orthodox position which must transcend Sabellianism and polytheism, see *e.g. De Trin.* 2, 23 (infra, 107 ff), 7, 2: *dum neque solitarius nobis Deus in confessione neque duo sunt. Et inter haec, unum neque negando neque confitendo, fidei conservata perfectio est, dum et quod unum sunt refertur ad utrumque et uterque non unus est*, cf. 7, 5; 8, 4 f; see however, *In Ps* CXXII 7 where there is no play upon the words *unum* and *unus*, but where it says: *Deus enim unus uterque est ... unus ex uno, et ambo unum*, cf. Novatian, *De Trin.* 27, 149: *Et quia dixit unum, intellegant haeretici, quia non dixit unus. Unum enim neutraliter positum societatis concordiam, non unitatem personae sonat. Unum enim, non unus esse dicitur, quoniam nec ad numerum refertur, sed ad societatem alterius expromitur*; 27, 148: *si enim erat, ut haeretici, putant, pater Christus, oportuit dicere: ego pater unus sum.* It is interesting that Hilary here rejects a divinity between a true God and a false one. That is the Arian position on Christ, who according to them is not truly God, but who is divine by participation. In the previous chapter Hilary had argued that a god who is not truly God is a false one and had therefore accused the Arians of teaching a false god (see *supra*, 56). In the present chapter he more or less acknowledges that the Arians do not teach a false god, but he also makes clear his opposition to this 'compromise'.

CHAPTER 18

Faith is a necessary condition for understanding anything of the divine truth.

Translation and Commentary:

(18) ''And you, whose ardour of faith and passion for the truth unknown to the world and its philosophers shall prompt to read this, must remember to cast away the weak and feeble opinions of earthly minds and in a devout expectation of learning break down the narrowness of imperfect knowledge.''

Here Hilary returns to his theme that God's infinity asks for an infinite faith which transcends all restrictions of the Divine to definitions and images (see *supra*, 33 ff). On the ardour of faith, see *De Syn.* 78: *O studiosi tandem apostolicae et evangelicae doctrinae viri, quos fidei calor in tantis tenebris haereticae noctis accendit*, but the *calor fidei* can also be impatient, see *De Trin.* 5, 12: *O impatiens fidei calor et desiderati sermonis incontinens silentium*; utterly rejectable is the *calor haereticus, De Trin.* 6, 15: *Sed inreligiosos aestus suos calor haereticus non continet.* – On the infirmity of human understanding see *infra*, 61 f, *De Trin.* 1, 19; on the expectation, the willingness to learn, *infra*, 60; on secular philosophy *infra*, 92 f.

> "For new faculties of a reborn mind are needed, so that everybody is enlightened by his own understanding according to the gift of heavenly origin."

In order to obtain true knowledge of God man must be reborn (see *supra*, 47, *De Trin.* 1, 12), then man knows that his gift of understanding is a divine gift (see *supra*, 16, *De Trin.* 1, 1) which should be used to know God.

> "First he must through faith, as the holy Jeremiah admonishes us to do, take his stand within the range of God's substance, in order that, since he is going to hear about the substance of God, he may direct his mind towards thoughts worthy of God's substance, directing it not with some understanding which means confining it, but with infinity."

The reference is to *Jer.* 23, 22, where the *Vulgata* reads *Si stetissent in consilio meo*, but where Hilary may have read something similar to the rendering of the LXX: εἰ ἔστησαν ἐν τῇ ὑποστάσει μού, since he says: *standum ... est ... in substantia Dei* (R. J. Kinnavey, *op. cit.*, pp 260 f, calls this an unusual adaptation of *substantia*, but gives no explanation of his own). In this context Hilary again stresses the infinity of God, and in the next sentence he speaks of himself as being *divinae naturae participem*. We take it that Hilary means to say that he who is conscious of being within the infinite range of God's substance does not confine God to any bounds set by the human mind (cf. *supra*, 33 ff).

> "Nay even, aware of the fact that he has been made a participant of the divine nature as the blessed apostle Peter (2 *Peter* 1, 4) says in his second epistle, let him not measure God's nature with the laws of his own nature, but gauge God's proclamations by the grandeur of God's testimony about Himself."

The right knowledge of God's infinity is made possible by the fact that man has become a participant of God's nature. In Greek words like μετέχειν can be used for the possession of knowledge, see J. H. Waszink, Bemerkungen zu Justins Lehre vom Logos Spermatikos, *Mullus, Festschrift für Theodor Klauser, Jahrbuch für Antike und Christentum, Ergänzungsband 1*, Münster i.W. 1964, p 388; cf. apart from the quotations given there Aristides, *Apol.* 2, 1, who speaks about μετέχειν τῆς ἀληθείας, Irenaeus, *Adv. Haer.* 4, 34, 6: μετοχὴ δὲ θεοῦ ἐστι τὸ γινώσκειν θεόν. Obviously the word *particeps* has here in Hilary the same meaning. On Hilary's opposition to measuring God with human laws see *infra*, 181 f, *De Trin.* 3, 26. On believing God's testimony about Himself see the last section of this paragraph.

> "For he is the best student who waits till the words reveal their own meaning rather than imposes it, who takes more from the words than (puts) into them, and who does not force a semblance of meaning on the words, which he had determined to be the right one before starting to read."

Hilary stresses repeatedly that one should not force a preconceived meaning on what one reads in Scripture or elsewhere, see *e.g. De Trin.* 7, 33: *Intellegentiae igitur sensum in consequentibus requiramus. Non enim fides ex arbitrio nostro, sed ex dictorum est ineunda virtutibus*; 11, 7: *eorum ipsorum dictorum ratio ex his ipsis dictis afferatur*, cf. 11, 24, *De Syn.* 6: *Iniquum est enim, non comperta usque ad finem ratione dictorum, praeiudicatam sententiam ex initiis quorum causa adhuc ignoretur afferre*, cf. 32. This implies insistence on an exegesis out of the context of the Biblical texts, see *infra*, 118, *De Trin.* 2, 31.

> "Since then we are going to speak of the things of God, let us leave to God knowledge of Himself and let us in pious reverence obey His words. For He is a fitting witness to Himself who is only known through Himself."

On the thought that God is only known to Himself and therefore can only be known by man if He gives testimony of Himself, cf. *De Trin.* 4, 14: *Ipsi de se Deo credendum est, et his quae cognitioni nostrae de se tribuit obsequendum*; 4, 36; 5, 21: *A Deo discendum est, quid de Deo intellegendum sit, quia nonnisi se auctore cognoscitur*; 6, 17: ... *nefas esset Deo de se non credidisse*; 7, 30: ... *cum dignum et iustum esset testanti de se Deo credere*; 7, 38: *Non relictus est hominum eloquiis de Dei rebus alius praeterquam Dei sermo*; Tertullian, *Apol.* 17, 2-3: *quod vero immensum est, soli sibi notum est. Hoc est quod Deum aestimari facit dum aestimari non capit; ita eum vis magnitudinis et notum hominibus obicit et ignotum* (cf. R. Braun, *op. cit.*, pp 53 ff); *Adv. Marc.* 18, 3: *Quomodo itaque revelatus est? Si per humanam coniecturam, nego Deum alias cognosci posse quam per semetipsum*; Irenaeus, *Adv. Haer.* 4, 34, 5: *Homo etenim a se non videt Deum. Ille autem volens videtur ab hominibus, a quibus vult, et quando vult, et quemadmodum vult.*

CHAPTER 19

The inadequacy of human speech about God.

Translation and Commentary:

> **(19)** "If in our discussion of the nature and birth of God we adduce certain analogies, let no one suppose that these are in themselves a perfectly certain argumentation. There can be no comparison between God and earthly things."

On the inadequacy of human or earthly comparisons for God see *De Trin.* 3, 1; 4, 2; 6, 9; 7, 28-30; Tertullian, *Adv. Marc.* 1, 4, 2: *De deo agitur, cuius hoc principaliter proprium est, nullius exempli capere comparationem.* That God cannot be compared with man is also constantly stressed by Athanasius, see *Contra Arianos* 1, 21, 23, 27, 28; 2, 34, 35; *De Syn.* 42; *De Decr.* 10, 11, 12, 20, 24; this fact makes images taken from earthly life inadequate, see e.g. *De Decr.* 12 (in connection with the image of the source): καὶ μικρὸν μέν ἐστι τὸ παράδειγμα καὶ λιὰν ἀμυδρὸν πρὸς τὸ ποθούμενον, cf. *Contra Arianos* 2, 17 (the word ἀμυδρός is the technical term in Middle Platonism for 'inadequate', see C. Andresen, *Logos und Nomos. Die Polemik des Kelsos wider das Christentum*, Berlin 1955, pp 338 f; J. Daniélou, *Message evangélique et culture hellénistique aux IIe et IIIe siècles*, Tournai 1961, p 50; J. H. Waszink, *Mullus*, p 386). – Although earthly images are inadequate they are necessary because of the weakness of the human mind:

> "But the weakness of our intellect forces us to seek for illustrations from a lower sphere as indications of higher realities, in order that we, on the instruction of the usual experience of ordinary things, might be led from the knowledge of our normal understanding towards forming an idea based on unusual understanding."

The weakness of human understanding is stated frequently by Hilary, as he himself says, *De Trin.* 12, 8: *Non praeiudicatur autem Deo, ut saepe iam diximus, per infirmitatem nostrae intellegentiae*, see further 1, 7, 15, 17, 18, 37; 2, 7; 3, 20; 4, 2, 14; 7, 1; 9, 40; 10, 53; 12, 50, 51. God adapts His revelation to human weakness, see *De Trin.* 3, 20: *Dominus ad omnem se intellegentiae nostrae inbecillitatem adcommodat*; 9, 40: *in tantum ad intellegentiam nostram sermones aptavit* (sc. *Dominus*), *in quantum naturae nostrae ferret infirmitas*, therefore man, conscious of his weakness, should not extend beyond what has been revealed to him, *De Trin.* 12, 51 (see further *infra*, 74 ff, *De Trin.* 2, 5 on curiosity). Since images are meant to help human weakness, man should cautiously use them as means towards some knowledge of the divine truth, not as the divine truth itself. (Similarly he had said in 1, 7, *supra*, 37 ff, that man can have a certain idea of God's beauty without being able to define this beauty.) The images lead the way from what is common to what is unusual, this is, according to Hilary, the ordinary way of instruction, see *De Trin.* 1, 34: ... *si qui diu tenui primum exercitatione longoque usu humilioris studii fuerunt eruditi, tum iam ad rerum ipsarum quibus inbuti sunt experimenta mittantur*, see also *De Trin.* 3, 2 where he says that before he can explain the very difficult question how the Father is in the Son and the Son is in the Father, he must first know the Scriptural doctrine of Father and Son, so that he may speak more clearly as dealing with familiar and accustomed matters: *Adque ut facilius intellegentiam difficillimae istius quaestionis consequi possimus, prius Patrem et Filium secundum divinarum scripturarum doctrinam cognosci a nobis oportet, ut de cognitis ac familiaribus absolutior sermo sit.* The same method in explaining difficult Biblical texts is advocated by Irenaeus, *Adv. Haer.* 2, 9, 1: *ea quae sunt talia* (sc. *aenigmata*) *ex manifestis et consonantibus et claris accipiunt absolutiones* and by Tertullian, *Apol.* 3, 2: *cum sit iustius occulta de manifestis praeiudicare quam manifesta de occultis praedamnare; De res. mort.* 21, 2: ... *incerta de certis et obscura de manifestis praeiudicari; Adv. Marc.* 1, 9, 4, 10 (cf. G. Quispel, *op. cit.*, p 25). Hilary will certainly have been influenced by Quintilian, *Inst.* 5, 10, 8: *per ea quae certa sunt fidem dubiis adferens ... neque enim certa incertis declarantur* (R. D. Sider, *Ancient Rhetoric and the Art of Tertullian*, Oxford 1971, p 50, supposes Quintilian's influence on Tertullian as well, but it seems more likely that Tertullian is here following a philosophical, Stoic, tenet, see E. P. Meijering, *Tertullian contra Marcion. Gotteslehre in der Polemik*, Leiden 1977, pp 30 ff.).

> "Therefore any comparison should be regarded as helpful to man rather than as appropriate to God, since it suggests rather than exhausts the sense we seek. Nor let it be thought to have been conceived in order to set side by side carnal and spiritual, invisible and palpable natures, since it avows itself to be both necessary to the weakness of human understanding and free from the envy of an imperfect example."

A comparison is only helpful, not exhaustive, it is not meant to put the divine and the earthly on one level. He who uses such a comparison realizes that it is necessary because of the weakness of understanding, but does not have any feelings of envy because of the imperfection of his example, *i.e.* he does not begrudge anybody perfect examples, since he knows that such perfect examples, which adequately describe God, do not exist. Hilary will accuse the Arians of treating images for the Divine incorrectly and therefore speaking about God, who is Spirit, in a corporeal way, see *infra*, 133.

> "So we shall continue to speak about God with words of God, nevertheless instructing our mind with illustrations drawn from human life."

The words of God must be understood by man and it is not enough just to quote them as authorities. For this understanding human analogies can be useful, see *infra*, 127 f, *De Trin.* 3, 1.

BOOK II

CONTENTS

I. THE SUFFICIENCY OF THE SCRIPTURAL DOCTRINE OF THE TRINITY
(1-5)

Christ's commandment to baptize in the name of the Father and the Son and the Holy Spirit contains the whole doctrine of the Trinity. So no human speculation should be added to this. The heretics, however, compel Hilary to speak about what is inexplicable. Doing this one is in real danger of transgressing the revelation given in Scripture, which is typical of the heretics, but in order to offer resistance to the audacity of the heretics it must be done, be it with the utmost caution.

The primary importance of these chapters lies in the fact that they reveal Hilary's attitude towards Scripture and towards speculation which go beyond Scripture, and they reveal in how far Hilary wanted to be a speculative theologian (not, however, in how far he actually *was* a speculative theologian).

CHAPTER 1

Christ's commandment to baptize in the name of the Father and the Son and the Holy Spirit ought to have been enough for the believers.

Translation and Commentary:

> **(1)** "For the believers the word of God should have been enough which on the testimony of the evangelist was with the very power of its truth transferred into our ears, when the Lord says: 'Go now and teach all nations, baptizing them in the name of the Father, and the Son, and the Holy Ghost, teaching them to observe all things whatsoever I command you; and lo, I am with you always unto the end of the world.'"

The revelation given in Scripture ought to have been sufficient, and the believers should not go beyond it, see on this important theme *infra*, 68 ff, *De Trin.* 2, 5, *infra*, 74 ff. – God speaks through the evangelist, cf. *De Trin.* 5, 33: *Omnia quidem per revelationem Christi apostolus didicit*, and *De Trin.* 3, 1, *infra*, 127 f; cf. on *Matth.* 28:19 as the core of the faith in the Trinity *De Syn.* 11, in connection with the authority of Scripture. Similarly Athanasius says that when the disciples heard this commandment of the Lord, they asked no curious questions about the Trinity, but believed as they heard; see *Ad Ser.* 4, 5: οἱ γοῦν μαθηταὶ ἀκούσαντες, βαπτίζοντες αὐτοὺς εἰς τὸ ὄνομα τοῦ Πατρὸς καὶ τοῦ Υἱοῦ καὶ τοῦ ἁγίου Πνεύματος, οὐ περιειργάσαντο διὰ τί δεύτερον ὁ Υἱὸς καὶ τρίτον τὸ Πνεῦμα ἢ διὰ τί ὅλως Τριάς, ἀλλ' ὡς ἤκουσαν ἐπίστευσαν (on Athanasius' views on *curiosity* see *infra*, 75 ff, *De Trin.* 2, 5).

"What element in the mystery of man's salvation is not concluded in His word? Or what has been left unsaid, or what is unclear?"

If anything of importance had been left unsaid, this would be an opportunity for heretical interpretation, cf. *De Trin.* 7, 20 where he asks, after quoting *John* 5:22-23: ... *quid reliquum est ad impietatem occasionis?* What has not been revealed by God is withdrawn from human understanding, see *De Trin.* 7, 38: *Non relictus est hominum eloquiis de Dei rebus alius praeterquam Dei sermo. Omnia reliqua et arta et conclusa et inpedita sunt et obscura.* So if anything of importance had been left unsaid and had not been revealed, the rash temerity of the heretics would get a chance. – Nothing in this word of Christ is unclear, – Hilary states explicitly that there is no obscurity in the divine words; if there is, the fault lies with the believers, see *De Trin.* 7, 38: *sit in fide nostra vitium, si in dictis Dei resedit obscuritas.*

"All is full as stemming from the full and perfect One."

In this sentence (*plena sunt omnia ut a pleno et perfecto profecta*) *profecta* seems indeed preferable to *perfecta*, since the reading *et a perfecto perfecta* could well be caused by the frequently used expression *perfectus a perfecto* (see *e.g.* 2, 8, 11, 20; 3, 3, this is directed against the Arians, see *De Trin.* 3, 8, *infra*, 141 f), but this applies to the perfect generation of the Son, not to the inspiration of Scripture.

"For it includes the indication of the words, the force of accomplishing these things, the order of the acts and the insight in what is."

Hilary means to say that the commandment of Christ contains the clear indication of the words to be used in baptism, it contains the force of implementing what is said (cf. *In Ps.* XIII 1: ... *nihil est verborum Dei quod non sit implendum; et omne quod dictum est, habet quandam iam efficiendi necessitatem, quia Dei verba decreta sunt.*), of the order of acts, *viz.*, the teaching and baptizing, and of the insight in what is or happens.

"He bade them baptize in the name of the Father and the Son and the Holy Ghost, that is in confession of the Source and of the Only-begotten and of the Gift. There is one Source of all things, for there is one God and Father, from whom are all things. And one Only-begotten, our Lord Jesus Christ, through whom are all things. And one Spirit, who is the Gift in all. So all are arranged according to their powers and merits: one Power from which are all things, one Offspring through which are all things, one Gift of perfect hope."

These words are a clear allusion to *Eph.* 4:4-6, a text which he calls in *De Trin.* 11, 1: *totum atque absolutum fidei evangelicae sacramentum.* On God the Father as the origin of all things see *infra*, 78 ff, *De Trin.* 2, 6; on Christ through whom all things were created see *infra*, 99 ff, *De Trin.* 2, 17 ff; on the Spirit as a gift see *infra*, 122 f, *De Trin.* 2, 33.

"And nothing will be found lacking in that supreme perfection which embraces, in Father, Son and Holy Spirit, infinity in the eternal, splendid appearance in the Image, fruition in the Gift."

The Father is of an infinite eternity, see *supra*, 33 ff, *De Trin*. 1, 6 and *infra*, 78 ff, *De Trin*. 2, 6. The splendid appearance of God which was discussed in *De Trin*. 1, 7, and of which it was said that it is beyond man's comprehension now appears to be in Christ as the Image of God, but Hilary stresses that Christ is the living Image and as such does not confine the Father to a human figure (see *supra*, 28, cf. J. Moingt S.J., La théologie trinitaire de S. Hilaire, *Hilaire et son temps*, p 172). The Spirit of God is God's gift which man can use; this is an allusion to I *Cor*. 12:7 which is quoted by Hilary in *De Trin*. 8, 29 in the following way: *Unicuique autem datur manifestatio Spiritus, ad id quod utile est*, and explained as: *in utilitatis datione manifestatio Spiritus* (*ibid*. and 8, 30), cf. J. Moingt's paraphrase: "L'incogniscibilité de Dieu est dans le Père, qui est sans principe; l'intelligibilité de Dieu, dans le Fils, image du Père; et la science de Dieu se trouve dans l'Esprit, qui est le don de la foi." (*op. cit.*, p 173).

CHAPTER 2

The heretics force Hilary to speak in his own words about the mystery of the Trinity.

Translation and Commentary:

(2)   "But we are forced by the sins of the heretics and blasphemers to deal with things which are not permitted to scale steep heights, to speak what is indescribable, to presume thoughts which have not been granted to us."

He is forced by the heretics to deal with things which are not permitted, etc. These things are human utterances which go beyond the revelation in Scripture, see *infra*, 74 ff, *De Trin*. 2, 5. The heretics force him to do so, since he has to refute their unscriptural doctrines, cf. *De Trin*. 5, 1; 6, 22; 8, 2; Irenaeus, *Adv. Haer*. 2, 46, 1: ... *uti et nos ad impietatem propter necessitatem sermonis devergamus ... sed nobis quidem propitius sit Deus*; Athanasius, *Contra Arianos* 1, 23; 3, 63; *Ad Ser*. 1, 16. – On the scaling of steep heights (*ardua scandere*) cf. *De Trin*. 7, 1; 10, 53. To go beyond the revelation given in Scripture is a sin, cf. his attack on the impious liberty in speculation, *infra*, 74.

"And whilst we ought to fulfil only by faith what is commanded, *viz*., to worship the Father, to give reverence to Him with the Son, to abound in the Holy Ghost, we are forced to stretch our humble language towards what is indescribable, we are forced to sin by the sin of others, so that what should have been contained in the piety of our minds is now exposed to the danger of human speech."

The commandment given in Scripture to worship the Trinity should have been enough. The heretics contradict Scripture, in refuting the heretics he is forced to do what in itself is not allowed, *viz.*, to go beyond Scripture. The divine revelation is inexplicable (*inenarrabilis*), cf. the definition given of this word in *De Trin.* 4, 2 where it says that it has no bound or limit of denoting, *i.e.* cannot be defined (*quod enim inenarrabile est, id significantiae alicuius finem et modum non habet*). Speech is below thought (see *supra*, 37 ff, *De Trin.* 1, 7). Therefore it is safer to venerate God in one's mind than to speak about God.

CHAPTER 3

The heretics' doctrine about God is not based on Scripture, but on erring human judgement.

Translation and Commentary:

> (3) "For there have arisen quite a number of people who received the simplicity of the heavenly words in an arbitrary way instead of in accordance with the perfection of the truth itself, interpreting them differently from what their sense required. For heresy stems from understanding, not from Scripture, the guilt lies in (human) understanding not in the (divine) word."

The words spoken by God have in themselves a simple meaning, Hilary stresses this simplicity of the divine revelation time and time again, sometimes adding that the heretics distort this simplicity, see *e.g. De Trin.* 9, 40; 10, 70: *In simplicitate itaque fides est*. But Hilary also stresses that faith needs understanding, the heretic who is without understanding is outside the simplicity of faith, see *De Trin.* 8, 34: *quia impietas, quae non capit intellegentiam, extra sermonis scientiam et extra simplicitatem fidei est*; for this reason the *simpliciores* under the believers have to be instructed, see *De Trin.* 12, 20, since the heretics constantly try to mislead the simple believers who have no knowledge, see *e.g. De Trin.* 4, 1; 5, 32; 7, 1, 30; 8, 2; 9, 5; 12, 18. The heretics do so with *subtilitas*, see 7, 1; this *subtilitas* they learned from the philosophers, see *De Trin.* 8, 3: *Iam vero hic quanta saecularis ingenii subtilitate contendunt*. Hilary is here in line with Tertullian, who contrasts the simplicity of the truth with the subtlety of the philosophers, see *Adv. Marc.* 5, 19, 8: *Hac simplicitate veritatis contraria subtililoquentiae et philosophiae nihil perversi possumus sapere* (for opposition against *subtilitas* or *minutiloquium* see further Irenaeus, *Adv. Haer.* 2, 18, 4; 2, 39, 1; Quintilian, *Inst.* 3, 11, 21, – see further *infra*, 74 ff, on curiosity). – The heretics interpret the simple divine words *pro voluntatis suae sensu, i.e.* in an arbitrary way. This meaning of *voluntas* as 'arbitrariness' is very clear in *De Trin.* 10, 1 where Hilary says that if *ratio* preceded *voluntas* in-

2,3   69

stead of the other way round, the truth would not be contradicted, since then one would not defend what one would like to be true, but one would begin to want what is true, see especially: *caeterum si non praeiret rationem voluntas, sed per veri intellegentiam ad velle id quod verum est moveretur: nunquam doctrina voluntatis quaereretur, si voluntatem omnem doctrinae ratio commoveret; essetque omnis sine contradictione veritatis sermo, cum unusquisque non quod vellet, id verum esse defenderet, sed quod verum est, id velle coepisset,* see further *e.g. In Ps.* I, 3; *De Trin.* 7, 23 (*mentium vaesanarum voluntas*), 6, 15 (*inreligiositatis voluntas ex inopia prudentiae est*); 8, 1 (*quae volunt sapiunt, et nolunt sapere quae vera sunt*). With their arbitrary interpretation the heretics give to the divine words a meaning which differs from their original one. – On Hilary's views on the exegesis of Biblical texts see *infra*, 118, *De Trin.* 2, 31. Heresy is thus caused by understanding, not by Scripture; this implies, of course, a wrong and arbitrary understanding of Scripture, cf. *De Trin.* 4, 1: ... *cognoscendum est ... qua interpretationum suarum arte veritatem divinorum dictorum virtutemque corrumpant*; 7, 4: *nec negari possit ex vitio malae intellegentiae fidei extitisse discidium, dum quod legitur sensui potius coaptatur quam lectioni sensus obtemperat*; 7, 33: *Non enim fides ex arbitrio nostro, sed ex dictorum est ineunda virtutibus*; 8, 10: *impiae intellegentiae crimen spem simplicem perdidit.*

> "Is not the truth indestructible, when the name 'Father' is heard? Is not the nature of the Son contained in His name? The Holy Ghost is mentioned by name, must He not exist? For it is impossible that fatherhood be not in the Father, sonship not in the Son, the gift not in the Holy Ghost."

What Hilary stresses is that the names Father, Son and Holy Ghost refer to realities and are not merely names, which, according to some heretics, they are, see *infra*, 98 ff, *De Trin.* 2, 15. On the actual existence of the Holy Ghost, who is received as a gift, see infra, 116 f, *De Trin.* 2, 29.

> "But evil men confuse and complicate all things and with the perversity of their understanding quarrel in order to change the nature, so that they take away fatherhood from the Father by wanting to take away sonship from the Son. And they take away the fatherhood when according to them the Son is not Son by nature, and He is not the Son by nature when the Begotten and the Begetter do not have the same nature in themselves. And He is not the Son, who has an essence different from and dissimilar to the Father. And how can God be the Father, if He does not perceive in the Son that essence and nature which He has in Himself?"

When the Son is not really the Son (and only by name), then the Father is not really the Father. If God is the Father by nature, then this implies that He is the Son by nature as well, and that Father and Son are of the same substance or nature. In denying that the Son is of the same substance as the Father, the Arians in fact deny the reality of God's Fatherhood. So, that God is the Father by nature implies that He is the

Son by nature, cf. *De Trin*. 8, 40: *quia cum Pater non nisi per Filium Pater sit, Filius per id significatur in Patre* (see C. F. A. Borchardt, *op. cit.*, p 64 n. 60, who further refers to Athanasius, *Contra Arianos* 3, 6, see also *Contra Arianos* 1, 17-18; 1, 20, where it says that without the Son the Father would be imperfect, and Athanasius' favourite argument that without the Logos the Father would be *alogos*, *Contra Arianos* 1, 14, 19, 24, 25; 2, 32; 3, 63; *De Decr*. 15.

CHAPTER 4

The heresies of Sabellius, Ebion (Photinus) and Arius.

Translation and Commentary:

> **(4)** "So although they can in no way deny Their existence, they never-theless come forward with new doctrines and human inventions."

Everybody has to accept the fact of the existence of the three Persons, the heretics do not deny it either, but they give a new interpretation to it, which is a human finding, and therefore cannot be orthodox. Hilary repeatedly attacks the novelty of the heresies, see *e.g. De Trin*. 11, 4: *Sed nunc hi novi Christi praedicatores, cuncta negando quae Christi sunt, alium Dominum Christum sicuti alium Deum patrem praedicant*; 12, 3: *... hi nunc novi apostolicae fidei emendatores ...*; cf. 6, 21, 37. This rejection of the novelty is in line with Irenaeus, see *e.g. Adv. Haer*. 3, 4, 2; 3, 12, 16; 5, 26, 2, 3, and partly in line with Tertullian. Tertullian is not consistent in his attitude towards novelty, but especially in doctrinal matters he usually attacks it, see *e.g. Adv. Marc*. 1, 9, 1; 4, 4, 1-2; *De praescr*. 31, 3 (cf. J. H. Waszink in his edition of *De anima*, p 359 and the extensive expositions given by J. C. Fredouille, *Tertullien et la conversation de la culture antique*, Paris 1972, pp 235 ff). The ironic remark made by Hilary that God postponed the revelation of the truth until now instead of granting it to Peter and the other apostles must be seen against the same background of suspicion of novelty, see *De Trin*. 6, 38: *Invidit, credo, hic Petro Deus, ut in tempora posteriora dissimulans haec nunc vobis novis praedicatoribus reservaret*! This is a favourite argument of Tertullian, see *Adv. Marc*. 1, 20, 1: *O Christe, patientissime domine, qui tot annis interversionem praedicationis tuae sustinuisti, donec scilicet tibi Marcion subveniret*, see further *Adv. Marc*. 4, 4, 5; 4, 19, 5; *De praescr*. 29, 2-3. Hilary should not, however, be regarded as an outright traditionalist who opposes any novelty. He concedes that there is always a good reason for any departure from the accustomed mode of expression and that verity may cause novelty, see *De Trin*. 5, 27: *Nunquam non ex causa est, cum consuetudo praedicationis exceditur; et rationem novitatis ratio veritatis inducit*; it would, of course, be impossible for Hilary to be a consistent traditionalist, since he is well aware that the term *homoousion* is not a Biblical term but a relatively new one. When he is confronted with this fact, he says that he would rather say something new than impiously reject it, and then he leaves the question of novelty out, see *De Syn.* 82: *Malo enim aliquod novum commemorasse quam impie respuisse. Praetermissa itaque quaestione novitatis* .... This is again in line with Tertullian, who also sometimes says that truth is beyond the antithesis of old and new, see *Adv. Marc.* 1, 8, 2: *viva et germana divinitas nec de novitate nec de vetustate, sed de sua veritate censetur, De virg. vel.* 1, 2: *Haereseis non novitas quam veritas revincit. Quodumque adversus veritatem sapit, hoc erit haeresis, etiam vetus consuetudo.*

> "So that Sabellius makes the Son an extension of the Father, and says that this confession is a matter of words rather than of realities, for he represents one and the same Person as the Son and also the Father."

On Sabellius see *supra*, 55, *De Trin.* 1, 16. The Arians accuse the orthodox saying that their doctrine of the *homoousion* is in fact Sabellianism, since it implies identity of Father and Son, see *De Trin.* 4, 4. Hilary rejects this accusation by making a distinction between *unio*, which means "oneness", and *unitas* which means "unity (of two)", see *De Trin.* 6, 11: *Et unionem destestantes unitatem divinitatis tenemus*, and he accuses the Arians of using the Sabellian doctrine of the identicalness of Father and Son as a means to undermine the belief in the unity of Father and Son, *ibid.*: *Idcirco autem unionis in Sabellio impietas praetenditur, ut ecclesiae fidei unitatis religio auferatur* (cf. 4, 42: *absolute Pater Deus et Filius Deus unum sunt, non unione personae sed substantiae unitate.*) In this use of *unio* and *unitas* Hilary differs from Tertullian, to whom these two words are synonymous, see J. H. Waszink's edition of *De anima*, p 208.

> "Hence Ebion allows no beginning to the Son of God except from Mary and represents Him not as first God and then man, but as first man and then God, and declares that the virgin did not conceive the pre-existent Word which was in the beginning with God and which was God, but that she gave birth to flesh through the Word, because in the pre-existent Word he does not mean the nature of the already existent only-begotten God, but only the edited sound of a voice."

Ebion, who is in fact Photinus (see *De Trin.* 7, 3, 7), was not mentioned in the first open attack on the heretics in 1, 16. He is attacked, together with Sabellius and Arius, in 2, 23 and 7, 3 ff.; 8, 40. He denies the pre-existence of Christ (and in this respect differs from the Arians, see *infra*, 72) and declares Him to be first man and then God (this is the adoptionist view), – see on Photinus G. Bardy, 'Photin', *D.T.C.*, 12, 2, pp 1534 f and A. Solignac, *Oeuvres de Saint Augustin (13), Les Confessions 1-7*, pp 694 f. On Christ as only a sound of voice, see *infra*, 96 ff, *De Trin.* 2, 15.

"So some preachers of our present time who come forward with an Image, Wisdom and Power of God created out of nothing and in time, in order to prevent that, if the Son is diminished from the Father, God is reduced to the level of the Son, because they harbour too great a fear that the Son, if generated by the Father, might empty the Father, and therefore they want to come to the rescue of God by declaring the Son to be a creature, by comparing Him to what has been created out of nothing, so that the Father may preserve the perfection of His nature, because nothing has been generated out of Him."

The Arians are, of course, his most important enemies, it is telling that Hilary does not mention their names whilst he does give the names of Sabellius and Ebion (Photinus); the same occurs in *De Trin.* 2, 23; 7, 6 (in 7, 7 the name of Arius is given), 8, 40; – behind this lies the idea: *nomina sunt odiosa.* – In 1, 17 Hilary said that the Arians' motive behind their declaring the Son to be a creature was that they wanted to deny the Son's divinity (see *supra,* 56); now he says that their motive is to save the Father from diminution to the level of the Son; on Hilary's opposition to diminution of the Father see *infra,* 106, *De Trin.* 2, 22; on his opposition to the Son as a creature see *infra,* 84 ff, *De Trin.* 2, 8. – In the beginning of the seventh book of the *De Trinitate* Hilary declares that the three heresies fight each other and help the church to triumph over all of them: the Arians prove against Sabellius that the Son was pre-existent before His birth (here, Hilary does not mention the fact that they deny Christ's *eternal* pre-existence), Sabellius proves against the Arians that Christ's works are the works of God, Photinus proves against Sabellius that the Son of God is a man, but the Arians prove against Photinus that He is more than merely a man, see *De Trin.* 7, 4-7; cf. the summary given in *De Trin.* 1, 26.

"So no wonder that their doctrine of the Holy Ghost should be different from ours, since they audaciously make the Giver of the Holy Ghost a creature and subject Him to change and non-existence, and so destroy the verity of this perfect mystery, by assigning different substances to matters which are common to such an extent, by denying the Father in robbing the Son of His sonship, by not knowing the Holy Spirit in being ignorant of its function and its Giver."

The Arians declare the Son to be a changeable creature. Since He is the Giver of the Holy Spirit, the Holy Spirit must be a creature as well. When they know neither the origin of the Spirit, *viz.,* the Son, nor its effect, *viz.,* that it is used as a gift, then they do not know the Spirit at all, cf. *De Trin.* 2, 29 where the existence of the Spirit is proved by he fact that it is given and received, see *infra,* 116 f. In a typically rhetorical way Hilary then accuses the Arians of dissolving the mystery of the divine truth by declaring to be of different substance what has in fact the same substance; – they have indeed done so by denying the Father in robbing the Son of what is typical of the Son, *i.e.* by denying that the Son is the eternal Son and thereby denying that the Father is the eternal Father. If the Father is not the eternal Father, the Son is merely a creature, and if the divine origin of the Holy Spirit and its effect are unknown, then the mystery of the one God, Father, Son and Holy Spirit, is gone and is replaced by a God who at a certain moment created a Son as an inferior being, a Son who then bestows men with a Holy Spirit.

> "Thus they ruin ill-trained souls, by affirming the logic of their pleading, and they deceive their hearers by robbing names of their reality, because they cannot rob reality of the names."

The Arians claim that their doctrine is logical, but Hilary will prove that this is not the case, see *infra*, 92 f. – The Arians use the names which are given by Scripture: Father, Son and Holy Ghost, but they say that these are mere names without reality. – This is not a correct interpretation of the Arian doctrine. The Arians do not say that these are names without reality, but that these names do not refer to one and the same divine reality, since Christ has been given the name of Son as there are more sons of God, see *e.g. De Trin.* 4, 3; against this Hilary argues that this name is an indication of His divine nature, *De Trin.* 7, 9 ff. In a typically rhetorical way Hilary argues that if the name 'Son' does not refer to the one divine reality, it refers to no reality at all; on this rhetorical method which confronts the opponent with a crude dilemma see G. C. Stead, Rhetorical Method in Athanasius, p 129.

> "I pass over the names of other dangers to man: the Valentines, Marcionites, Manicheans, and other plagues, who every now and then catch the attention of ill-trained men and infect them by the contagiousness of their contact. And all of them become one plague when the illness of the teachers affects the minds of the hearers."

The Arians deny that their doctrine has anything in common with the one held by Valentinus who, according to them, regards the Son as a *prolatio* of the Father, see *De Trin.* 6, 5. According to Hilary they only dissociate themselves from Valentinus, because they regard *prolatio* as the same as *nativitas*, and because they want to deny the *nativitas*, see *De Trin.* 6, 9. The Arians also deny that their doctrine has anything in common with the one held by the Manicheans, who say that the Son is a part of the same substance with the Father, see *De Trin.* 6, 5. According to Hilary they dissociate themselves from this doctrine in order to be able to deny the *nativitas* of the Son and to deny that the Son is of the same substance as the Father (implying that for the Son to be a *pars* or *portio* of the same substance is the same as the Son being of the same substance), see *De*

Trin. 6, 10; – one may agree with, amongst others, G. C. Stead, *Divine Substance*, p 243, that this Arian reference to the Manicheans is an artifice of controversy. (Opposition to the Manichean and Marcionite separation of the Old and the New Testament is expressed by Hilary in *In Ps.* LX-VII 15, 17). – On the heresies as a plague see further *De Trin.* 6, 1: ... *multis iam ... ecclesiis morbo pestiferae huius praedicationis infectis*; 6, 3: *Emersit enim pestifera et letalis populis proxime lues*, 8, 1 and *De Syn.* 2, on the heretics becoming *one* plague cf. *infra*, 105 f, *De Trin.* 2, 22.

CHAPTER 5

The heretics force Hilary to speak about the divine mystery.

Translation and Commentary:

> (5) "So their unbelief leads us into uncertain and perilous ground, so that it is necessary to utter words about such great and mysterious matters, words which go beyond the heavenly command."

The special danger of speaking about these matters seems to be that according to Hilary all words are liable to be opposed, see *De Trin.* 10, 1: *Non est ambiguum, omnem humani eloquii sermonem contradictioni obnoxium semper fuisse.* This is already the case with the words uttered in Scripture, and certainly so with human words. – Scripture is here called *praescribtum coeleste*, this is because Hilary in this context primarily has in mind the risen Christ's commandment to baptize in the name of the Father, Son and Holy Ghost, see *supra*, 65 f, *De Trin.* 2, 1. – Hilary says repeatedly that man should not go beyond what has been revealed to him in Scripture, see *De Trin.* 4, 14: *cessent itaque propriae hominum opiniones, neque se ultra divinam constitutionem humana iudicia extendant*; 9, 44 where he accuses the Arians: *Et tu qui ultra evangelia sapis*; 11, 1: ... *ut sapere nos, nisi ad id tantum quod praedicatum a se fuerat, non sineret* (sc. *Apostolus*); 12, 26: *confiteri necesse est in quo nos apostolicarum ac propheticarum praedicationum dicta concludunt; In Matth.* 20, 10: *quamquam ultra evangelicam veritatem non necesse sit opinari; In Ps.* I 3 where he says of the heretics: *Nec Novi nec Veteris Testamenti legibus continentur.* Scripture sets clear bounds to *libertas intellegentiae, i.e.* uninhibited speculation, see *De Trin.* 7, 16: ... *ex ipsis dictis dominicis huius quoque sermonis nostri fides adfirmanda est, ne temeritas contradicendi sub libertate diversae in hominibus intellegentiae audeat professionibus divini de se testimonii contraire*; 9, 42: *Concludit autem audacissimum impietatis tuae furorem apostolica fides, ne quo licentia liberae intellegentiae evageris*; 11, 1: ... *statutis per se et oppositis obicibus libertatem intellegentiae voluntatisque concludens* (sc. *Apostolus*), cf. also 8, 20. Speculation which goes beyond the revelation and which wants to investigate the causes of God's actions is *curiosity*, this applies especially to the wonders of God's creation. Here man can perceive the effect without knowing the cause; he should, if he cannot know the causes, bow before God's inscrutable wisdom, see *e.g. De Trin.* 12, 53: *Multa enim istius modi in rebus humanis praestitisti, quorum cum causa ignoretur, effectus tamen non nescitur. Et religiosa fides est, ubi est etiam naturalis inscientia. Nam cum erexi in caelum tuum hos luminis mei infirmes oculos, nihil aliud esse quam caelum tuum credidi*; – beyond man's understanding are the movements of the heavenly bodies, further the sea-tides (cf. *In Ps.* CXX-IX 1, where more examples of unknown natural causes are given). Investigations into the natural causes cannot contradict the faith that the world was created by God, that the soul is immortal, that there is a resurrection of the flesh and that there is divine providence, see *In Ps.* LXIII 9. He who tries to find these causes of God's creation is compared to a man who out of curiosity wants to find the cause of the light of the sun and in doing so is blinded by the light of the sun, *De Trin.* 10, 53: *Quod si contuentibus solis claritatem virtus intenti luminis obstupescit, ut si quando causam radiantis lucis sollertius acies curiosae contemplationis inquirat, usque ad emortuum videndi sensum oculorum natura revocetur ... quid nobis in Dei rebus et in sole iustitiae expectandum est? Nonne incumbet volentibus supersapere stultitia?* In this respect there is a striking similarity between Hilary and Irenaeus. Irenaeus, too, says that man should not go beyond the revelation given in Scripture, see *Adv. Haer.* 2, 40, 1: *sensus autem sanus ... et religiosus ... quae quidem dedit in hominum potestatem Deus ... haec prompte meditabitur ... Sunt autem haec, quae ante oculos nostros occurrunt, et quaecumque aperte, et sine ambiguo ipsis dictionibus posita sunt in Scripturis*; 2, 41, 1: *... Scripturae quidem perfectae sunt, quippe a Verbo Dei et Spiritu eius dictae.* Man can try to find natural causes and in many words explain them, but only God the Creator really knows them, see *Adv. Haer.* 2, 41, 2: *Multa quidem dicimus, et fortassis suasoria, fortassis autem non suasoria: quod autem verum est, et certum, et firmum, adiacet Deo ... In his omnibus nos quidem loquaces erimus, requirentes causas eorum: qui autem ea facit solus Deus veridicus est.* – Tertullian opposes curiosity (at least the wrong curiosity) as well, but he does not regard Scripture as the barrier against speculation, but the *regula fidei* (on this subject see J. H. Waszink in his edition of *De anima*, pp 113 f, J.-C. Fredouille, *op. cit.*, pp 412-432, E. P. Meijering, *Calvin wider die Neugierde. Ein Beitrag zum Vergleich zwischen reformatorischem und patristischem Denken*, Nieuwkoop 1980, pp 8 ff), see especially Tertullian's famous remark, *De praescr.* 14, 5: *Cedat curiositas fidei ... adversus regulam nihil scire omnia scire est.* – Athanasius seems to regard Scripture as the barrier against curiosity, he says that one should simply believe Christ when He says: "I am in the Father and the Father is in Me" instead of asking curious questions about it, see *Contra Arianos* 3, 1; the disciples did not ask curious questions when they heard the commandment to baptize in the name of the Father and the Son and the Holy Ghost, *Ad Ser.* 4, 5 (the quotation is given *supra*, 65). One should not in too great a temerity try to think of new words which deviate from Scripture to explain the Trinity, *Ad Ser.* 1, 17: Ἔδει δὲ αὐτοὺς ... τὸ γεγραμμένον ἐπιγιγνώσκειν καὶ τῷ Πατρὶ συνάπτειν τὸν Υἱὸν καὶ τὸ Πνεῦμα μὴ διαιρεῖν ἀπὸ τοῦ Υἱοῦ. Ἔστι μὲν γὰρ πᾶσι τοῖς γενητοῖς, μάλιστα δὲ ἡμῖν τοῖς ἀνθρώποις ἀδύνατον ἐπαξίως εἰπεῖν περὶ τῶν ἀπορρήτων. Τολμηρότερον δὲ πάλιν μὴ δυναμένους λέγειν ἐπινοεῖν ἐπὶ τούτων καινοτέρας λέξεις παρὰ τὰς τῶν Γραφῶν. *Ad Ser.* 1, 18: Ὦ ἀνόητοι καὶ πάντα τολμηροί, διὰ τί μὴ μᾶλλον ἐπὶ τῆς ἁγίας Τριάδος παύεσθε περιεργάζομενοι καὶ μόνον πιστεύετε ὅτι ἔστιν; cf. also *Contra Arianos* 2, 36. – Closely connected with curiosity are the so-called *quaestiones*, see on this *infra*, 154.

> "The Lord had said that the nations were to be baptized in the name of the Father and the Son and the Holy Ghost. The formulation of faith is fixed, but with all the heretics the meaning is uncertain."

Again, as in *De Trin.* 2, 1, Hilary refers to Christ's commandment of baptism as the core of the Christian faith, see *supra*, 65. This commandment is called *forma fidei*, "formulation of faith", cf. *De Trin.* 8, 8: *Non nostra loquimur, neque ad illudendas audientium aures corrupto dictorum sensu aliqua ex his ementita compingimus: sed sanae doctrinae formam tenentes, quae sincera sunt sapimus, et praedicamus;* In Matth. 12, 24; 16, 4 (See R. J. Kinnavey, *op. cit.*, p 284); on the similar use of *forma* by Tertullian see J. H. Waszink's edition of *De anima*, p 101. On the uncertainty of the meaning of Biblical texts in the interpretations given by the heretics see *supra*, 68 f, *De Trin.* 2, 3.

> "So nothing may be added to the divine commandments, but a limit has to be set to audacity, so that we come forward with the nature of the divine names, because malice, inspired by the devil's cunning, robs the divine things of their reality by coming forward with the reality behind the names, and so that, the dignity and function of the Father, Son and Holy Ghost having been explained in such Scriptural words as we shall find, the words are not robbed of the essential qualities of the divine nature, but that these qualities are by these words confined to their essential meaning."

What he is going to say is not meant as an addition to Christ's commandment, but as a limit to the temerity or audacity of the heretics. On the heretics' audacity or temerity see *supra*, 54, *De Trin.* 1, 15. The reason why it is necessary to say things in defence of Christ's commandment against audacious misinterpretation is that the heretics try to dispose of the realities of Father, Son and Holy Ghost by saying that these are merely names given to the divine nature, see *supra*, 69 f, *De Trin.* 2, 3, and *infra*, 96 ff, *De Trin.* 2, 15. Against this Hilary wants to state that these names imply reality, the essential qualities of the divine nature. This means that Father, Son and Holy Ghost are not merely names but refer to essential qualities of the divine nature (on this use of *proprietas* for a Person of the Trinity see R. J. Kinnavey, *op. cit.*, p 134).

> "I do not know what manner of mind have those who think about these things differently, who corrupt the truth, who darken the light, divide what is indivisible, rend what is incorruptible, dissolve what is perfect unity."

In *De Trin* 2, 11 Hilary says that the Son is not a *divisio* or *discissio* from the Father, but *perfectus a perfecto, totus a toto,* see *infra,* 90. So here in *De Trin.* 2, 5 he may suggest that the heretics with their doctrine make the Son a *discissio* or *divisio* from the Father.

> "It may be easy to them to tear in pieces what is perfect, to impose a law on Omnipotence, a limit on the Infinite, as for me, in answering them there is certainly anxiety in my concern, trembling in my mind, amazement in my intellect, in my speech I shall confess no longer my weakness, but my dumbness. And certainly to want this is forced out of me, since it means resisting audacity, guiding the error and looking after ignorance."

Whilst the heretics find it easy to place themselves above God, it is with the greatest reluctance that Hilary says things which go beyond Scripture, the only reason he does so is that he has to resist the heretics. – Hilary draws a distinction between resisting audacity, *i.e.* willful unbelief of the heretics which goes beyond Scripture, and error caused by ignorance, see *De Trin.* 6, 15: *Sed si quos timor Dei et intellegentiae ignoratio, non impietatis voluntas, per stultitiae sensum detinuerit in errore, spero ut ad emendationem proclives sint ...* – On imposing a law on God omnipotent see *infra,* 176 ff, *De Trin.* 3, 24; on imposing a limit on the Infinite see *supra,* 33 ff, *De Trin.* 1, 6; on the weakness of speech (implying that words inadequately express thoughts) see *supra,* 37 ff, *De Trin.* 1, 7.

> "What is demanded is immense, the object of our venture is incomprehensible to speak about God in terms which go beyond what God had determined beforehand. God has given as names of His reality the names Father, Son and Holy Ghost. Words cannot express, mind cannot pursue and intellect cannot comprehend what is further sought. It is ineffable, unattainable, incomprehensible. The nature of the divine matter itself annihilates the indicative power of the words, the imperspicable light blinds the gazing of the eye of the mind, what is contained by no limit exceeds the capacity of intellect."

Here again Scripture is set as the barrier to human intellect. If the theologian goes beyond Scripture it is not with the intention to receive more revelation than given there, but it is a reluctant attempt to understand what has been revealed in Scripture. – On the ineffability of God see further *supra,* 33 ff, *De Trin.* 1, 6-7. On God as a blinding light see the quotation from *De Trin.* 10, 53, given *supra,* 75; this is a commonplace, see *e.g.* Novatian, *De Trin.* 2, 15: *Nam si ad solis aspectum oculorum nostrorum*

acies hebetescit ... hoc idem mentis acies patitur in cogitatione omni de deo et, quanto
ad considerandum deum plus intenditur, tanto magis ipsa cogitationis suae luce
caecatur and, apart from the parallels quoted by H. Weyer, *Novatianus, De*
Trinitate, Über den dreifaltigen Gott. Text und Übersetzung mit Einleitung und
Kommentar, Darmstadt 1962, p 48, further Irenaeus, *Adv. Haer.* 4, 45, 1,
Minucius Felix, *Oct.* 32, 5 f.

> "But asking Him, who is all this, forgiveness for this necessity, we will ven-
> ture, enquire and speak and – the only promise we can make in a matter of
> such importance – we shall believe what will be indicated to us (by Scrip-
> ture)."

On the necessity (imposed on him by the heretics) to speak see *supra*, 67,
De Trin. 2, 2. Again Hilary stresses that the goal of speaking is to express
faith in revelation given to him and nothing beyond this.

II. THE FATHER, SON AND HOLY GHOST
(6-35)

A) God the Father (6-7)

God the Father, the origin of all things, is infinite, beyond time and
beyond space. At the same time He is in His totality everywhere. As such
the Father is ineffable.

CHAPTER 6

The infinity of God the Father.

Translation and Commentary:

> **(6)** "It is the Father to whom all that has come into being owes its origin.
> In Christ and through Christ He Himself is the origin of all things."

On God as the Creator through Christ see *infra*, 99 ff, *De Trin.* 2, 17 ff.

> "But He is self-existent, He does not draw His being from without but He
> possesses what He is from Himself and in Himself."

God is self-caused, cf. *De Trin.* 3, 2: *... non aliunde quid sumens.* This is the
answer to the question of heretical and philosophical gainsayers quoted
by Tertullian, *De praescr.* 7, 5: *unde deus?*, cf. *infra*, 154.

> "He is infinite, because He Himself is not inside anything, but all things
> are inside Him. He is always outside space, because He is not contained.
> He is always before time, because time has been created by Him. Let your
> thoughts range if you think that there is a limit to him: you will always find
> that He is, for however far you may strain, there is always towards which to

strain. Always to strain towards His space is the same to you as it is to Him to be without limit. Words will fail with Him, His nature will not be circumscribed. Again, revolve the times, and you will always find that He is, and whilst the number of count may fail to be expressed, God nevertheless does not fail to possess eternal being.''

What is said here about God's infinity in space is a repetition of what was said in *De Trin.* 1, 6, see *supra*, 33 ff, with this small difference that there Hilary stated that God is outside and inside all things at the same time, and here he says that God contains all things without Himself being contained. Time is created by God, see on this *infra*, 99, *De Trin.* 2, 17. Therefore God in His eternity is still beyond time, however far we try to go back in time, cf. *De Trin.* 12, 26: *Aeternum autem est, quidquid tempus excedit*; 12, 24: *id quod infinitum in Deo est, semper se infiniti sensus nostri recursui subtrahat: ut ante id, quod proprium Deo est, semper esse, aliquid aliud intentio retroacta non capiat; quia nihil aliud ultra ad intellegentiam Dei, aeternitate procedendi, quam Deum semper esse semper occurrat.* God's infinity in time is described in the same way as God's infinity in space.

> ''Gird up your intellect and try to comprehend the totality (of God) in your mind, you grasp nothing. This totality has a rest, but this rest is always in the totality. So there is neither totality where there is a rest, nor is anything which is total a rest. For a rest is a part, but totality is the whole. But God is everywhere and is in His totality wherever He is. So He exceeds the range of our intellect, outside whom there is nothing and whose eternal characteristic is to be eternal.''

If man tries to think God in His totality, he will fail completeley. For God's totality still includes more than that which is grasped by human mind, and what is not grasped by it is also in God's totality. So if man only grasps a part, he does not grasp totality. Furthermore God's totality knows no parts, for God in His totality is everywhere. Against this argument the following logical objection can, of course, be made: First Hilary says that if man believes that he has grasped God's totality, there is still something left which man has not grasped. This implies that God can only be grasped partially, i.e. that God does have parts. Then Hilary says that God has no parts but is in His totality everywhere. Then the question can be asked: if God is in His totality everywhere and, wherever He is, is in His totality, why is He not in His totality in the human mind which tries to comprehend Him but can only grasp a part of Him? This would not imply that God is enclosed by the human mind, for whilst He is in His totality in the human mind, He can still be in His totality everywhere else as well. One cannot maintain at the same time that God is in His totality everywhere and that only a part of God can be grasped. – That God has no parts is an important element in Hilary's discussion of the relationship between Father and Son, see *infra*, 90 f, *De Trin.* 2, 11.

That God is in His totality where He is, is an idea frequently expressed by Hilary, see *e.g. In Ps.* CXVIII XIX 8: *Adest ubique, et totus ubicumque est: non pro parte usquam est, sed in omnibus omnis est*; CXLIV 21. God is in His totality in all actions, see *In Ps.* CXXIX 3: *Deus autem, qui et ubique et in omnibus est, totus audit, totus videt, totus efficit, totus incedit*; cf. *De Trin.* 9, 72. The same idea appears already in Irenaeus, *Adv. Haer.* 1, 6, 1: ὃς ἅμα τῷ νοηθῆναι καὶ ἐπιτετελεχέναι τοῦθ' ὅπερ ἠθέλησε καὶ ἅμα τῷ θελῆσαι καὶ ἐννοεῖται τοῦθ' ὅπερ καὶ ἠθέλησε, τοῦτο ἐνοούμενος ὃ καὶ θέλει καὶ τότε θέλων ὅτε ἐννοεῖται, ὅλος ἔννοια ὢν ὅλος θέλημα ὅλος νοῦς ὅλος ὀφθαλμὸς ὅλος ἀκοὴ ὅλος πηγὴ πάντων ἀγαθῶν, see further 2, 15, 3; 2, 16, 4; 2, 42, 2; 4, 21, 2; R. M. Grant traces this back to the famous line of Xenophanes οὖλος ὁρᾷ οὖλος δὲ νοεῖ οὖλος δέ τ' ἀκούει, Diels F.V.S. 1, 24, see R. M. Grant, Early Christianity and Pre-Socratic Philosophy, *H. A. Wolfson Jubilee Volume, American Academy for Jewish Research*, Jerusalem 1965, pp 376 ff, cf. also Novatian, *De Trin.* 6, 36: *Ceterum ipse totus oculus, quia totus videt; et totus auris, quia totus audit; et totus manus, quia totus operatur: et totus pes, quia totus ubique est. Idem enim, quicquid illud est totus, aequalis est et totus ubique est*; Athanasius, *Contra Gentes* 28: ὁ γὰρ θεὸς ὅλον ἐστὶ καὶ οὐκ μέρη.

> "This is God's true mystery, here we have in the Father the imperspicable name of His nature: God invisible, ineffable, infinite, speech must be silent when it wants to express Him, mind must be blunted when it wants to investigate Him, intellect must be constrained when it wants to embrace Him. Nevertheless He has the name of His nature in the name 'Father', but He is only Father. For He does not, in a human way, receive His fatherhood from elsewhere."

God's mystery is God's incomprehensible infinity. Hilary goes on to dwell on God's fatherhood: The name 'Father' is an indication of God's nature, this means that God is eternally the Father and does not at a certain moment become the Father. This is particularly stressed in the twelfth book of the *De Trinitate*, see *e.g.* 12, 25: *Ex aeterno autem nihil aliud quam aeternum. Quod si non aeternum, iam nec pater qui generationis est auctor aeternus est. Quod cum illi patrem semper esse, atque huius filium semper esse sit proprium esse, et in eo quod est, significatur aeternitas*; 12, 32: *Aut enim non semper Pater, si non semper et Filius; aut si semper Pater, semper et Filius*; cf. 12, 21, see on the subject of the eternal generation further P. Smulders, *La doctrine trinitaire*, pp 172 ff. This is also an answer to the Arian objection that if Father and Son are of the same substance, then they participate in a substance which is anterior to them, see *De Trin.* 4, 4: *Sequens illa est* (sc. *falsitas eorum*) *quod adfirment id enuntiationem homousii significare, quod rei anterioris adque alterius communio sit duobus et tamquam prior substantia vel usia materiae alicuius extiterit, quae participata duobus et in utroque consumpta utrumque illum et naturae anterioris et rei esse testetur unius* (the same objection is quoted by Athanasius, *Contra Arianos* 1, 14 and *De Synodis* 51). Against this Hilary can state that the Son is generated eternally out of the Father who has no beginning. Athanasius argues in a similar way, see *Contra Arianos* 1, 14: οὐ γὰρ ἔκ τινος ἀρχῆς προϋπαρχούσης ὁ Πατὴρ καὶ ὁ Υἱὸς ἐγεννήθησαν, ἵνα καὶ ἀδελφοὶ νομισθῶσιν, ἀλλ᾽ ὁ Πατὴρ ἀρχὴ τοῦ Υἱοῦ καὶ γεννήτωρ ἐστί, καὶ ὁ Πατὴρ πατήρ ἐστι καὶ οὐχ υἱός τινος γέγονε, καὶ ὁ Υἱὸς δὲ υἱός ἐστι καὶ οὐκ ἀδελφός. Εἰ δὲ ἀΐδιον γέννημα τοῦ Πατρὸς λέγεται καλῶς λέγεται. The eternity of Father and Son prevent, according to Athanasius, a theogony in which, in a human way, in the course of time one father begets the other, *i.e.* a father begets a son who in his turn begets a son who in his turn will become a father as well, see *Ad Ser.* 1, 15-16; 4, 6.

> "He is unbegotten, eternal, eternally having in Himself His eternal existence."

On God's selforiginated existence see *supra*, 78, and *infra*, 82, *De Trin.* 2, 7.

> "Only to the Son is He known, for no one knows the Father save the Son and he to whom the Son wants to reveal Him, nor yet the Son save the Father (*Matth.* 11:27). They have a mutual knowledge, and their mutual knowledge is perfect. And since no one knows the Father save the Son, let our thoughts of the Father be at one with the Son, the only faithful Witness (*Rev.* 1:5), Who reveals Him."

On *Matthew* 11:27, see *infra*, 83. The Arians deny that the Son has a perfect knowledge of the Father, see Athanasius, *Contra Arianos* 1, 6: ... ἔθηκεν (sc. ὁ ῎Αρειος) ἐν τῇ θαλείᾳ ὡς ... οὔτε γινώσκειν τελείως καὶ ἀκριβῶς δύναται ὁ Λόγος τὸν ἑαυτοῦ Πατέρα. This insistence that only the Son has a perfect knowledge of the Father leads to what will now be stressed again: God is ineffable.

CHAPTER 7

The ineffability of the Father.

Translation and Commentary:

> **(7)** "And I should rather think this about the Father than say it. For I am well aware that all speech is too weak to express the things of God. He must be known who is invisible, incomprehensible, eternal. But to say that He is self-originating and self-existent, that He is invisible, incomprehensible and eternal, in these words there is a confession of His glory, an indication of the idea we have, some sketch of our view, but our speech is inferior to nature and our words do not explain reality as it is."

On speech which is below thought and therefore inadequately expresses thought see *supra*, 37 ff, *De Trin.* 1, 7, cf. also *De Trin.* 1, 6, *supra*, 33 ff, and 2, 6, *supra*, 78 ff.

"For when you hear that He is Himself, this contradicts human reason, for we make a distinction between possessing and being possessed, and what is and that in which it is are two things. Again, if you hear that He is out of Himself, nobody is the giver and the gift at the same time."

When God is out of Himself, then God is Himself the Giver of a Gift which is His own life, *i.e.* which He is Himself. This is a similar paradox as when it says that God is in Himself. That God is self-originating was already said in *De Trin.* 2, 6, now it is explained why this is in fact beyond human understanding and not a plausible statement at all. If God causes His own life, then He is the Giver and Receiver at the same time, which is impossible in the created sphere which we know. – For the meaning of *absolutio*, 'explanation', see R. J. Kinnavey, *op. cit.*, p 83 (the examples listed under b), not under c)). It was already said that in God there is no distinction between *habere* and *haberi*, when the paradox was referred to that God is at the same time inside and outside all things; see *De Trin.* 1, 6, *supra*, 33 ff. In explaining *John* 5:26 ("As the Father has life in Himself, He has granted to the Son to have life in Himself") Hilary says that in God there is no difference between what He has and what He is, but His total being is life, see *De Trin.* 8, 43: … *non humano modo ex compositis Deus est, ut in eo aliud sit quod ab eo habetur, et aliud sit ipse qui habeat: sed totum quod est, vita est.* This identity of Giver and gift, of cause and what is caused is beyond human understanding.

"If you hear that He is immortal, then it follows that there is something not originated by Him, to which He is not subject according to this word used by you. And this is not the only thing which because of the use of this word is claimed by somebody else."

The first thing mentioned was that God causes Himself, this is beyond human understanding. Now a second thing which is beyond human understanding is mentioned: God is immortal – this sounds plausible, but it in fact means, according to Hilary, that death does not find its origin in God. As Watson, *op. cit.*, p 54 n. 5, suggests, this seems incompatible with the statement that God is the cause of all things, so God is at the same time the cause of, *inter alia*, death, and He is not the cause of death. Watson may also be right in saying that what is further excluded from God by the word 'immortal' are disease and pain.

"If you hear that He is incomprehensible, it follows that He is nowhere, since it is denied that He can be touched."

So the seemingly plausible word 'incomprehensible' implies that God is *nowhere*, since what cannot be grasped or touched is nowhere, but this is incompatible with what was said in the previous chapter, *viz.*, that God is *everywhere*, see *supra*, 78 ff. Hilary must, of course, realize here as well that this implies a bodily, human way of speaking about God. What can be touched is bodily, cf. Tertullian, who in *De anima* 5, 6 and *Adv. Marc.* 4, 8, 3 (see J. H. Waszink's edition of *De anima*, p 130) quotes a line of Lucrece: *tangere enim et tangi nisi corpus nulla potest res*. Hilary himself attacks the Arians for speaking in a bodily way about God, see *infra*, 133. What Hilary wants to show here is that the seemingly plausible word 'incomprehensible' for God can, if it is used on the bodily level, lead to the absurd consequence that God is nowhere. Man must realize that when he applies this word to God it transcends the bodily level and therefore is not easily understood.

> "If you hear that He is invisible, then what does not visibly exist, is devoid of its own existence."

The seemingly plausible word 'invisible' implies that God does not exist, but this is incompatible with the fact that God is self-existing and self-originating, see *supra*, 78 ff.

> "So our confession fails in our speech, and whatever word will be used for Him, it cannot express how God is and how great He is."

All the plausible and usual words for God end up in contradictions, when they are used as in the bodily sphere. When man realizes that God is beyond this sphere, he realizes that God is also beyond these words.

> "Perfect knowledge is to know God in such a way, that you know that He is, although not unknowable, nevertheless ineffable. He has to be believed, understood, adored, and in doing this expressed."

God is not unknowable, but He is ineffable, – Hilary is not consistent in his use of *ignorabilis* for God, in *De Trin.* 6, 26 he says in explaining *Matth* 11:27: *Tam ignorabilis est Filius quam et Pater*. Here in *De Trin.* 2, 7 he wants to say that the inadequacy of human speech does not lead to the consequence that God cannot be known at all, *i.e.* that there is no revelation. Without revelation God is *ignorabilis*, see *De Trin.* 11, 33: ... *quia cessante in nobis fide Filii, ignorabilis Pater est, non adituris ad paternam religionem, nisi prius Filii veneratione suscepta*. On the ineffability of God see the definition of *inenarrabilis* given in *De Trin.* 4, 2: *Quod enim inenarrabile est, id significantiae alicuius finem et modum non habet*. Ineffability does not imply unknowability, see *De Syn.* 79: *Numquid si inenarrabilis est* (sc. *generatio Filii*), *ideo et ignorabilis est?* On faith and intellect see *supra*, 40, *De Trin.* 1, 7.

B) God the Son (8-28)

1) The eternal generation of the Son (8-23)

The Son is the perfect offspring of the Father. The 'how' of this generation remains unknown to man, so does the 'moment' of generation. This is discussed extensively with the help of the first verses of the Prologue of the fourth gospel, and defended against the misinterpretations by the heretics.

CHAPTER 8

The Son as the perfect offspring of the Father.

Translation and Commentary:

> (8) "We have sailed from a harbourless coast into a stormy open sea, and we can neither safely retreat nor safely advance, yet what lies before us has more difficulties in store than what is behind."

The metaphor of the sea-voyage (which is a common one, see *supra*, 5 f, and further E. R. Curtius, *Europäische Literatur und lateinisches Mittelalter*, Bern/München 1967⁶, pp 138 ff; T. Janson, *Latin Prose Prefaces. Studies in Literary Conventions*, Stockholm 1964, pp 146 ff) occurs repeatedly, but not always consistently, in the *De Trinitate*, see further *De Trin.* 1, 37 (*supra*, 5 f), where he says that he is about to start his voyage; here in 2, 8 he says that he has left behind the harbourless coast, in 7, 3 again he says that he is leaving the harbour, in 10, 67 he says that faith always calls itself back into the harbour of its religion (on truth as a safe harbour see further *supra*, 26), and finally in 12, 1-2 where he says that the Holy Ghost will finally lead him to the safe harbour. – On the statement here in 2, 8 that the voyage ahead is more difficult than the one behind cf. Quintilian who says that the voyage in its course has become more difficult, Proem to book 12 of *Inst. or.*

> "The Father is as He is and He has to be believed to be as He is. The mind shrinks from contacting the Son and every word trembles to give itself away."

The Father cannot adequately be expressed by human language and can only be believed. Similarly the Son is beyond human mind and *a fortiori* beyond human speech. This is the reason why the voyage will be more difficult than it has been until now: now he will not only have to deal with the Father, who is ineffable, but also with the Son, who is ineffable as well.

> "For He is the Offspring of the Unbegotten, One from One, true from true, living from living, perfect from perfect, the Power of Power, Wisdom of Wisdom, Glory of Glory, Image of the invisible God, Likeness of the unbegotten Father. But in what sense can we conceive that the Only-begotten is the Offspring of the Unbegotten? For repeatedly the Father cries from heaven: 'This is my beloved Son in whom I am well pleased'?"

That the Son is the offspring of the Father implies that He shares with the

Father unity, verity, life, perfection, power, wisdom and glory. But the Son is only-begotten, the Father is unbegotten, so here there is a difference, but how can He then still be the offspring of the Father? (The Arians claim that in this case the Son ought to be unbegotten as well; see *infra*, 90 f, *De Trin.* 2, 11). But in the gospel the Father declares repeatedly (at Jesus' baptism and His transfiguration) that Jesus is His Son, *i.e.* Offspring. In *De Trin.* 6, 24 Hilary gives as the reason of this repetition: ... *ut id firmius crederetur ad vitam, quod non credidisse mors esset* (for Hilary's views on repetition in general see *infra*, 143 ff, *De Trin.* 3, 9). This declaration of the Father is, according to Hilary, made in order to distinguish Jesus from the sons of God through adoption: only this man is called "My Son", *De Trin.* 6, 23: *Alios quidem cognominatos habeo in filios, sed hic Filius meus est; donavi adoptionis plurimis nomen, sed iste mihi Filius est,* cf. 6, 27. (On the difference between generation and adoption see further P. Smulders, *La doctrine trinitaire,* pp 151 ff.) The words "This is My Son" are a declaration of the Son's nature, the words (spoken at the transfiguration) "listen to Him" are an indication of the reason for His descent from heaven, see *De Trin.* 6, 28: *Ut enim in eo quod ait Pater: 'Hic est Filius meus' naturae demonstratio est, et in eo quod subiecit: 'Hunc audite' sacramenti et fidei ob quam e caelis venit auditio est*; cf. Athanasius who explains this verse as an indication that the Son is out of the substance of the Father, *Contra Arianos* 1, 15, *De Syn.* 35.

> "He is no rending or division, for He who begot Him cannot suffer, and He who was generated is the image of the invisible God, and He testifies: 'Because the Father is in Me and I am in the Father?'"

The Son cannot be a rending or division of the Father, since the Father is without passion, this is said time and again by Hilary, see *e.g. De Trin.* 3, 3; 5, 2, 37; 6, 35; 7, 11; 8, 41. This is in fact more a remark made in defence of the orthodox doctrine against an Arian accusation, than an accusation against an Arian doctrine, since the Arians oppose the *homoousion* for this very reason, see *De Trin.* 4, 4: ... *hanc inprobandi homousii causam comminiscuntur, quod secundum verbi huius significationem ex divisione paternae substantiae esse Filius existimetur: tamquam desectus ex eo fuerit ita ut in duos sit res una divisa ... nec posse in Deum cadere divisionis passionem* (cf. 6, 10). – Athanasius opposes a desection in God for the same reason, see *Contra Arianos* 1, 16, 28; 2, 34; *Ep. ad ep. Aeg. et Lib.* 16 (cf. G.-L. Prestige, *Dieu dans la pensée patristique* (trad.), Paris 1955, pp 29 ff.). It is also a philosophical tenet that division implies passion or affection, see Porphyry, *De Sent.* 21, Proclus, *Elem. theol.*, prop. 69 and 80. – On Christ's words "The Father is in Me and I am in the Father" see *infra*, 127 ff, 133, *De Trin.* 3, 1, 4.

> "He is not adopted, for He is the true Son of the Father and cries: 'He that has seen Me has seen the Father also.' "

The words of the Father spoken at Jesus' baptism and transfiguration exclude, according to Hilary, that He is merely an adopted son, see *supra*, 85; Christ's words spoken here exclude this as well, cf. *De Trin*. 8, 48.

> "But neither was He commanded to come into existence as the other creatures. For He is the Only-begotten of the One, and He has life in Himself, as has life in Himself He who begot Him, for He says: 'As the Father has life in Himself, so He gave to the Son to have life in Himself' (*John* 5:26)."

Hilary here opposes the Arian doctrine that Christ is a (be it: outstanding) creature of God, who came into being through the will of God; naturally he attacks this doctrine frequently, see *e.g. De Trin*. 3, 22; 4, 3, 4, 11; 6, 1, 18, 28, 38 f; 10, 3; 11, 4; 12, 1 f, 5 f. Like Athanasius (see *e.g. Contra Arianos* 3, 60, 61) Hilary makes a clear distinction between creation and generation (creation having a beginning in time, generation being eternal), see *De Trin*. 11, 4; 12, 1 f. But here we find a difference between Athanasius and Hilary as well: Athanasius distinguishes between "creation through will" and "generation out of substance" (Athanasius denies that the Son has been generated through the will of the Father), Hilary distinguishes between "creation through will" and "generation through will" (Hilary says that the Son has been generated through the will of the Father), see on this difference between Hilary and Athanasius *infra*, 134 f, *De Trin*. 3, 4.

> "But there is not a portion of the Father in the Son either. For the Son testifies: 'All things that the Father has are mine', and again, 'And all things that are mine are Thine, and Thine are Mine.' The apostle, too, testifies: 'For in Him dwells all the fulness of the Godhead bodily.' And it is impossible that a portion be the whole. He is the perfect One from the perfect One, for He who has all has given all. And we must not imagine that He (the Father) did not give because He still has, nor that He does not have because He gave."

The Arians, too, reject as Manichean the doctrine that the Son is a portion or part of the Father, see *De Trin*. 6, 10, *supra*, 73 f. Biblical texts show that the Father has given the totality of His being to the Son without, in doing so, losing the totality of His being, cf. *De Trin*. 6, 12: ... *sine detrimento suo naturam suam praestat ex sese, ut det quod habet et quod dederit habeat ...*; 7, 20: *quia et omnia habere sola natura possit indifferens, neque nativitas aliquid possit habere nisi datum sit*, cf. 9, 31; 11, 29; *De Syn*. 16: *Non enim aliud habet quam dedit: et sicut vitam habens, ita habendam dedit vitam*; Athanasius, *Contra Arianos* 3, 36. This implies that there is no diminution of the Godhead in the generation of the Son, see on this *infra*, 106, *De Trin*. 2, 22.

CHAPTER 9

The Son's generation is only known to the Father and the Son. Man does not even know his own generation.

Translation and Commentary:

> **(9)** "So both of them keep the secret of this generation. And if by chance somebody blames his lack of understanding that he cannot get hold of the mystery of this generation, whilst nevertheless the Father as such is known and the Son as such as well, then he will hear with even greater pain that I do not know it either. I do not know, and I do not investigate. And nevertheless I shall comfort myself: The archangels do no know it, the angels have not heard it, the ages do not comprehend it, the prophet has not perceived it, the Apostle has not asked about it, the Son Himself has not revealed it."

It is not entirely clear whether the 'greater pain' is felt by him who hears that Hilary does not know the mystery of the Trinity, or by Hilary himself because he does not know it. The latter possibility could be suggested by the fact that Hilary declares that he derives comfort for his ignorance from the fact that even the angels and apostles do not know it. But it is more likely that Hilary wants to say that somebody who thinks that he knows the Father and the Son, and who regrets that he does not know the way of generation, will be even more disappointed when he hears that Hilary cannot tell him about it. Hilary does not claim to know the Father and the Son perfectly (see *De Trin.* 2, 6-8, *supra*, 78 ff), so he cannot deplore his ignorance even more than he who wrongly presumes to know the Father and the Son perfectly. – To say that the generation of the Son is an unknown secret, was a commonplace amongst early Christian theologians (cf. C. F. A. Borchardt, *op. cit.*, pp 75 f, who refers as a parallel to Athanasius, *Contra Arianos* 2, 36), see *e.g.* Irenaeus, *Adv. Haer.* 2, 42, 4: *Si quis itaque nobis dixerit: Quomodo ergo Filius prolatus a Patre est? dicimus ei quia ... generationem ... nemo novit ... neque angeli, neque archangeli, neque principatus, neque potestates, nisi solus qui generavit Pater et qui natus est Filius*; Novatian, *De Trin.* 31, 183: *cuius sacrae et divinae nativitatis arcana nec apostolus didicit nec prophetes comperit nec angelus scivit nec creatura cognoscit, filio soli nota sunt, qui patris secreta cognovit*; Lactance, *Inst.* 4, 8; Athanasius, *De Inc.* 37. Hilary stresses the secret of the generation of the Son time and again, see *e.g. De Trin.* 2, 21; 6, 9, 16, 35; 7, 27; 10, 7; 11, 46 ff; 12, 26.

> "Let the painful complaints stop! Whoever you are, who are making enquiries into this, I am not calling you back into height, I am not stretching you out into breadth, I am not leading you into depth. You do not mind that you do not know the generation of the Creator, if you do not know the origin of creatures, do you?"

It would be useless to call the man who wants to know the manner of generation to the height, breadth and depth of creation, since he will

know that he cannot know the origin of creation. Then he should ac-
quiesce in not knowing the generation of the Creator either. Here the
argument is *a minore ad maius*. On the uselessness of questions regarding
the origin of creation cf. *In Ps.* I 2: *Cum enim quaeras, cur mundus, et quando,
et in quantum? ... circa haec impietatis suae consilia agitur semper, et vadit, loco
consistendi in his consiliis non reperto*, cf. Irenaeus, *Adv. Haer.* 2, 41, 4; 2, 42,
4, see on this matter especially G. C. Stead, *Divine Substance*, pp 195 ff.

> "I am only asking you this question: Do you understand your own birth
> and do you comprehend what has been born out of you? I am not asking
> you whence you drew your understanding, whence you obtained your life,
> whence you received your intellect, what is the nature of your senses of
> smell, touch, sight, hearing. Surely everybody knows what he does. I am
> asking you: whence do you give this to your children, how do you insert the
> faculty of perception, lighten the eyes, implant the heart? Tell me this, if
> you can. So you have powers which you do not know, you impart what you
> do not understand; you do not mind your ignorance in what is your own,
> but impudently you do not want to be ignorant in the things of God.

As he does not want to ask for an explanation of the origin of creation, he
does not ask his opponent to give an explanation of his own birth. His opponent knows about his existence and about his powers, without being
able to explain how this came into being, since in the earliest stages of his
life he was unconscious of all this. So Hilary asks a seemingly easier question: how does he impart to his own children what he himself received but
is unable to explain? Now he is in a stage of his life in which he should be
able to explain this. If he acquiesces in this lack of knowledge, then he
should not impudently enquire into the generation of the Son, his
Creator. Again the argument is *a minore ad maius*. Hilary's scepticism
about knowledge of how man imparts his powers to his children shows
that he was obviously not impressed by theories as put forward by Tertullian, *De anima* 25-27 about the simultaneous origin and growth of body
and soul in the embryo, see J. H. Waszink's edition, pp 318 ff, and by
Lactance, *De op.* 12, who begins his discussion about the uterus and conception with saying that, although these are in a hidden place, they cannot escape our sense and understanding: ... *quae quamquam in operto latent,
sensum tamen atque intellegentiam latere non possunt* (see on this chapter M.
Perrin, *Lactance, L'ouvrage du Dieu Créateur, II, Introduction, Texte critique,
Traduction*, Paris 1974 (S.C. 214), pp 355 ff). Hilary expresses a similar
ignorance about the movement of his mind, *De Trin.* 12, 53: *nam
diiudicantis mentis meae aut motum aut rationem aut vitam et non intellegens sentio,
et sentiens tibi debeo* ... and about his rebirth, and there, too, his ignorance
implies no doubt about its reality, see *De Trin.* 12, 56: *Regenerationis meae
fidem obtinens nescio, et quod ignoro iam teneo. Sine sensu enim meo renascor, cum
efficientia renascendi.*

CHAPTER 10

The generation of the Son remains a secret.

Translation and Commentary:

> **(10)** "So listen to the unbegotten Father, listen to the only-begotten Son. Hear: 'The Father is greater than I.' Hear: 'I and the Father are one.' Hear: 'He that has seen Me has seen the Father also.' Hear: 'The Father is in Me and I am in the Father.' Hear: 'I went out from the Father.' And: 'All that He has, He has delivered to Me.' And: 'The Son has life in Himself, as the Father has life in Himself too.' Hear that the Son is the Image, Wisdom, Power, and Glory of God. And notice that the Holy Spirit proclaims: 'Who shall declare His generation.' And rebuke the Lord when He testifies: 'No one knows the Son save the Father, neither does anyone know the Father save the Son and he to whom the Son wants to reveal Him.' "

These Biblical texts make a distinction between the unbegotten Father and the only-begotten Son, but they also say that the Son reveals the Father perfectly, cf. *supra*, 84 ff, *De Trin.* 2, 8. These Biblical texts declare the generation of the Son to be a mystery. It is somewhat strange that Hilary all of a sudden says 'Rebuke the Lord', *obiurga Dominum*; this can, as R. J. Kinnavey suggests, only be understood as being intensely ironical, *op. cit.*, p 152 (on irony in Hilary see M. F. Buttell, *op. cit.*, p 89).

> "Penetrate into this mystery, and between the one unbegotten God and the one only-begotten God plunge into the secret of the unconceivable generation. Begin, go on, persevere. Although I know that you will not reach the goal, I congratulate you on making progress. For he who with piety pursues the infinite, though he never reaches the goal, nevertheless will profit from going on. Intelligence here makes a halt at the limit set by the words (of the Bible)."

The right knowledge of God is to know that He is infinite and to pursue Him infinitely, realizing that one will never reach Him, see *supra*, 33 ff, *De Trin.* 1, 6. The heretics make the mistake of wanting to embrace the Infinite with their thoughts, see *supra*, 54 f, *De Trin.* 1, 15. Hilary exhorts his opponent to think endlessly about the mystery of the generation of the Son without ever solving it. But in the end human understanding can never go beyond the Scriptural revelation.

CHAPTER 11

The Son is the perfect Offspring of the Father.

Translation and Commentary:

> **(11)** "The Son is from the Father who truly *is*, the only-begotten from the

unbegotten, Offspring from Parent, Living from Living. As the Father has life in Himself, even so life in Himself was given to the Son.''

The Son is from the Father who truly is, this is an allusion to *Exodus* 3:14. In *De Trin.* 12, 24 f Hilary says that this implies the eternity of the Son: 12, 24: *Nam secundum ad Moysen dictum, Misit me ad vos is qui est, Deo proprium esse id quod est, non ambiguus sensus est*; 12, 25: *Erat igitur atque est* (sc. *Filius*): *quia ab eo est, qui quod est semper est*; this is opposition against the Arian tenet that God, who *is*, creates the Son who was not, see *e.g.* Athanasius, *Contra Arianos* 1, 24: ὁ ὢν τὸν μὴ ὄντα (πεποίηκεν). On the life of the Father and the Son see *infra*, 91.

"He is the Perfect from the Perfect, since He is the Whole from the Whole."

On the Perfect from the Perfect see *supra*, 66, *De Trin.* 2, 1 and *infra*, 141, *De Trin.* 3, 8. On the Whole from the Whole cf. 8, 56 where it appears that this is directed against the theory that the Son is a part of the Father: ... *intellege ... ex toto totum ... Huius itaque divinitas corporalis in Christo est, non ex parte, sed tota*; see further 9, 61 and *supra*, 78 ff, *De Trin.* 2, 6.

"There is no division or rending, for each is in the other, and the fulness of the Godhead is in the Son. Incomprehensible from Incomprehensible, for nobody knows them, they only know each other."

For opposition against a division in God see *supra*, 85, *De Trin.* 2, 8. Not only the Father is incomprehensible, see *supra*, 78 ff, *De Trin.* 2, 6-7, but also the Son, see *supra*, 84 ff, *De Trin.* 2, 8. On the mutual knowledge of Father and Son see *supra*, 81, *De Trin.* 2, 6.

"Invisible from Invisible, because He is the Image of the invisible God and because he that has seen the Son has also seen the Father."

On the Son as the Image of the Father see *supra*, 28, *De Trin.* 1, 4.

"The One is from the Other, for they are Father and Son. There is no difference in the divine nature, for both are one."

The distinction is stressed against the Sabellians, who identify Father and Son; the difference in nature is excluded against the Arians; see *supra*, 56, *De Trin.* 1, 16 and *supra*, 72, *De Trin.* 2, 4.

"God from God, the only-begotten God from the one unbegotten God, not two gods, but one from one, not two unbegotten gods, because one is born from the unborn."

One of the Arian objections against the doctrine that Father and Son are of the same substance is that in that case both ought to be unbegotten, see *De Trin.* 10, 6 and 4, 33 where Hilary says that the equality of Father and

Son does not follow from the fact that the Son is *innascibilis* like the Father, cf. Athanasius, *Contra Arianos* 1, 21, who opposes the Arian objection that if the Son is the Image of the Father, the Son ought to generate and become a Father as well, in the latter case it is not said that there should be two Unbegotten Ones, but two Begetters.

> "The One is from the Other without diversity, for the Life of the Living is in the Living."

On the subject that the Son receives the totality of life from the Father see *supra*, 86, *De Trin.* 2, 8 and 7, 39; 8, 53; 9, 53, 69; 10, 6; 11, 5 and Novatian, *De Trin.* 14, 76, see C. F. A. Borchardt, *op. cit.*, p 103, n. 221.

> "This is what we just touch upon regarding the divine nature, not getting hold of a total understanding, but realizing that what we are talking about is incomprehensible."

In *De Trin.* 2, 7, *supra*, 82 f, it was said that God, since He is incomprehensible, cannot be touched. Here this is slightly modified and it is said that human mind can only touch upon the divine nature without being able to enclose it. This is again in line with the idea that the infinite mind can always pursue the infinite God without ever reaching full knowledge of Him, *De Trin.* 1, 6, *supra*, 33 ff.

> "So, you object, there is no service of faith, if nothing can be comprehended? On the contrary, let faith profess this service, that it knows that it cannot comprehend that from which the enquiry arises."

On this confession of faith see *supra*, 40, *De Trin.* 1, 8.

CHAPTER 12

When was the Son generated?

Translation and Commentary:

> **(12)** "There is still something to be said about the inexplicable generation of the Son. Or rather this 'something' is the whole matter."

After it has been made clear that the manner in which the Son was generated cannot be known, it will now be made clear that the time when the Son was generated cannot be known, since this generation is beyond time.

> "I waver, I am disturbed, my mind fails and I do not know where to begin."

On this rhetorical figure of *diaporesis*, where one pretends to be at a loss where to begin or end, a hesitation which must lend an impression of truth to one's words, see M. F. Buttell, *The Rhetoric of St. Hilary of Poitiers*, The Catholic University of America, Washington, D.C., 1933, p 93.

> "For I do not know when the Son was generated, and at the same time it is not allowed for me to be ignorant of the fact that He was generated. Whom shall I call upon, whom ask for help? From what books shall I take the words in order to explain so great a difficulty? Shall I read through the whole philosophy of Greece? But I have read: 'Where is the wise? where is the enquirer of this world?' In this matter the philosophers of the world and the wise men of Paganism are dumb: for they have rejected the wisdom of God."

He must know that the Son has been generated, since this is taught by Scripture. The answer to the question, when the Son was generated, will be taken from the Prologue of the fourth gospel (see *infra*, 94 ff, *De Trin.* 2, 13 ff). First other sources are taken into consideration and rejected. Greek philosophy cannot provide an explanation for the divine generation, since it has rejected the wisdom of God (I *Cor.* 1, 19, see *infra*, 176 f, *De Trin.* 3, 24). This again shows that Hilary had hardly any knowledge of Neo-Platonism, since there he could have learned about an eternal generation, as Augustine rightly says (see *supra*, 43 f, *De Trin.* 1, 10). – The philosophers are referred to as *sophistae* (cf. *De Trin.* 3, 10); on this contemptuous description see J. H. Waszink's edition of Tertullian, *De anima*, pp 356 f. – Hilary quite often makes statements about the value of Greek philosophy. Usually these are negative: philosophers try to make the Christian confession about God the Creator ridiculous, *In Ps.* LXIII 5, they are offended by the cross, death and resurrection of Christ, *In Ps.* LXVII 21, *De Trin.* 3, 25 (see *infra*, 178 ff), philosophy does not lead to knowledge of God, *De Trin.* 5, 21, crafty philosophy comes forward with intricate questions, *De Trin.* 12, 19 (on the *quaestiones* see *infra*, 154, *De Trin.* 3, 14). The most dangerous aspect of philosophy is that the heretics take their inspiration from it. In *De Trin.* 3, 8 Hilary says that the philosophers argue that one cannot be generated out of one, but only out of two, in *De Trin.* 8, 3 he says that the Arians argue in this way with the subtlety of a Pagan mind (see *infra*, 141), in *De Trin.* 7, 1 it is said that the Arians adapt their doctrine to Pagan philosophy. It is a commonplace amongst early Christian writers to trace heresies back to philosophy, see *e.g.* Irenaeus, *Adv. Haer.* 2, 18, 2; Tertullian, *Adv. Marc.* 1, 13, 3; 4, 25, 3; *De praescr.* 7, 3; *Adv. Herm.* 1, 3; 8, 3; 44; *De anima* 3, 1 (see J. H. Waszink's edition p 115); Athanasius, *De Decr.* 28, *Contra Arianos* 1, 30; 2, 14. But Hilary also wants to fight the heretics with their own philosophical weapons: in *De Trin.* 7, 4 he expresses the hope that he can make it clear to Pagan philosophy, which does not accept the mystery of faith, that the church does preach the truth against the heretics, *i.e.*, that the orthodox doctrine is superior to the heretical one: *Sed eam, ut spero, ec-clesia doctrinae suae lucem etiam imprudentiae saeculi invehit, ut licet fidei sacramentum non suscipiat, tamen adversum haereticos veritatem sacramenti a nobis intellegat praedicari.* This in fact implies that the heretical doctrines are worse than the philosophical ones. This, too, is a commonplace amongst early Christian writers, see *e.g.* Irenaeus, *Adv. Haer.* 2, 18, 1; 2, 8, 2; 3, 39, 41; Tertullian, *Adv. Marc.* 1, 13, 3; *De anima* 23, 5; Athanasius, *De Decr.* 28 (see on this text *infra*, 106, *De Trin.* 2, 22)). Therefore heresy and philosophy should not be shunned, but refuted (with reasonable arguments), since the apostle has not left us with a faith void of reason, see *De Trin.* 12, 20: *Cavendum igitur adversum philosophiam est, et humanarum traditionum non tam evitanda sunt studia, quam refutanda ... oportet eos, qui Christum praedicant mundo, irreligiosis mundi imperfectisque doctrinis per scien-tiam sapientis omnipotentiae contraire ... Fidem non nudam Apostolus atque inopem rationis reliquit*; cf. J. E. Emmenegger, *op. cit.*, p 70.

> "Shall I consult the Scribe of the Law? But he does not know, for the cross of Christ is an offence to him."

See on the offence the Jews take at the cross *infra*, 178 ff, *De Trin.* 3, 25. – So according to Hilary neither the philosophers nor the scribes can help to give an answer to the question of when the Son was generated. In *De Trin.* 8, 52 he says that both the Synagogue and philosophy do not understand that the perfect generation of the Son implies no diminution of the Father: *Hoc Ecclesia intellegit, hoc Synagoga non credit, hoc philosophia non sapit, unum ex uno, et totum a toto, Deum et Filium, neque per nativitatem Patri ademisse quod totum est, neque hoc ipsum totum non secum nascendo tenuisse*, cf. J. E. Emmenegger, *op. cit.*, p 71 (see on this subject of diminution fur-ther *infra*, 106, *De Trin.* 2, 22).

> "Shall I by chance bid you to connive and be silent (in the face of heresy), because sufficient veneration is shown to Him, who is preached, if one believes that the lepers were cleansed, that the deaf heard, the lame ran, the paralysed stood, the blind received sight, the man blind from birth had eyes been given to him, demons were routed, the dead came to life? But the heretics confess all this and yet they perish."

The miracles are not sufficient proof of Christ's divinity, since the heretics, too, believe in Christ's miracles without adhering to the or-thodox doctrine of Christ's divinity; in *De Trin.* 7, 6, *e.g.*, Hilary says that the miracles lead Sabellius to the identification of the Father and the Son. Similarly Tertullian says (*Adv. Marc.* 3, 3) that the miracles are not suffi-cient legitimation of Christ, since Christ Himself says that many would come and perform great miracles (*Matth.* 24:24). – It is interesting that the cure of the man born blind is mentioned separately, after the blind in general who received eye-sight. The story of the cure of the man born blind (*John* 9:1 ff) is treated separately by Hilary in *De Trin.* 6, 48 where he says that not the gift of eye-sight won the man eternal life, but the confession of Jesus as the Son of God and not merely as the Christ (as also the heretics believe Him to be). The underlying idea is obviously that miracles can merely lead to the belief in a Christ who is not truly divine, as the Arians have it. So the miracles are believed by Sabellians and Arians, yet they have the wrong doctrine of Christ. – The fact that Hilary here mentions the cure of the man blind from birth separately could be caused by the fact that he already knows that he will discuss this story in the course of his treatise (which would be a further indication that the contents of the whole treatise was more or less preconceived by Hilary right from the beginning).

CHAPTER 13

The poor fisherman, the evangelist John, can teach him about the generation of the Son.

Translation and Commentary:

(13) "So expect nothing less than lame men running, blind men seeing, flight of demons, the coming to life again of the dead."

This is a *litotes*, since he must expect more than these miracles, if he wants to be instructed adequately about the generation of the Son; – on the *litotes* in Hilary see M. F. Buttell, *op. cit.*, pp 87 f.

"There stands by my side, to help me through the difficulties mentioned above, a poor fisherman, unknown, uneducated, fishing-lines in hand, clothes dripping, muddy feet, every inch a man who has just left the boat."

It is a commonplace in early Christian writers to boast about the fact that the apostles were poor fishermen and that this was a proof of their wisdom being divinely inspired, see Tertullian, *De anima* 3, 3 and the parallels quoted by J. H. Waszink in his edition, p 119, to which can be added Augustin, *De civ.* 10, 29, 2; Athanasius, *De Inc.* 47, 50; it is interesting that Cicero lists the fishery amongst the vulgar occupations, *De off.* 1, 42, 150. – Hilary refers to John as a fisherman repeatedly in this section, in *Ad Const. Aug.* (II) 8 he refers to the apostles as *indocti piscatores*. The special relationship between the apostle John and Jesus is stressed in *De Trin.* 6, 43, cf. Tertullian, *De praescr.* 22, 5.

"Consider and decide, whether it was a greater miracle to have raised the dead or to have imparted to an uneducated man the knowledge of this (divine) doctrine. For he says: 'In the beginning was the Word.' What does this mean, 'in the beginning was'? Times are passed by, centuries are left behind, ages removed. Fix in your mind a beginning, whatever you want, you will not get hold of that beginning in time, for then the beginning we are speaking about already was.''

The evangelist transcends time when he says that the Word was in the beginning, therefore no moment of time can be fixed as this beginning, since the beginning in which the Word was transcends time. This was already said about the Father and it is now repeated about the Son, see *De Trin.* 2, 6; cf. for this use of *John* 1:1 as a proof of Christ's eternity, Athanasius, *Contra Arianos*: 1, 11: οὐδεμία γὰρ τῶν ἁγίων Γραφῶν τοιοῦτόν τι (sc. ἦν ποτε ὅτε οὐκ ἦν) περὶ τοῦ Σωτῆρος εἴρηκεν, ἀλλὰ μᾶλλον τὸ ἀεὶ τὸ ἀΐ-διον καὶ τὸ συνεῖναι ἀεὶ τῷ Πατρί, this is followed by a quotation of *John* 1:1.

> ''Turn your attention upon the world, see what is written about it: 'In the beginning God made heaven and earth'. So what is created comes into being in the beginning, and you can get hold of in time that which is stated in the beginning to have come into being.''

Unlike the Word, the world *was* not in the beginning, but *came into being* in the beginning, *i.e.* it has a temporal beginning. In *De Trin.* 12, 16-17 he argues that it is typical of created things once not to have been, but *not* of the only-begotten Son, who always was. In *De Trin.* 2, 17 Hilary argues that time was created by the Word as well. This must logically lead to the consequence that there was no time before the world, in which case it cannot be said of the world either that it was 'once' not, since 'once' is a temporal category. Hilary does not seem to have been aware of the difficulties which are hidden here, see *infra*, 99 ff.

> ''But my fisherman, unlettered, uninstructed, is free from time and ages. He has surpassed every beginning: for what is, was already and what was in the beginning rather than came into being in the beginning is not limited by some temporal beginning.''

The unlettered fisherman can transcend all time, because he is instructed by the Word which is beyond time.

CHAPTER 14

The eternal Word is not a solitary God.

Translation and Commentary:

> **(14)** ''But perhaps we shall find that our fisherman has departed from the order of the proposed subdivision of discussion. For he has set the Word free from the limitations of time, and that which is free is entirely its own and alone and obedient to nobody.''

The discussion is about the one God who is the Father of the Son, and especially about the manner and time of generation, both of which are unknown. It now seems as if the evangelist comes forward with the doctrine about the divine Word which is in complete isolation without any relation to the Father. For it seems that by setting the Son free from time the evangelist suggests that the Son is not obedient to anybody. This would mean that this statement made by the evangelist has nothing to do with the generation of the Son by the Father. (On Christ's obedience to the Father see *infra*, 142 f, *De Trin.* 3, 9).

> "Let us prick up our ears to what follows. He says: 'And the Word was with God.' That which was before the beginning is already without a beginning with God. So the Word is since all past with God, and He whose existence cannot be specified in time is not without Origin."

The Son is before the beginning of heaven and earth, and therefore of time, which was made simultaneously with the world, see *infra*, 99, *De Trin.* 2, 17. So the Son is beyond time, but this does not mean that He is without a relation to the Father, since the Father is His eternal origin, cf. *supra*, 95, and *De Trin.* 9, 53: *Non enim suae originis est Filius, neque nativitatem sibi non exstans ipse conquisivit ex nullo. Sed ex vivente natura vivens natura exstans ...*; and 4, 17 and 4, 19 where the plural in *Genesis* 1:26 is interpreted as a proof that the Father is not alone.

> "For this once our fisherman has escaped. But perhaps he will be at a loss in what follows."

CHAPTER 15

The Word is not merely a sound of voice and expression of thought.

Translation and Commentary:

> **(15)** "For you will say: 'The word is a sound of voice, a naming of things, a verbalisation of thoughts. This Word was with God and was in the beginning, because the expression of thought is eternal, since He who thinks is eternal."

So the objection is made against the eternal generation of the Son, that the Word is merely the eternal expression of God's eternal thought. As appears from *De Trin.* 2, 4 this objection is made by an Ebionite, see *supra*, 71, and is meant as a denial of a real pre-existence of Christ, see further *De Trin.* 10, 21: *Sed volentes unigenitum Deum, qui in principio apud Deum erat Deus Verbum, non substantivum Deum esse, sed sermonem vocis emissae; De Syn.* 46: *Haeretici perimentes, quantum in ipsis est, Dei filium, verbum esse tantum confitentur, prodeuntem scilicet loquentis ore sermonem, et insubstantivae vocis incorporalem sonum,* cf. *De Trin.* 7, 11. As appears from Tertullian, *Adv. Prax.* 7, 5-8 the Sabellians make a similar objection (cf. J. Moingt, La théologie trinitaire de Saint Hilaire, p 162). In itself Hilary agrees with the statement that a word is the (inadequate) expression of thought, see *supra*, 37 ff, *De Trin.* 1, 7. What he denies is that the Word spoken of by the evangelist John is this kind of word.

> "First I will give you a brief answer on the fisherman's behalf, before we see how he defends his own simplicity."

That the language of the fisherman should be simplicity (*rusticitas*) is, of course, ironical, cf. *supra*, 89, *De Trin.* 2, 11. On Hilary's view on brevity see *infra*, 143 ff, *De Trin.* 3, 9.

> "The nature of a word is that it first is potentially, then it will have been, but it only *is* when it is being heard. And how 'was in the beginning' what exists neither before a certain moment nor after it? And I do not know whether it can at all be in time: the word of the speakers is not before they speak and it will not be when they have spoken, and in that which they actually say that with which they began will not be any more when they finish. This reply is given by me as a bystander."

A transitory sound once was and once will not be. How then can the eternal Word be such a word? Even in the process of speaking the human word seems not to be, since the successive sounds constantly put an end to each other. For this reason the divine Word cannot be compared with a human word. Hilary says that this argument could have been put forward by anybody else, in other words that it is common one; cf. Athanasius, *Contra Arianos* 2, 35: καὶ ὁ μὲν τῶν ἀνθρώπων λόγος ἐκ συλλαβῶν ἐστι συγκείμενος ... καὶ μόνον ἐξῆλθε καὶ παρῆλθε μηκέτι φαινόμενος ἐπειδὴ οὐδὲ ἦν ὅλως πρὶν λαληθῇ, and Augustine, *Conf.* 11, 34.

> "But the fisherman will defend himself differently. And he will begin by reproving you that you did not listen attentively. For although you as an inexperienced listener have lost the first sentence 'In the beginning was the Word', why do you complain about the following one: 'And the Word was with God'? You did not hear 'in God', so that you took it to be the word of a hidden thought, did you? Or did the difference between 'to be in' and 'to be with' escape the simple mind of the evangelist? For that which was in the beginning is not preached to be *in* the other, but *with* the other."

The Word can only be interpreted as the utterance of a thought if it were said that the Word was *in* God, but the evangelist says that it was *with* God. This difference may have escaped the critical questioner but certainly not the divinely inspired fisherman.

> "But I do not argue from the previous words. Let what follows speak for itself. Wait for the rank and name of the Word. For the evangelist says: 'And the Word was God'. Gone is the sound of voice and the verbalization of a thought. This Word is a reality, not a sound, a being, not a speech, God, not an emptiness."

The evangelist's statement that the Word was God excludes the idea that as a mere sound it is in fact an emptiness. In similar words Tertullian opposes the same idea, *Adv. Prax.* 7, 8: *Vacua et inanis res est sermo Dei, qui Filius dictus est? Qui ipse Deus cognominatus est?* On the opposition *natura – nomen* or *sermo* cf. Hilary, *De Trin.* 4, 26 where he says that a name is applied to a nature, not the other way round a nature to a name: *Nomen enim naturae, non nomini natura componitur,* cf. *De Syn.* 20 where it is said of the heretics: *Patrem et Filium solis nominibus, non etiam per veritatem naturalis et genuinae essentiae praedicantes.* Here Hilary is in line with Tertullian, who says that he lays claim to supreme greatness not for the *name* of a God either spoken or written, but for that *substance* to which this name is applied, *Adv. Marc.* 1, 7, 3; *Ita ego non nomini dei nec sono nec notae nominis huius summum magnum in creatore defendo, sed ipsi substantiae cui nomen hoc contigit.* The same idea that substances rank above names also occurs in Athanasius, *Contra Arianos* 2, 3: οὐ γὰρ αἱ λέξεις τὴν φύσιν παραιροῦνται, ἀλλὰ μᾶλλον ἡ φύσις τὰς λέξεις εἰς ἑαυτὴν ἕλκουσα μεταβάλλει, καὶ γὰρ οὐ πρότεραι τῶν οὐσιῶν αἱ λέξεις, ἀλλ᾿ αἱ οὐσίαι πρῶται καὶ δεύτεραι τούτων αἱ λέξεις, see further *infra,* 118, *De Trin.* 2, 31 on exegesis.

CHAPTER 16

Nevertheless there is only one God.

Translation and Commentary:

(16) ''But I tremble in hearing this, the unusual word astounds me. I hear 'And the Word was God', I to whom the prophets announced one God.''

The Old Testament had taught him that Pagan polytheism is utterly rejectable and that there is only one God (see *supra,* 30 ff, *De Trin.* 1, 5 f); now this monotheism is in danger because of the doctrine of the Word which is also God.

''But lest my trembling should be carried further, my fisherman, explain this great mystery. And you bring all things back to one God, without any blasphemy, without any robbing of reality, timeless. He says: 'And the Word was in the beginning with God'. Because this Word was in the beginning, it is not limited by any time. Because it is God, it cannot be reduced to a mere sound. Because it is 'with God', it is in no respect confused with or separated from (the Father), for it is not abolished into the other, and it is preached to be with the one unbegotten God out of whom it is itself the one only-begotten God.''

J. C. M. van Winden proposes to read *nihil nec confunditur* (as is testified by J) instead of *nihil nec offenditur.* This corresponds with *nam nec aboletur* and is a polemical remark against the Sabellian doctrine, similarly the words *nec aufertur* correspond with the statement that the only-begotten One is with the unbegotten Father, and these corresponding statements are made against the Arians. The Sabellians confuse the Father and the Son by abolishing the Son so that He is no longer an entity of His own, the Arians take away the divinity of the Son so that He is no longer God with God. Both the Sabellian and the Arian doctrine are an offence against the Son, as was stated earlier in this chapter with the word *contumelia*. The word *contumelia* is likely to have caused the reading *offenditur*.

CHAPTER 17

That the Word was in the beginning means that the Word was always.

Translation and Commentary:

> **(17)** ''We still expect from you, fisherman, completeness. He was in the beginning (you have said), but (one may say) He might not have been before the beginning. Here, too, I produce an argument on behalf of my fisherman. What *was* could not not have been, for 'was' does not imply not to have been in time.''

Just as in *De Trin.* 2, 15 (*supra*, 96 ff) first a reasonable argument is given: 'was' cannot mean that it ever was not, since then one would expect: in the beginning the Word came into being, see *supra*, 94 ff, *De Trin.* 2, 13.

> ''But what does the fisherman say for himself? 'All things were made through Him.' So if nothing is without Him through whom the universe came into being, then the Word through whom all that is was made must be infinite. For time is a measure of an extension which abides not in space but in duration. And when all things are made by Him, there is no thing which has not been made by Him and therefore time, too, is made by Him.''

The difference between the Creator and creation is that the former is infinite and the latter has a temporal beginning. Since the Word causes the temporal beginning of all creation, it must itself be without a temporal beginning, *i.e.* infinite; cf. Novatian, *De Trin.* 31, 190: *... cum id sit principium ceteris, quod innatum est.* Time itself is a measure, *i.e.* has a beginning and an end, which means that it is finite. As such a finite creature time has been been created by the Word as well, cf. *De Trin.* 4, 42; 12, 34; *In Ps.* II 23, 43; – this is a commonplace amongst Christian theologians and amongst Platonists, see W. Beierwaltes, *Plotin über Ewigkeit und Zeit. Text, Übersetzung, Kommentar*, Frankfurt/M. 1967, p 277.

CHAPTER 18

The principal Author of creation and His Companion.

Translation and Commentary:

> **(18)** ''But somebody may say to you, my fisherman: 'Here you were too quick and indiscriminate. That 'all things were made by Him' does not

> have a restriction. But there is the unbegotten One who has been made by
> nobody, there is also He Himself, begotten by the unbegotten One. 'All
> things' means without exception, leaving nothing outside.''

The objection made here is that it seems that everything has been made
by the Son; this would imply that the Father was made by Him as well.

> ''But whilst we dare say nothing more, or whilst we perhaps try to say
> something, help us, fisherman: 'And without Him was nothing made'. You
> have restored (the Father as) the Author in proclaiming His companion. For
> when nothing is without Him, I understand that He is not alone, – 'by
> whom' and 'not without whom' are two, with these two expressions a
> distinction is drawn between Him who intervenes and Him who acts.''

Hilary continues his *diatribe*. In it he pretends reluctance to discuss this
objection. But he immediately receives help from the evangelist, who according to Hilary makes a distinction between 'by Him' which Hilary interprets as the Father and the Son and 'not without Him' which Hilary
interprets as the Son. It may seem strange that the instrumental *per* is
used for the Father, but in *De Trin.* 2, 17 the *omnia per eum facta sunt* was
also interpreted as *ab eo omnia*, see also *De Trin.* 10, 70: *Jesum … suscitatum
a mortuis per Deum credere.* – Hilary reads *John* 1:3: *Omnia per ipsum facta
sunt, et sine ipso factum est nihil* (see *De Trin.* 1, 10, – on the interpretations
given to *John* 1:3-4, interpretations which vary on account of different
punctuations, see P. Lamarche, Le Prologue de Jean, *Recherches de Science
Religieuse* (52) 1964, pp 514 ff). Hilary takes *per eum* to refer to the Father
and the Son, *non sine eo* to the Son.

CHAPTER 19

The creation through the Father and not without the, Son.

Translation and Commentary:

> **(19)** ''When I was concerned about the Author, who is the One unbegot-
> ten, lest in your assertion 'all' nothing was omitted, you dispelled my fears
> by saying: 'And without Him nothing was made'.''

In the previous chapter the fear was expressed that the words 'And by
Him (*i.e.* the Word) all things were made' implied that the Father was
made through Him as well. This fear disappeared when it became clear
to him that there is a distinction between 'by Him' (*i.e.* the Father and
the Son) and 'not without Him' (*i.e.* only the Son).

> ''But I am confused and disturbed by this 'nothing was made without
> Him'. So there is something made by somebody else, which nevertheless
> was not made without Him. And if something was made by somebody else,
> be it not without Him, then no longer has all been made by Him: because
> there is a distinction between to have made and to have intervened in the
> making.''

Here Hilary is confronted with the difficulty that the distinction he has made between 'by Him' and 'not without Him' (the former referring to the Father and the Son, the latter to the Son), and between 'to make' and 'to intervene in the making' might imply that not all things have been made by the Son, as was the assumption in *De Trin.* 2, 17, before this distinction was made. Therefore 'by Him' and 'not without Him' asks for further consideration.

> "Here, my fisherman, I can produce no argument of my own, as I could with the other objections. I immediately have to answer with your words: 'All things have been made by Him'. I can see it, for the apostle taught: 'Things visible and things invisible, whether thrones or dominions or principalities or powers, all are through Him and in Him'."

Already in the previous chapter he had given no answer of his own, but produced a text from the evangelist, but then he at least tried to formulate his own answer (see *supra*, 100). Now even such an effort is not made. The Johannine doctrine, that all things are made by Him, is referred to the Father, and to the Son, because the 'by Him' is interpreted with the help of the Pauline text that all things are made *in* the Son. This will be further explained in the next chapter.

CHAPTER 20

In the eternal generation of the Son, who is Life, the Father has potentially created the world.

Translation and Commentary:

> **(20)** "So when all things are by Him, come to our help and tell us what was not made without Him. 'What was made in Him was life.' So this is not without Him that was made in Him. For that which was made in Him was also made through Him. For 'all things have been created in Him and through Him'. They were created in Him, because He was born as God Creator."

That all things were created in the Son means that they were not created without Him. The creation *in* the Son is said to be the creation *through* the Son, *i.e.* in so far as the creation was created in the Son and not without the Son it can be said to have been created through the Son as well (as was said in *De Trin.* 2, 17, *supra*, 99). The creation in the Son is given with the fact that the Son was born as God Creator. Watson is right in suggesting that the generation of the Son is also the potential creation.

> "But also for this reason nothing is made without Him that was made in Him, because as the begotten God He was life, and He who was life was not made life after he had been generated. For in Him there is no difference between that which was born and that which He received after having been born. There is no interval between generation and further growth."

First it was said that in (the generation of) the Son the world was potentially created. Now this is further elaborated with the statement that the
Son was generated as life, and did not at a certain moment after His
generation become life. There is no interval between generation and further growth – this is, in fact, an understatement, since Hilary denies any
growth in God on the ground that God is fullness, see *De Trin.* 11, 44,
especially: *Et haec quidem de Deo ita opinandi piae intellegentiae species est, Deo
nihil deesse, plenumque esse*; 11, 47: *Manet itaque ut est semper Deus, nec profectu
eget qui ad id quod est, ex se ac sibi semper est*, cf. for this thought Athanasius,
Contra Arianos 1, 14, 17, 18, 20, 21; *Ad Ser.* 4, 7; Plotinus, *Enn.* 3, 7, 6, 37
ff; 3, 7, 4, 15-16 (see further W. Beierwaltes, *op. cit.*, pp 210, 182). – The
concept of the potential creation of the world in the Son, who was eternally generated as life, is to Hilary, as to many other early Christian
theologians, a means to avoid the crude consequence that God at a certain moment suddenly decided to create a world, which is the famous
Epicurean objection against a creation by gods (see *e.g.* Lucrece, *De rer.
nat.* 5, 168 ff, Cicero, *De nat. deor.* 1, 9, 21), see *De Trin.* 12, 39: *Cum enim
praeparetur coelum, aderat Deo* (sc. *sapientia*). *Numquid coeli praeparatio Deo est
temporalis ut repens cogitationis motus subito in mentem tamquam antea torpidam
stupentemque subrepserit, humanoque modo fabricandi coeli impensam et instrumen-
ta quaesierit*, cf. *In Ps.* LXVII 29 ... *quia rerum subitarum in Deum non cadit
nova repensque molitio: cuius scientiam non subterfugiant quae gerenda sunt, quia
natura eius universa quae erunt, virtutis suae potestate complexa est*, cf. Tertullian,
Adv. Marc. 2, 3, 3-4, where the idea of a sudden goodness of God is rejected, and *Adv. Prax.* 6 where the planning of the world in the divine
mind is discussed, see J. H. Waszink's edition of *De anima*, p 470 and H.
A. Wolfson, *The Philosophy of the Church Fathers* I, Cambridge (Mass.)
1970, pp 265 f; see on this subject more in general J. C. M. van Winden,
The Early Christian Exegesis of 'Heaven and Earth' in Genesis 1, 1,
Romanitas et Christianitas, Studia ... J. H. Waszink oblata, Amsterdam-
London 1973, pp 371 ff.

> ''But nothing of the things that were created in Him were created without
> Himself: because He is the life in which they were created, and the God who
> was born from God came into existence as God not after He had been
> generated but by virtue of His generation.''

In the generation of God the Son the world was potentially created. This
doctrine safeguards the fact that both Father and Son created the world.
The world was created by (*per*) the Father in the Son and not without the
Son, and because it was created in the Son and not without the Son it can
also be said that the world was created by the Son. By means of this ar-
tificial exegesis Hilary can maintain that all things were created by the

Son, without the Son being unborn like the Father: His generation implies that He is God's eternal companion in the act of creation.

> "Being generated as the Living from the Living, as the True from the True, the Perfect from the Perfect, He was generated in full power of His own birth, so that He did not understand His generation later on, but He was conscious of His divinity by the very fact that He was generated God from God."

Man knows little or nothing about the process of his birth (see *supra*, 87 f, *De Trin.* 2, 9); in the mystery of the divine generation the Son is perfectly conscious of His generation as God from God. On 'the Living from the Living' etc. see *supra*, 91, *De Trin.* 2, 11.

> "This is implied by the words 'the Only-begotten from the Unbegotten', and 'The Father and I are one'. This is the One God in the confession of the Father and the Son."

The problem was how the Father and the Son could be the one God, especially how the Son could be fully God without putting the unity of God at risk – this problem has, according to Hilary, now been solved.

> "This is implied in the words 'The Father is in the Son and the Son is in the Father'."

These words will again be discussed extensively in *De Trin.* 3, 1 ff, see *infra*, 127.

> "Hence 'He that has seen Me has seen the Father also'. Hence 'All that the Father has, He has given to the Son'. Hence 'As the Father has life in Himself, so He has given to the Son to have life in Himself'. Hence 'No one knows the Son save the Father, no one the Father save the Son'. Hence 'in Him dwells all the fullness of the Godhead bodily'."

The texts quoted at the beginning of this section, *viz.*, in *De Trin.* 2, 8 (cf. 2, 10), are here referred to again, and what has been said in the chapters in between is meant as an explanation of these texts.

CHAPTER 21

Man should accept this mystery of the divine generation as it is revealed in Scripture and not try to investigate into it.

Translation and Commentary:

> **(21)** "This life is the light of men, this is the light which lightens the darkness. In order to comfort us that we are, as the prophet says, unable to describe His generation, the fisherman added: 'And the darkness comprehended Him not'."

Hilary had already comforted himself for the inability with the thought that even the archangels etc. do not know the generation of the Son, see *De Trin.* 2, 9, *supra*, 87 ff. Then certainly the realm of darkness cannot comprehend it. "As the prophet says" is an allusion to *Is.* 53:8.

> "Language has here given way to reality and it cannot be prolix."

Words are inadequate to express this mysterious reality and it is impossible to give long expositions about it: H. Kling, *op. cit.*, p 22 refers as parallels to *sermo non habet quo excurrat*, to Quintilian, *Inst. or.* 4, 3, 14 and Cicero, *De or.* 3, 190.

> "And nevertheless the fisherman, lying on the bosom of the Lord, received this mystery."

The unenlightened man cannot expect to be in such a close relationship to the Lord as John, cf. *De Trin.* 6, 43 where he ironically asks the Arians whether their doctrine was revealed to them by the Lord when they were lying intimately on his bosom: *Anne secreto tibi hoc per familiaritatem amoris recumbenti in pectus suum Dominus ostendit?*

> "This is not the language of the world, because it deals with a reality not of this world. Let it be said, if in the meaning of the words something can be found which contains more than what has been said, and if there are any other words for the reality elicited by us, let them be made public."

Hilary states two possibilities: the language of the apostle could still have a hidden meaning which has not yet been expressed in the quotations from the apostle. This would, however, mean that Scriptural revelation is not clear in this respect, an idea to which Hilary is opposed, see *De Trin.* 2, 1 and 2, 5, *supra*, 65 ff, 74 ff; the other possibility is that non-scriptural words can be used in order to speak about this divine reality; about this, too, Hilary is highly sceptical, see *De Trin*, 2, 5, *supra*, 75 ff, and the now following sentence.

> "If there be none indeed, or rather because there are none, let us accept with admiration this doctrine of the fisherman, and let us understand in him the words of God."

On the apostles as spokesmen of God see *De Trin.* 2, 1, *supra*, 65.

> "Let us cling in adoration to the confession of the Father and the Son, the Unbegotten and the Only-begotten, a confession which is inexplicable and transcends all grip both of language and thought. Let us, following the example of John, lie on the bosom of the Lord Jesus, so that we can understand and speak about these things."

He who follows the example of John clings to the revelation of God and adores what he receives there and realizes that his knowledge of and speach about the divine revelation can never define it, cf. *supra*, 37 ff, 78 ff, and *De Trin.* 12, 56: *Cum his ego proprie electis tibi viris* (sc. *Paulo et Joanne*) *haec ita sentiam, ut sicut nihil aliud ultra sensum intellegentiae meae secundum eos de Unigenito tuo dicam, quam esse natum; ita quoque ultra ingenii humani opinionem secundum eos aliud de sancto Spiritu tuo loquar, quam Spiritum tuum esse.*

CHAPTER 22

The one faith is a cure of all heresies. The true confession of the generation of the Son.

Translations and Commentary:

> **(22)** "This faith is in its purity commended to us by the authority of the gospels, the teaching of the apostles and the unavailing deceitfulness of the heretics, who make disturbing noises from every corner."

Hilary often makes a distinction between the gospels, which contain the words of the Lord, and the doctrine of the apostles, see *e.g. De Trin.* 11, 41; 4, 1; 5, 6, 35, 37; 6, 8 (cf. Irenaeus, who in *Adv. Haer.* 3 refutes the heretics with words of the apostles and in *Adv. Haer.* 4 does so with words of the Lord). – It is interesting that according to Hilary the deceit of the heretics recommends the true faith; here he is in line with Tertullian who, with reference to I *Cor.* 11:19 says, *De praescr.* 4, 6: *et ideo haereses quoque oportebat esse ut probabiles quique manifestarentur* (see for further examples J. H. Waszink's of *De anima*, pp 114 f). (On the noise made by the heretics cf. Tertullian, *Adv. Marc.* 1, 20: *Huic expeditissimae probationi defensio quoque a nobis necessaria est adversus obstrepitacula diversae partis*). The heretics are a threat to peace and quietness in the church, cf. *supra*, 53 f.

> "This foundation stands firm and unshaken in face of all kinds of winds, rains, torrents, it cannot be overthrown by storms, dripping water cannot penetrate into it, floods cannot sweep it away. And that is of highest quality which, although assailed by many, can be destroyed by nobody."

The verses *Matthew* 7:24-25 also refer to the unshakable faith of the church in *In Ps.* CXXVIII 10. Cyprian was particularly fond of this use of these verses, see *De hab. virg.* 2, *De mort.* 1.

> "Just as certain types of remedies are so composed as to be of value not only to single diseases, but to cure all and to be of universal efficacy; similarly the catholic faith, too, provides the cure of a universal medicine not (only) for single plagues, but for all diseases; this faith cannot be weakened by any kind of disease, it cannot be defeated by any number of diseases, it cannot be misled by the diversity of diseases."

This is a common comparison, see H. Kling, *op. cit.*, p 21 for places in Lactance. – Since the heresies become one plague (see *De Trin.* 2, 4, *supra*, 74) the catholic faith can provide one cure against them. Further-

more the various heresies are according to Hilary no threat to the orthodox faith, since they destroy each other, see *supra*, 72.

> "One and the same it stands firm against every single disease and all
> diseases together. For it is marvellous that in that one faith there are as
> many remedies and that there are as many principles of truth as there are
> contrivances of falsehood. Let the heretics, whatever they are called, come
> together and let all their schools come forward."

These are indeed the schools of heretics, not of philosophers, cf. *De Trin.*
8, 19: *Excutiat ingenii sui aculeos omnis haereticorum schola.*

> "Let them hear that there is one unbegotten God the Father and one only-
> begotten Son of God, the perfect offspring of the perfect Father, not
> generated by way of diminution of the Father,"

Hilary repeatedly expresses opposition against the idea that the generation of the Son implies any diminution of the Father, see *e.g. De Trin.* 6,
12, 17; 7, 11, 39; 8, 18. This idea is also rejected by Athanasius, who in
De Decr. 28 says explicitly that the Greeks (which in this case means: the
Neo-Platonists) do not teach that the *Nous* and the *Psyche* diminish the
Good, this despite the fact that they say that the *Nous* is out of the Good
and the *Psyche* is out of the *Nous* (this is a correct interpretation of the way
the second hypostasis proceeds from the One, see A. H. Armstrong,
Plotinus, *The Cambridge History of Later Greek and Early Medieval Philosophy*,
Cambridge 1970², pp 239 ff, and H. Dörrie, Emanation, Ein un-
philosophisches Wort im spätantiken Denken, *Parusia. Studien zur
Philosophie Platons und zur Problemgeschichte des Platonismus. Festgabe für Johan-
nes Hirschberger*, Frankfurt/Main 1965, pp 135 ff). – On the Son as the
perfect offspring of the Father see *supra*, 84 ff.

> "not in some part cut off from the whole (of divinity), but that He who
> possesses all things begot Him who received all things,"

On the rejection of the idea that the Son was cut off from the Father and
on the Father as giving all things to the Son whilst retaining all things see
supra, 85, *De Trin.* 2, 8.

> "not deduced from the Father by way of emanation or outflowing, but that
> He was generated out of all things and in all things by Him who does not
> cease to be in all things in which He is."

This, again, is opposition against any emanation which implies diminution of the Father. Sometimes rejection of emanation and diminution
goes together with the affirmation of divine power, see *De Trin.* 5, 37 and
7, 28: *neque ex derivatione sed ex virtute nativitas est*; on the generation as a
manifestation of divine omnipotence see further *infra*, 139.

> "But that He is free from time and ages, He through whom all things were
> made, for He could not belong to those things which were made by Him."

As the Creator of time, the Word must be beyond time, see *supra*, 99, *De Trin.* 2, 17.

> "This is the catholic and apostolic confession based on the gospel."

CHAPTER 23

Refutation of the heretics with Biblical texts.

Translation and Commentary:

> **(23)** "Let Sabellius, if he dare, preach that the Father and the Son are one and that He has received the two names, so that with him both are not a unity, but one person."

See on this Sabellian doctrine *supra*, 55 ff, 71, *De Trin.* 1, 16-17 and 2, 4.

> "He will have a prompt answer from the Gospels, not once or twice but frequently repeated: 'This is my beloved Son, in whom I am well pleased'."

See on this text and the frequency with which it occurs *supra*, 85, *De Trin.* 2, 8.

> "He will hear: 'The Father is greater than I', and 'I go to the Father', and 'Father, I thank Thee', and 'Glorify Me, Father' and 'Thou art the Son of the living God'."

These texts must show, against the Sabellians, that the Son is an entity on His own besides the Father. Some of these texts are used by the Arians as proofs against the orthodox doctrine, see *De Trin.* 9, 39 ff; 9, 55 ff; 11, 10 ff. It is Hilary's view that the heretics, in fighting each other, fight the battle of the church, see *supra*, 72, so it is understandable that Hilary comes forward against Sabellius with texts which the Arians use against the orthodox.

> "Let Ebion come in creeping, who allows the Son of God His existence since His birth out of Mary and recognizes Him as the Word since the days of His appearance in the flesh."

See on Ebion and his doctrine *supra*, 71, *De Trin.* 2, 4.

> "Let him read again: 'Father, glorify Me with Thee in that glory which I had with Thee before the world was'. And: 'In the beginning was the Word, and the Word was with God, and the Word was God'. And: 'All things were made by Him'. And: 'He was in the world, and the world knew Him not'."

These texts must prove the eternal pre-existence of Christ as God, cf. *supra*, 89 ff.

> "Let the preachers of the new apostleship – who stem, however, in fact from the Anti-Christ – come forward, mocking the Son of God with all kinds of insult."

Again, the most important heresy is referred to without its name being given, cf. *supra*, 72, *De Trin.* 2, 4; on the novelty of the heresy, cf. *supra*, 70 f. Athanasius calls the Arian heresy the forerunner of the Anti-Christ, *Contra Arianos* 1, 1.

> "And they will hear: 'I came out from the Father', and: 'The Son is at the bosom of the Father', and: 'I and the Father are one' and 'I am in the Father and the Father is in Me'."

These texts must prove the unity (not the identicalness) of the Father and the Son, cf., *supra*, 56 ff, *De Trin.* 1, 17.

> "And finally let them rage together with the Jews, because Christ in confessing God as His own Father made Himself equal with God, and let them hear together with them: 'Believe because of My works, that the Father is in Me and I am in the Father'."

Elsewhere, *De Trin.* 6, 50, Hilary says that the Arians are worse in their blasphemy of the Son than the Jews: both reject Jesus as the Son of God, but the Jews do so without knowing about Jesus' virgin birth: *Eadem enim Filium Dei eum esse impietate tu negas. Illi tamen eo crimine minore, quod nesciunt. Nesciunt enim de Maria Christum, sed Christum Dei Filium esse non ambigunt. Tu, quia Christum non potes nescire de Maria, Christum tamen Dei Filium esse non praedicas. Illis in eo quod nesciunt, potest adhuc in tuto salus esse, si credant. Tibi iam omnia clausa sunt ad salutem, qui negas quod ignorare iam non potes*; cf. *De Trin.* 7, 23: *Quanto tu inreligiosior Iudaeo! Lapides ille in corpus elevat, tu in Spiritum; ille in hominem, ut putabat, tu in Deum, ille in deversantem in terris, tu in throno virtutis sedentem; ille in ignoratum, tu in confessum, ille in moriturum, tu in iudicem saeculorum.* According to Athanasius the Arians do the same as the Jews, see *Contra Arianos* 3, 28.

> "So this is the one immovable foundation, this is the one blissful rock of faith, which is confessed through the mouth of Peter. 'Thou art the Son of the living God', containing in itself as many arguments of truth as perverse objection and unfaithful slanders can be made."

On this rock of confession see further *De Trin.* 6, 36-37; on the idea that it contains as many proofs of the truth as objections can be raised against it, see *De Trin.* 2, 22, *supra*, 105.

2) The Incarnation of the Son of God (24-28)

On behalf of mankind God the Son assumed a human body. Through this assumed state of humility the Son promoted man to the state of glory.

CHAPTER 24

The Son of God assumed the universal human nature.

Translation and Commentary:

(24) "In what remains there is the economy of the divine will."

'In what remains' refers to all that is said about the Son apart from His divine generation and nature, so to His life as man. In this the divine economy is revealed. There is one much discussed question in early Christian theology in this respect: Why did God not want the incarnation to take place much earlier, why did the Son of God appear so late? This was an objection made by Celsus against Christianity as a whole, see Origen, *Contra Celsum* 4, 7; 6, 78. Irenaeus and Tertullian make similar objections against the Gnostics and Marcion, see *Adversus Haereses* 2, 3, 3; 2, 4, 3, 4; 2, 22, 5; 4, 11, 1; *Adversus Marcionem* 1, 17, 2-4; 1, 22 ff (cf. J.-C. Fredouille, *op. cit.*, pp 271 ff); similarly Novatian asks the Christ of Marcion, *De Trin.* 10, 50: *Quare nunc venire voluisti?* This is a question in which Hilary shows hardly any interest, he merely refers the moment of the incarnation to Christ's own will, see *De Trin.* 10, 69: *Sacramentum suum est, et in tempore, et in opere. Neque quia modo venit, deductus per alterum esse credendus est: nec temporalis eius adventus potestati deducentis subditus intellegendus est.* (This is the only place we found in Hilary in which this question is discussed, it is indicative of Hilary's opposition against curiosity that he is not interested in this kind of question, cf. *supra*, 74 ff, *De Trin.* 2, 5). – Athanasius tries to justify the moment of the incarnation by saying that it could have taken place earlier, but that God postponed it to the benefit of the whole creation, see *Contra Arianos* 1, 29: Καὶ ὥσπερ δυνάμενος καὶ ἐξ ἀρχῆς ἐπὶ τοῦ Ἀδὰμ ἢ ἐπὶ Νῶε ἢ ἐπὶ Μωϋσεως ἀποστεῖλαι τὸν ἑαυτοῦ Λόγον, οὐκ ἀπέστειλεν εἰ μὴ ἐπὶ συντελείᾳ τῶν αἰώνων, τοῦτο γὰρ εἶδε λυσιτελεῖν πάσῃ τῇ κτίσει.

"The virgin, the birth and the body, and then the cross, death, the visit to the lower world, all this is our salvation."

For similar statements see *De Trin.* 5, 18; 6, 23; 9, 51. What our salvation consists of will be discussed in this and the following chapters.

"For on behalf of mankind the Son of God was born of the Virgin and of the Holy Ghost. In this work He ministered to Himself, and because His own power – namely the power of God – overshadowed her He sowed for Himself the beginning of His body and created the first stage of His flesh."

Hilary says repeatedly that the Son wrought His own human body, see *De Trin.* 10, 15 ff, 35, 47 (cf. L. F. Ladaria, *El Espiritu Santo en San Hilario de Poitiers*, Madrid 1977, p 113), see also Athanasius, *De Inc.* 8: αὐτὸς γὰρ δυνατὸς ὢν καὶ δημιουργὸς τῶν ὅλων ἐν τῇ Παρθένῳ κατασκευάζει ἑαυτῷ ναὸν τὸ σῶμα καὶ ἰδιοποιεῖται τοῦτο ὥσπερ ὄργανον.

> "So that, having become man from the Virgin, He might receive the nature
> of flesh in Himself, and so that in Him the body of the whole mankind was
> sanctified by this union."

Christ assumed the universal human nature in order to save all mankind,
cf. *De Trin.* 11, 16; *In Ps.* LI 16: *Natus enim ex Virgine Dei filius ... naturam
in se universae carnis assumpsit, per quam effectus vera vitis, genus in se universae
propaginis tenet* (cf. on this subject more in general R. M. Hübner, *op. cit.*,
pp 232 ff).

> "So that in the way in which all were created in Him through His ap-
> pearance in a body, in the same way He may be reproduced in all through
> His unseen existence."

By His assuming the body of the universal human nature, the whole
human race was identified with Christ, and since Christ in His appearance in man also remained God (see *supra*, 50 ff, *De Trin.* 1, 13), the
benefits of Christ's divinity were bestowed on all men. The 'invisibility of
Christ' is here undoubtedly His divine nature.

> "So the invisible image of God did not refuse the shame of a human begin-
> ning, He passed through conception, birth, wailing, cradle, through all
> humiliations of our nature."

Christ is here called the invisible Image of God, since at the very beginning of His life as man His divinity was not visible to anybody. On these
stages of humiliation see further the next two chapters.

CHAPTER 25

In the incarnation Christ remained in His infinite divinity. He assumed humility in order to bestow nobility upon men.

Translation and Commentary:

(25)   "What worthy return can we make for so great a condescension?"

No such return can be made, since men are all sinners who cannot
honour God properly, see *De Trin.* 3, 7, *infra*, 140.

> "The one only-begotten God, who has an inexplicable origin in God,
> entered the holy Virgin's womb and in His growth took the frame of a weak
> human body. He who contains everything, and in whom and through
> whom all things are, was brought forth by the law of a human birth."

It is important to Hilary that Christ, whilst growing as man, was nevertheless fully God, see *De Trin.* 10, 54: *puer crescit, sed plenitudinis Deus per-
manet.* Christ was in the incarnation not confined to a human body, but
remained as God omnipresent, see *De Trin.* 10, 16: *... non se ex infinitatis
suae virtute intra regionem definiti corporis coartavit,* cf. Athanasius, *De Inc.* 17:

οὐ γὰρ δὴ περιχεκλεισμένος ἦν ἐν τῷ σώματι· οὐδὲ ἐν σώματι μὲν ἦν ἀλλαχόσε
δὲ οὐκ ἦν, ἀλλὰ τὸ παραδοξότατον, Λόγος ὢν οὐ συνείχετο μὲν ὑπό τινος
συνεῖχε δὲ τὰ πάντα μᾶλλον αὐτός.

> "And He at whose voice archangels and angels tremble, heaven and earth
> and all the elements of this world will be melted, is heard in childish
> wailing."

It is important that all this is said in the present tense: whilst Christ is
wailing as a new-born baby, the archangels tremble at His voice as the
Word of God, cf. *De Trin.* 10, 54: *Vagit infans, sed in coelo est; In Ps.* II 11:
*Non abest ergo a coelo, quia cum de coelo descenderit, filius hominis manens atque lo-
quens, est tamen, cum haec loqueretur, in coelo.* On the angels as the obedient
ministers see *infra*, 140, *De Trin.* 3, 7.

> "He who is invisible and incomprehensible, who cannot be gauged by vi-
> sion, sense and touch, is wrapped in a cradle."

If sense or vision could perceive God, then God would not be infinite, see
De Trin. 1, 6, *supra*, 133 ff. Whilst remaining infinite, Christ is nevertheless wrapped in a cradle, cf. *De Trin.* 9, 4: ... *contrahere se usque ad con-
ceptum et cunas et infantiam, nec tamen Dei potestate decedere.*

> "If somebody regards all this as unworthy of God, then he will confess
> himself indebted to a benefit which is all the greater according to the degree
> in which this less benefits the majesty of God."

Ever since Marcion deleted the story of Christ's birth from the gospel as
unworthy of God, the real birth had to be defended, see Irenaeus, *Adv.
Haer.* 1, 25, 1, as in itself perhaps unworthy of God's majesty, but as
necessary to man's salvation and therefore a great miracle, see *e.g.* Tertullian, *Adv. Marc.* 2, 27, 1: ... *vim maiestatis suae, intolerabilem utique
humanae mediocritati, humilitate temperaret, sibi quidem indigna, homini autem
necessaria, et ita iam Deo digna, quia nihil tam dignum Deo quam salus hominis.*
The same idea is expressed by Hilary in *De Trin.* 5, 18, see further *infra*,
145 ff, *De Trin.* 3, 10.

> "There was no need to become man for Him, through whom man was
> made, but it was necessary for us that God became flesh and dwelt amongst
> us, *i.e.* that He made all flesh His home by assuming the flesh of one. His
> humility is our nobility. His shame is our honour."

On the idea that there was no need for God to become man, cf. *De Trin.*
3, 7, *infra*, 139, and *De Trin.* 11, 43: *nec sermo istud, nec sensus rationis capax
loquitur, ut naturali quadam necessitate ad consulendum nobis obnoxius Deus.* On
the assumption of the universal human nature by God see *supra*, 110, *De
Trin.* 2, 25. God's humility and shame are our nobility and honour, cf.
De Trin. 9, 4: *Neque assumptio nostra Deo profectus est: sed contumeliae suae*

voluntas, nostra provectio est; Irenaeus, *Adv. Haer.*, Praef. ad V; *Adv. Haer.* 3, 11, 1; 3, 20, 1; Tertullian, *Adv. Marc.* 2, 27, 7: *Totum denique dei mei penes vos dedecus sacramentum est humanae salutis ... Deus pusillus inventus est, ut homo maximus fieret*; Athanasius, *Ad Max.* 4: Καὶ δέδεικται πᾶσιν ὅτι οὐ δι' ἑαυτὸν ἀλλὰ δι' ἡμᾶς ὑπέμεινε πάντα ἵν' ἡμεῖς τοῖς ἐκείνου παθήμασιν ἀπάθειαν καὶ ἀφθαρσίαν ἐνδυσάμενοι διαμείνωμεν εἰς ζωὴν αἰώνιον. - Again it is very important to Hilary that Christ's state of humility did not disrupt His unity with the Father, see *De Trin.* 9, 53: *Et hoc quidem Patri debitum reddens, ut oboedientiam suam mittentis deputet voluntati, non tamen ut naturae unitatem oboedientia humilitatis infirmet*; cf. 6, 25.

> "What He is as God through His existence in flesh, this is what we in return are when we have been renewed from the flesh to God."

On this theme of man's deification through Christ's incarnation see *supra*, 49 ff, *De Trin.* 1, 13.

CHAPTER 26

The dignity of Christ's conception.

Translation and Commentary:

> (26) "But lest by any chance the thoughts of scrupulous minds are detained by cradle, wailing, birth, and conception, God's dignity must be given to each of them, so that the display of His power precedes the humility of His will and His dignity remains in His (state of) condescension."

Christ's birth is then not a stumbling-block for faith in His divinity, if it is recognized that prior to Christ's humble obedience as man is His powerful honour as God, and that in His state of condescension He does not lose His divine majesty; – this was explained in the two previous chapters, see further *De Trin.* 5, 18 f; 9, 4 and *In Ps.* CXXXVIII 19, where he says that Christ was God before the incarnation and after it (*i.e.* since His resurrection), He was God and man during the incarnation.

> "So let us see who were the attendants of His conception. An angel speaks to Zacharias, fertility is given to the barren, the priest comes forth dumb from the place of incense, John bursts forth into speech while yet confined within his mother's womb."

The events in connection with Christ's birth must show that divine dignity accompanies the divine condescension. In *Luke* 1:41 it only says that the baby John stirred in his mother's womb, but already Irenaeus amplifies this by saying that John at that moment greeted Jesus, who was also still in his mother's womb, see *Adv. Haer.* 3, 17, 4: *Ipse igitur erat Christus ... quem Joannes, cum adhuc in ventre matris suae esset, et ille in vulva Mariae, Dominum cognoscens, exsultans salutabat.* Hilary provides a similar amplification, and goes so far as to call him a prophet already in his mother's womb, see *De Trin.* 6, 27: *Iohannes ... iam ab utero profetans ...*, cf. 2, 32, *infra*, 121 f.

> "An angel blesses Mary and promises that she, a virgin, will be the mother of the Son of God. Conscious of her virginity she is distressed by the difficulty of this event. The angel explains to her the efficient power of the divine working by saying: 'The Holy Ghost shall come from above into thee, and the power of the Most High shall overshadow thee'. The Holy Ghost, descending from above, sanctified the virgin's womb, and, breathing therein – for the Spirit blows where it wills – united Himself with the nature of human flesh and assumed with His own force and power that which was alien to him."

Because of the virgin birth Christ is free from sin, cf. *supra*, 50, and L. F. Ladaria, *op. cit.*, p 114. Both Christ's eternal generation and His birth are according to Hilary the product of divine omnipotence, see *De Trin.* 3, 5-6, *infra*, 136 ff. The free breathing of the Spirit is to Hilary an indication of the absolute liberty of the Spirit, see *De Trin.* 12, 56 where after a quotation of *John* 3:7-8 Hilary says: *Modus autem Spiritui nullus est loquendi cum velit, quod velit, ubi velit.*

> "And lest because of the weakness of the human body anything be at variance (with this working of the Spirit) the power of the Most High overshadowed the virgin, strengthening her feebleness in semblance of a cloud cast around her, that the shadow of the divine power might put her bodily substance in the right condition to receive the procreative power of the Spirit entering into her. This is the dignity of the conception."

CHAPTER 27

The dignity of Christ's birth.

Translation and Commentary:

> (27) "Let us now see which dignity accompanies the birth, the wailing and the cradle. The angel tells Joseph that the virgin will bear a son and that He who will be born shall be named Emmanuel, which is 'God with us'. The Spirit proclaims it through the prophet, the angel testifies to it: He who is born is God with us. A new light of a star is shown from heaven to the Magi, a heavenly sign escorts the Lord of heaven."

It is important to note that according to Hilary the new-born baby is at the same time the Lord of heaven, see *supra, De Trin.* 2, 25.

> "An angel announces to the shepherds that Christ the Lord is born, the Saviour of the world. A multitude of the heavenly host flock together in order to praise the new-born child, and the rejoicing of the divine company proclaims the mighty work. Then glory to God in heaven and peace on earth to men of good will is proclaimed."

So the events at Christ's birth show that He is Lord and God, cf.
Irenaeus, *Adv. Haer.* 3, 17, 4: ... *quem pastores cum vidissent, glorificabant
Deum.*

> "Then the magi come and worship Him wrapped in swaddling-clothes, and
> after that hidden operation of their vain science they bow their knees before
> Him who is laid in the cradle."

In *De Trin.* 4, 38 Hilary says that the journey of the magi, their adoration
and offering of gifts fulfils the prohecy in *Is.* 45:14: *Laboravit Aegyptus et
mercatus Aethiopum et Sabain. Viri excelsi ad te transibunt ... et adorabunt te.* The
myrrh is offered to Christ as man, the gold (to Christ) as king, the incense
(to Christ) as God, see *In Matth.* 1, 5. This interpretation goes back to as
early as Irenaeus, *Adv. Haer.* 3, 10 and is fairly common, see Ch. Kan-
nengieser, L'exégèse d'Hilaire, *Hilaire et son temps*, p 132. – According to
Tertullian, *De idol.* 9 the story of the magi shows that astrology was a
science which was allowed until Christ, see on this matter P. G. van der
Nat, *R.S.F. Tertulliani De idolatria. Edited with Introduction and Commentary*,
Part I, Leiden 1960, p 118. According to Athanasius the magi prove the
divinity of the new-born child, *Ad Max. Phil.* 4: Ταῦτα τοίνυν κατανοῶν ὁ
ἄπιστος μαθέτω ὅτι βρέφος μὲν ἦν ἐπὶ φάτνης τοὺς δὲ μάγους ὑπέταξε
προσκυνούμενος ὑπ᾽ αὐτῶν.

> "Thus the dirt of the cradle is adored by the magi. Thus the wailing is
> honoured by the divine rejoicing of the angels. Thus the proclamation of the
> Spirit through the prophet, the announcement by the angel and the star
> with the new light serve the birth. Thus the Spirit coming from above and
> the overshadowing by the power of the Most High create the beginning of
> birth. There is a difference between what is understood and what is seen,
> what is perceived by the eyes and what by the mind. The virgin bears, the
> birth is from God. The child wails, the praise of the angels is heard. The
> swaddling-clothes are dirty, God is adored. Thus the majesty of power is not
> forfeited whilst the humility of flesh is assumed."

These sentences summarize what has been said since *De Trin.* 2, 24. The
sentence "There is a difference between what is understood and what is
seen, what is perceived by the eyes and what by the mind" raises difficulties: the miraculous events around Christ's birth are, of course,
regarded by Hilary as historical events which could be seen. To the
Christian believers in Hilary's days no more faith is required for the lying
in the cradle than for the praise by the angels. Only the magi can perhaps
be regarded as people who adored what they understood without seeing
it, but they had been led to the cradle by the new star. It seems that
Hilary here wants to say that Christ's divinity must be believed behind
His human appearance, which can be seen (cf. *De Trin.* 7, 34 ff), without
realizing that the miracles cause His divinity to be seen just like His
humanity.

CHAPTER 28

In the works during all His life Christ appears as God who assumed a human body.

Translation and Commentary:

(28) "The course of His further life was also similar. For the whole time He passed in (the form of) a man was filled with works of God. I have no time to deal with each separately. Only this must be observed in all kinds of powerful works and healings, that He appears as a man by virtue of the assumption of flesh, but as God by virtue of His deeds."

In itself belief in Christ's miracles is not enough, since the heretics believe in them as well, see *De Trin.* 2, 12. But once the doctrine of the eternal generation of the Son has been established, and once it has become clear that Christ's life on earth was an act of condescension, the miracles can be a proof that in His condescension He did not lose His divinity; for further instances in Hilary where Christ's miracles are seen as proof of His divinity see L. F. Ladaria, *op. cit.*, p 125 n. 98, cf. Athanasius, *De Inc.* 18 f, *Contra Arianos* 2, 12; 3, 31 f; *Ad Ser.* 4, 16, and on this subject more in general, R. M. Grant, *Miracle and Natural Law in Graeco-Roman and Early Christian Thought*, Amsterdam 1952, pp 188 ff.

C) God the Holy Ghost (29-35)

The Holy Ghost has to be confessed with the Father and the Son, for He is given and received, there can be no doubt about His existence. When the Father or the Son are called "Spirit" this is no indication that the Spirit is not an entity of His own, it indicates the invisibility and omnipresence of the whole divine Being. A distinction must be made between God who in His nature is Spirit, and God's Spirit as a gift to the believers. But the Spirit as a Gift is also fully God and is therefore omnipresent like the Father and the Son. This means that the Spirit as a Gift cannot be confined to the believers. It is in Its totality everywhere, but not all men receive Him. Those who do not receive Him remain below the level of the destination of man. Those who do receive Him lastingly overcome the fear of death, if they retain the Spirit by observing God's commandments.

CHAPTER 29

The Holy Spirit is, since He is attested by the Father and the Son, and since He is God's gift to the believers.

Translation and Commentary:

> **(29)** "I ought not to be silent about the Holy Spirit, but there is no necessity to speak about Him either. But because of those who are in ignorance we cannot be silent about Him. But it is not necessary to speak about Him, who has to be confessed on the authority of Father and Son."

These remarks seem contradictory; twice it is said that he ought not to be silent about the Holy Spirit, and twice it is stressed that there is no necessity to speak about Him either. Bearing in mind what Hilary's views on human speech about God are (see *De Trin.* 2, 1-5, *supra*, 65 ff) he apparently means to say this: One cannot be silent about the Holy Spirit since He has to be confessed according to Scripture. In itself it is not necessary to go beyond Scriptural revelation about the Holy Spirit, but the heretics who do not know the Spirit force him to do this to a certain degree. So there is a distinction between speaking about the Holy Spirit for the purpose of refuting the heretics and confessing the Holy Spirit according to Scripture; for the believer the latter ought to be enough and would mean that he is not silent about the Holy Spirit.

> "I think it not necessary to deal with the question whether He exists. For He does exist, since He is given, received and retained."

The question whether the Spirit is, is answered affirmatively with a reference to the function of the Spirit. Here Hilary is in line with a rhetorical argument which also appears in Tertullian, who says that the question whether a god is, must be answered according to his actions, see *Adv. Marc.* 1, 17, 1: *Primo enim quaeritur, an sit, et ita, qualis sit. Alterum de operibus, alterum de beneficiis dinoscetur*; on the rhetorical background, *viz.*, the *status coniecturalis* see G. C. Stead, Divine Substance in Tertullian, *Journal of Theological Studies* (14), pp 57 ff, see Quintilian, *Inst.* 3, 6, 80 ff.

> "And He who is connected with the confession of the Father and the Son cannot be separated from the confession of the Father and the Son. A totality is imperfect to us if that totality is lacking in something."

Father, Son and Holy Spirit are the one divine perfection, see *De Trin.* 2, 1, *supra*, 66; God is what He is in His totality and He does not consist of parts, see *De Trin.* 2, 6, therefore the Holy Spirit must be believed just as the Father and the Son.

> "If somebody wants to know how we understand this, he as well as we can read in the apostle: 'Because ye are sons of God, God has sent the Spirit of His Son into our hearts, crying: Abba, Father'. And again: 'But we have not received the Spirit of this world, but the Spirit which is of God, that we may know the things that are given to us by God.' And again: 'But ye are not in the flesh, but in the Spirit, if it so be that the Spirit of God is in you. But if any man has not the Spirit of Christ, he is not His.' And again: 'But if

the Spirit of Him that raised up Jesus from the dead dwells in you, He that raised up Christ from the dead shall quicken also your mortal bodies through His Spirit which dwells in you'.''

These texts make it clear that the Spirit is of the Father and the Son and that He is given and received, as it was said in the beginning of this chapter.

"On account of this, since the Spirit is and is given and is possessed and is of God, let the detractors stop talking. When they say (ask), through whom He is, to what end He exists, or how He is, and if our answer: 'Through whom are all things and out of whom are all things and the Spirit is God's gift to the faithful' does not please them, let then also the apostles and prophets displease them, who only say this about Him that He is. And then also Father and Son will displease them.''

Hilary had dismissed the question *an sit* concerning the Holy Spirit by referring to the Father's and the Son's testimony about Him and by referring to His function as God's gift to the believers. So the answers to rhetorical questions about the cause behind a thing and about what a thing causes and how a thing is according to Hilary are answers to the question *an sit* and need now no longer be discussed. (On these rhetorical questions see Quintilian, *Inst.* 3, 6, 80 f, who distinguishes between *an sit, quid sit, quale sit*, and says that the question *an sit* must be answered affirmatively before the next two questions can be discussed; but he also says that the answer to *an sit* is not yet an answer to the following questions, cf. H. Lausberg, *op. cit.*, p 83). Here Hilary differs from Tertullian, who treats the questions *an sit* and *qualis sit* separately, see *Adv. Marc.* 1, 17, 1-2, *supra*, 116 (for an example of the question regarding the *causa ob quam sit* see Tertullian, *De praescr.* 1, 2-3). Since to Hilary these are questions about the same matter, it is fruitless to discuss any further questions if the answers to the question *an sit* are not accepted.

CHAPTER 30

Both the Father and the Son are Spirit and holy and named as such in Scripture.

Translation and Commentary:

(30)   "I believe that on account of this certain people remain in ignorance or doubt, that they see this third being 'Holy Spirit' often understood as the Father or the Son. There is no difficulty in this: whether it is Father or Son, He is also a Holy Spirit.''

Some of these texts are discussed in *De Trin.* 8, 23 ff, see *infra*, 118 ff, *De Trin.* 2, 31. Hilary cannot mean that Father and Son are the Holy Spirit, since this would mean that the Holy Spirit would not be a reality on His own, but merely another name for the Father and the Son, an idea to which Hilary is obviously opposed, see *De Trin.* 2, 4, *supra*, 69 ff. Watson's translation 'whether it be Father or Son, He is Spirit, He is holy' seems the correct interpretation (though not a correct translation), see *infra, De Trin.* 2, 31.

CHAPTER 31

The definition 'God is Spirit' implies God's omnipresence. The distinction between God's nature as Spirit and the Spirit as a gift.

Translation and Commentary:

(31)   "But what is read in the gospel 'Because God is Spirit' needs careful examination as to its precise formulation and meaning. For all that is said has a cause to be said, and the meaning of what is said must be understood from the intention of the speaker, lest because of the response given by the Lord 'God is Spirit', therefore with the name of the Holy Spirit also its fruition and gift are denied."

It seems as if the definition 'God is Spirit' implies that the Holy Spirit is no entity on its own and therefore cannot be received and given. Careful exegesis of this text must show that this is a misinterpretation of this text. Hilary says repeatedly that in interpreting a text one should pay attention to the cause of it, the words must be interpreted in the light of this cause and not the other way round; this cause can be found by observing *inter alia* the time in which a statement was made, see *e.g. De Trin.* 1, 30: ... *omnes dictorum causas ex his ipsis vel interrogationum vel temporum vel dispensationum generibus adtulimus, causis potius verba subdentes, non causas verbis deputantes*; 4, 14: *Intellegentia enim dictorum ex causis est adsumenda dicendi, quia non sermoni res sed rei est sermo subiectus*, cf. Athanasius, *Contra Arianos* 1, 54; 2, 7; *De Decr.* 14; as G. C. Stead, Rhetorical Method in Athanasius, p 123, has shown, it was typical in ancient rhetoric to develop an argument by reference to a list of *staseis*, relevant factors, such as the person concerned, the action, the place, the time, the manner and matter or cause. – The motive of a saying must be understood from the meaning of the words, cf. *De Trin.* 5, 7: *Sensus rationis est motus ... ex sensu rationem intellegamus*. This also implies that the reader should not apply a preconceived meaning to the words, see *De Trin.* 1, 18, *supra*, 60. Hilary accuses the Arians of interpreting Biblical texts completely out of context, see *De Trin.* 9, 2, cf. C. F. A. Borchardt, *op. cit.*, p 49.

"The Lord was speaking with a woman of Samaria, for the redemption of all men had come. He had talked with her at length about the living water and her five husbands and him whom she then had, but who was not her husband, and the woman answered: 'Lord, I perceive that Thou art a

prophet. Our fathers worshipped on this mountain, and ye say that in
Jerusalem is the place where men ought to worship.' The Lord replied:
'Woman, believe Me, the hour comes when neither on this mountain nor in
Jerusalem shall ye worship the Father. Ye worship that which ye do not
know, we worship that which we know, for salvation is from the Jews. But
the hour comes and now is, when the true worshippers shall worship the
Father in the Spirit and in truth, for the Father seeks such to worship Him.
For God is Spirit, and they that worship Him must worship in the Spirit and
in truth, for God is Spirit'.''

Hilary has made it clear that the context of the definition 'God is Spirit' is
that it is an answer to the question where God ought to be worshipped. So
this definition is caused by a specific question, cf. *De Trin.* 9, 15: *Omnis
responsionum ratio necesse est, ut ex interrogationum causis proficiscatur. Ad id enim
respondebitur, unde quaeretur.*

"So the woman, conscious of inherited traditions, thought that God had to
be worshipped either on a mountain, as in Samaria, or in a temple, as in
Jerusalem, for Samaria in disobedience to the law had chosen a mountain as
the place to worship God, whilst the Jews thought that the temple built by
Solomon was the place of their religion. The prejudice of both confined
God, inside whom are all things and outside whom nothing can grasp Him,
to the crest of a hill or to a vault of a building.''

The 'disobedience to the law' of the Samarians is a reference to the fact
that in the books of Kings in the Old Testament the worship of God is
confined to Jerusalem and that worship on the mountains is forbidden. –
Both Samarians and Jews make the mistake to confine God who embraces all things and cannot be embraced by anything, see on this subject
especially *De Trin.* 1, 6; 2, 6; *supra,* 33 ff, 78 ff. – Novatian, too, stresses
that the building of the temple, which was allowed by God, did not confine God to the narrowness of the temple; God is not narrow, but the
power of understanding of the people is, see *De Trin.* 6, 32: *sic et templum
exstruitur, nec tamen deus intra templi angustias omnino saepitur ... nec angustus
deus, sed rationis populi angustus est intellectus habitus.*

"So because God is invisible, incomprehensible, immeasurable, the Lord
says that the time has come when God should be worshipped neither on a
mountain nor in a temple, because God is Spirit, and a Spirit cannot be
cabined or confined, it is by the power of its nature everywhere, and it is
nowhere absent, abundantly present in all men. And that therefore these are
the true worshippers, who will adore in the Spirit and in truth.''

God is Spirit, therefore He is not somewhere in a bodily way, cf. *De Trin.*
8, 24, *In Ps.* CXXIV 6: *Spiritus namque est omnia penetrans et continens. Non
enim secundum nos corporalis est, ut cum alicubi adsit, absit aliunde*; see also *In
Ps.* CXXIX 3 where *John* 4:24 is quoted as a proof that God's nature is
incorporeal and infinite. With a similar reference to *John* 4:24 Novatian
argues the same, *De Trin.* 6, 33.

"And in the case of those who will adore God the Spirit in the Spirit, the one is in the act of worship, the other is the object of worship, for a distinction has been made (between the Holy Spirit as God and the Spirit) in which each (divine Person) has to be adored. The words 'God is Spirit' do not alter the fact that the Holy Spirit has a name of His own and is a gift to us."

Here a clear distinction is made between God who in His nature is Spirit and object of worship, and the Spirit as a gift to the believers, who enables man to worship. Because of this gift of the Spirit men can know God as Spirit.

"To the woman who wanted to confine God to a temple and mountain, the answer was given that all things are in God, that God is in Himself and that He who is invisible and incomprehensible must be adored in what is invisible and incomprehensible."

Here Hilary works with the well-known tenet of the knowledge of the like by the like, see on this matter in general: A. Schneider, Erkenntnis des Gleichen durch Gleiches in antiker und patristischer Zeit, Beiträge zur Geschichte der Philosophie des Mittelalters, Supplement-Band II (Festgabe zum 70. Geburtstage Clemens Baeumkers, Münster i.W., 1923, pp 61-76 and J. H. Waszink, Timaeus a Calcidio translatus commentarioque instructus, Leiden 1962, p 100.

"And thus the nature of the gift and of the object of reverence is indicated, when the Lord taught that God who is Spirit has to be adored in the Spirit, thereby showing the liberty and knowledge of the adorers and the infinity of adoration, because God the Spirit is adored in the Spirit."

The liberty and knowledge of the adorers is a gift of the Holy Spirit, see De Trin. 2, 33-34, infra, 122 ff. The words 'adorandi infinitas' can either be translated as: 'infinity of Him who has to be adored' or as 'infinity of adoration'; both translations have parallels, see De Trin. 1, 6: ... in tantum omnem persequentis se naturae infinitatem infinitas inmoderatae aeternitatis excederet. As God's infinity requires an infinite stretching of the mind which tries to know Him, so it requires an infinite adoration. - Those who adore God as the Spirit in the Spirit are, of course, the Christians, see De Trin. 4, 6: Novit (sc. ecclesia) in Spiritu Deum Spiritum inpassibilem et indesecabilem.

CHAPTER 32

Although there is a distinction between God's nature as Spirit and the gift of the Spirit, the Spirit as Gift is fully God and omnipresent.

Translation and Commentary:

(32) "Something similar is said in the well known word of the Apostle: 'For the Lord is Spirit, and where the Spirit of the Lord is, there is liberty.'

In order to make his thought clear he distinguished between Him who is Spirit and Him of whom is the Spirit. For Proprietor and Property are not one and the same, and 'He' and 'of whom' do not have the same meaning."

The distinction between God who is Spirit and the Spirit of God as a gift to the believers is further elaborated. The distinction between *habere* and *haberi* was already made in *De Trin.* 2, 7, where *habere* was identified with *quod est* and *haberi* with *in quo est* (cf. *De Trin.* 1, 6 where – in a chiastic construction – *habet* is the same as *excedit exterior* and *habetur* is the same as *inest interior*). Here in *De Trin.* 2, 32 *habere* applies to God who is Spirit and *haberi* to the Spirit of God who is God's gift to and in the believers. – On the distinction between 'He' and 'His' see *De Trin.* 4, 23, where in 'the Angel of God' a distinction is made between *ipse qui est, viz.*, God in His manifestation, and *ille cuius est*, the angel whose duty it is to serve God; – cf. *De Trin.* 5, 11 where a distinction is made between the *officium* of an angel (as a messenger) and the *natura* of that Angel who is called God (see also 5, 22).

"So when he says: 'The Lord is Spirit', he reveals His infinity, but when he added: 'Where the Spirit of the Lord is, there is liberty', he indicates Him who is His, because both is the case: the Lord is Spirit and where the Spirit of the Lord is, there is liberty."

The definition of God as Spirit implies God's infinity, which embraces all things, see *supra*, 118 ff, *De Trin.* 2, 31 and *supra*, 33 ff, *De Trin.* 1, 6 on God who embraces (*habet*). If God's Spirit is somewhere, then it means that it is obtained and possessed (*habetur*), see *supra*, 33 ff, *De Trin.* 1, 6 and God who is also embraced (*habetur*). In *De Trin.* 1, 6 and *De Trin.* 2, 7, where the distinction between *habere* and *haberi* was already made, it was also made clear that in God these two go together. This will now be made clear here in *De Trin.* 2, 32 as well:

"These things have not been said because the subject matter requires it, but only lest there remained any obscurity in these things."

This remark takes up what was said in the beginning of *De Trin.* 2, 29, *viz.*, that in itself a discussion of the Holy Spirit is unnecessary, since He is clearly revealed, but that the ignorance of the heretics force him to say something about the Holy Spirit, see *supra*, 116.

"For the Holy Spirit is One everywhere, illuminating all patriarchs, prophets and the whole company of the Law, inspiring John even in his mother's womb, given in due time to the apostles and other believers, that they may know the truth given (to them)."

In *De Trin.* 2, 7 it was already said that God is Giver and Gift at the same time, and in *De Trin.* 1, 6 it was stressed that God, whilst He is embraced, nevertheless embraces at the same time. Similarly it is now argued that God is Spirit by nature and as a gift at the same time. As a gift God is not confined to certain believers, but He is according to His nature everywhere, illuminating and inspiring potentially (see *infra*, 124, *De Trin.* 2, 35) all men. So the Spirit given to men is not an inferior divine being, but is fully God, fully sharing in God's omnipresence, which is implied in the fact that God is Spirit. – On the function of the Holy Spirit in the history of Israel, in John the Baptist and the church see further L. F. Ladaria, *op. cit.*, pp 55 ff, 80 f, 166 ff, cf. *De Trin.* 2, 26, *supra*, 112 f.

CHAPTER 33

Christ's words about the work of the Holy Spirit in the believers.

Translation and Commentary:

> (33)   "Let us hear from the Lord's own words what is His work in us. For He says: 'I have yet many things to say unto you, but you cannot bear them now. For it is expedient for you that I go. When I have gone, I will send you the Advocate'. And again: 'I will ask the Father, He says, and He will send you another Advocate, the Spirit Paraclete. He will glorify Me'. And again: 'I will ask my Father, and He will send you another Advocate, that He may be with you forever, the Spirit of truth. He will guide you into all truth, for He will not speak from Himself, but whatsoever He will hear, He will speak, and He will declare unto you the things that are to come. He will glorify Me, for He will take of Mine'."

These texts express the work of the Spirit which is received together with the liberty in the gift of the Spirit, as was already briefly indicated in *De Trin.* 2, 31, see *supra*, 120.

> "These words were taken from a larger number of texts, in order to pave the way to understanding, and in these words are contained the will of the Giver and the nature and condition of the gift: so that, since our weakness cannot comprehend the Father and the Son, the gift of the Holy Spirit may illuminate, by way of some bond of His intercession, our faith which has difficulties with God's incarnation."

The texts discussed are a selection from a larger number of texts, this selection must pave the way to understanding, cf. *De Trin.* 10, 57: *Non inopiae necessitate, vel dictorum ignoratione de multis pauca memoramus, sed ut absolutam expositionem ratio non morosa commendet.* – Here Christ (and not the Father) is called the Giver of the Spirit; in *De Trin.* 2, 4 this is also the case (cf. L. F. Ladaria, *op. cit.*, pp 288). – The finite human mind cannot grasp the infinite nature of the Father and the Son, and it cannot believe in the incarnation of the Son, therefore the Spirit gives them the possibility to believe, cf. *De Trin.* 2, 31, *supra*, 118 ff.

CHAPTER 34

The apostle Paul's words about the work of the Holy Spirit in the believers.

Translation and Commentary:

> **(34)** "The next logical step is to listen to the apostle's account of the power and function of this gift."

A reference to the relevant texts from the gospels is followed by a reference to the relevant texts from the apostle, see on this *supra*, 105, *De Trin.* 2, 22.

> "For as many as are led by the Spirit of God, these are sons of God. For ye received not the Spirit of bondage again unto fear, but ye received the Spirit of adoption in which we cry 'Abba, Father'. And again: 'For no man by the Spirit of God says anathema to Jesus, and no man can say: 'Jesus is Lord, but in the Holy Spirit'. And again: 'Now there are diversities of gift, but the same Spirit, and diversities of ministrations, but the same Lord, and diversities of workings, but the same God who works all things in all. But to each one is given the enlightenment of the Spirit, to profit withal. Now to one is given through the Spirit the word of wisdom, to another the word of knowledge according to the same Spirit, to another faith in the same Spirit, to another gifts of healing in the same Spirit, to another workings of miracles, to another prophecy, to another discerning of Spirits, to another kinds of tongues, to another interpretation of tongues. But all these works are given by one and the same Spirit'. So we have the cause of this gift and we have its results. And I do not know what kind of doubt can remain about Him whose cause, nature and power are so certain."

After the quotations from Paul a conclusion is drawn from the whole discussion on the Holy Spirit since *De Trin.* 2, 29. It is clear what the cause of the Spirit as a gift is: God the Father and the Son; it is clear what the effects of this gift are: the believers are sons of God, they know Jesus as their Lord and have various gifts of faith. In these effects the motive behind the gift of the Spirit and the power of the gift are manifest and so, as was said right in the beginning of the whole discussion (*De Trin.* 2, 29, *supra*, 116), there can remain no doubt about the existence of the Holy Spirit.

CHAPTER 35

Exhortation to use the gift of the Spirit.

Translation and Commentary:

> **(35)** "So let us make use of these magnificent benefits and let us seek the use of this most necessary gift. For, as we already showed, the apostle says: 'But we have not received the Spirit of this world, but the Spirit which is of

> God, that we may know the things that are given to us by God'. So He is
> received because of knowledge.''

The earlier reference to this Pauline text was in *De Trin.* 2, 29; on the
function of the Spirit to provide knowledge see *De Trin.* 2, 31 and 2, 32,
supra, 118 ff, 120 ff.

> ''For as the nature of the human body is idle when there are no causes to ex-
> ercise its function – for the eyes cannot exercise their function without light,
> be it artificial or natural, the ears will be ignorant of their function unless a
> voice or sound is heard, the nostrils will be unconscious of their function
> unless some scent be breathed. Not that their nature is absent, because there
> is no reason to exercise it, but because the nature is experienced by a cause –
> similarly the human mind will have the natural faculty to know God, but
> will not have the light of knowledge unless it has, through faith, received the
> gift of the Spirit. But that gift which is in Christ is offered in its totality as
> one to all men. And that which is present everywhere is given to that degree
> in which anyone is willing to receive it, and it remains with the believer to
> the degree in which anyone wants to merit it.''

In *De Trin.* 2, 32 it was argued that the Spirit as a gift was not confined to
a believer, but that it is everywhere. But it is also obvious that not all men
receive this gift. Therefore it is now stressed that the gift is available
everywhere, but that it depends on man's free will whether he wants to
receive it. As an idle human nature remains below the level of life destin-
ed for man, so a human mind which can know God but does not receive
God's Spirit, remains below its destination as well. This was already expressed in the Prologue, where a life was discussed in which no proper
use is made of the gift of understanding, see *supra*, 16 ff, 26 ff.

> ''This gift is with us until the end of the world, this is the solace of our
> expectation, this is through the workings of the gifts the assurance of our
> future hope, this is the light of the minds, the sun of our souls. This Holy
> Spirit we must seek, we must earn, and then retain by faithful observation
> of the commandments.''

The fear of death, as was stated in the Prologue (see *supra*, 45 f), can only
lastingly be overcome if human mind wants to receive the Holy Spirit,
and only through the right religious conduct of life the gift of the Spirit
can be retained, cf. *De Trin.* 1, 11 where the men becoming sons of God
are made dependent upon men's right use of their free will. But also the
beginning of book II is picked up again, especially the promise given in
Matth. 28:20 that Christ will be with the believers until the end of the
world and the exhortation to keep all His commandments, see *De Trin.* 2,
1, *supra*, 65.

BOOK III

CONTENTS

1.

The meaning of the text 'I am in the Father and the Father is in Me'
(1-4)

Human mind cannot comprehend that the Father is in the Son and
that at the same time the Son is in the Father. Bearing in mind that both
the Father and the Son have the same eternal, infinite and spiritual
nature it is possible to understand the mutual indwelling of the Father
and the Son in a non-bodily way. Hilary here repeats what was discussed
extensively in the previous books. He adds one statement which is of importance if one wants to determine the differences between Hilary's
theology and Athanasius' theology. According to Hilary the Son is
generated through the eternal will of the Father. Here he adopts a tenet
which was normal in pre-nicene theology, but which under the influence
of the Arian controversy was rejected by Athanasius, who declared the
Son to *be* the Will of God and not *caused by* the will of God. Athanasius
feared that this latter position gave room to the Arian doctrine that the
Son is a creature with a temporal beginning.

Chapter 1

The difficulty of the text 'I am in the Father and the Father is in Me'.

Translation and Commentary:

(1) "When the Lord says: 'I am in the Father and the Father is in Me'
these words cause a great number of people uncertainty."

As we have already seen, *supra*, 66, *De Trin.* 2, 1, the uncertainty does not
lie with God's revelation, but with the difficulties men can have in
understanding it. On Hilary's exegesis of this text see *infra*, 133, *De Trin.*
3, 4.

"And rightly so. For the nature of human understanding cannot grasp the
meaning of this text. For it seems impossible that the very thing which is in
something else should equally be outside that thing, and it seems – since it is
necessary that the Beings of whom we are speaking are not isolated – that
they, retaining their own position, cannot nevertheless contain each other;
so that He who has something else inside Himself lastingly and in this way is
always exterior, should on the other hand equally be always interior to Him
whom He has inside."

It had been laid down in *De Trin.* 2, 14, *supra*, 133, that the divine Persons are not isolated Beings. Hilary had already stated that God is inside

and outside all things, see *supra*, 33 ff, 78 ff, *De Trin.* 1, 6 and 2, 6 (cf. *infra*, 127, *De Trin.* 3, 2). This could give room to the Arian claim that the Son is in the Father in the same way as all men are in God, see Athanasius, *Contra Arianos* 3, 1, who quotes the Arians as saying: ῍Η τί θαυμαστὸν εἰ ὁ Υἱὸς ἐν τῷ Πατρί, ὅπουγε καὶ περὶ ἡμῶν γέγραπται· Ἐν αὐτῷ γὰρ ζῶμεν, καὶ κινούμεθα καί ἐσμεν. Hilary will escape this conclusion by pointing out that the Son is mysteriously omnipresent in the same way as the Father, see *infra*, 133 ff, *De Trin.* 3, 4. – If the mutual indwelling of the Father and the Son is understood in a bodily way, this is an impossibility. The Arians understand it in such a way by rejecting a mutual indwelling and by saying that the Father, who is more than the Son, cannot be in the Son who is less than He; see the quotation from the Arians given by Athanasius, *Contra Arianos* 3, 1: ῍Η πῶς ὅλως δύναται ὁ Πατὴρ μείζων ὢν ἐν τῷ Υἱῷ ἐλάττονι ὄντι χωρεῖν; Athanasius retorts that it is wrong to speak about God in such bodily way (see *infra*, 133), and Hilary, too, accuses the Arians of subjecting God to the laws of the realm of creation (see *infra*, 176 ff, 181 f, *De Trin.* 3, 24 and 3, 26).

> "Human mind will not understand this, and a comparison taken from human existence will not provide an analogy for the divine existence."

In *De Trin.* 1, 19, *supra*, 61, Hilary had said that certain inadequate images can be taken from the realm of human life as an indication of divine life, but with respect to the mutual indwelling of the Father and the Son this is not possible, since man is only somewhere, which implies that he is not somewhere else as well, see *De Trin.* 8, 24: *Homo enim ... cum alicubi erit, tamen alibi non erit: quia id, quod est illic, continetur ubi fuerit, infirma ad id natura eius, ut ubique sit, qui insistens alicubi sit.*

> "But what man cannot understand, God can have."

On God's being which transcends human understanding see *supra*, 30 ff, *De Trin.* 1, 5-6; for this particular statement, cf. Athanasius, *Ad Ser.* 1, 17: ... οἱ τὰ Ἀρείου φρονοῦντες ... μηδὲ ἅπερ αὐτοὶ μὴ δύνανται νοεῖν ταῦτα λεγέτωσαν μηδὲ εἶναι δύνασθαι.

> "Let this not be said by me in such a way, that the mere authority of God's having said something is enough to indicate the meaning of this word. So we have to know and to understand what this means: 'I am in the Father and the Father is in Me', if at least we are able to understand this as it is, so that the divine truth may achieve what the nature of things is believed to be unable to permit."

It is Hilary's view that the authority of God makes it necessary to believe what God says, but God also wants man to understand the meaning of what he believes, see *De Trin.* 8, 52: *Namque cum credendi necessitatem dicti dominici auctoritas sola praestaret, tamen sensum nostrum per intellegentiam editae rationis instituit* (see on this text J. E. Emmenegger, *op. cit.*, pp 75 f), cf. *De Trin.* 3, 20 where he describes himself as somebody who believes God in all things as they have been said by God, see *infra*, 165 ff (on the relation between faith and understanding see *supra*, 40, 83, 91).

CHAPTER 2

The infinite nature of the Father.

Translation and Commentary:

> **(2)** "And in order to be able to obtain more easily an understanding of this most difficult question, we must first know the Father and the Son according to the doctrine of the divine Scriptures, so that we speak with more certainty as dealing with known and familiar matters."

In this chapter and the following one Hilary will repeat what he has already said about the nature of the Father and the Son. Once the knowledge of this nature has been refreshed it can cast light on the difficult question of how the Father and the Son can mutually be in each other; on this way of arguing (where what is difficult is explained with what is clear) see *supra*, 61, *De Trin.* 1, 19. It is interesting to see that Hilary here does try to find an answer to a *difficillima quaestio*, whilst he often expresses scepticism about answering *quaestiones*, see *infra*, 154 f, *De Trin.* 3, 14.

> "The eternity of the Father, as we discussed in the previous book, exceeds space, time, appearance and all of that kind that can be conceived by human thought."

The reader is referred back to *De Trin.* 2, 6, *supra*, 78 ff, but see also *De Trin.* 1, 6-7, *supra*, 33 ff. 'Eternity' here has the meaning of 'infinity', since not only time is exceeded, but also space and appearance; the same is stressed in the chapters just mentioned.

> "He is outside and inside all things, embracing all things, embraced by nobody."

See again *De Trin.* 1, 6 and 2, 6, further 2, 7, 31.

> "He is incapable of change by increase or diminution."

On the rejection of increase in God see *supra*, 102, *De Trin.* 2, 20; of diminution see *supra*, 106, *De Trin.* 2, 22. As to all early Christian theologians the notion of God's unchangeability is very important to Hilary (see on this subject in general W. Maas, *Unveränderlichkeit Gottes. Zum Verhältnis von griechisch-philosophischer und christlicher Gotteslehre*, München-Paderborn-Wien 1974; E. P. Meijering, *God Being History.*

Studies in Patristic Philosophy, Amsterdam-Oxford 1974, especially pp 135
ff). Hilary stresses the unchangeability of God in the generation of the
Son, see *infra*, 131 f, *De Trin.* 3, 3, and in the incarnation of the Son. This
incarnation does not imply that God changed into a man. The objection
against the incarnation, that this implies a change of God (which is unacceptable) was already made by Celsus, see Origen's quotation given in
Contra Celsum 4, 14: εἰ δὴ εἰς ἀνθρώπους κάτεισι (sc. ὁ θεός), μεταβολῆς αὐτῷ
δεῖ, μεταβολῆς δὲ ἐξ ἀγαθοῦ εἰς κακόν ... καὶ μὲν δὴ τῷ θνητῷ μὲν ἀλλάττεσθαι
καὶ μεταπλάττεσθαι φύσις, τῷ δ᾽ ἀθανάτῳ κατὰ τὰ αὐτὰ καὶ ὡσαύτως ἔχειν.
Against this kind of objections Hilary states firmly that God in the act of
the incarnation does not change into a man, but that He, remaining
God, assumes a human body, see *e.g. De Trin.* 9, 66: ... *non ut in naturam
infirmam natura indemutabilis sit redacta, sed ut in natura indemutabili susceptionis
esset sacramentum, De Trin.* 11, 48, *De Syn.* 48 (cf. further *supra*, 108 ff).

> "But He is invisible, incomprehensible, full, perfect, eternal, not deriving
> anything from elsewhere, but self-sufficient in what He always is."

On God's invisibility, incomprehensibility see *supra*, 81 ff, *De Trin.* 2, 7;
on His fulness and perfection see *supra*, 84 f, *De Trin.* 2, 8; on His eternity
and self-sufficiency *supra*, 78 ff, *De Trin.* 2, 6.

CHAPTER 3

Through the eternal generation the Son shares the full divinity of the
Father. The act of the incarnation takes place on behalf of man's salvation.

Translation and Commentary:

> **(3)** "So He, who is unbegotten, begat before all time a Son from Himself,
> not from any already existing matter, because all things are through the
> Son."

On the generation before time see *supra*, 99, *De Trin.* 2, 17. That the Son
is not created out of any already existing matter, because all things have
been created through the Son, which implies that such an already existing matter would have been created through the Son as well and
therefore could not possibly be the Son's origin, is stated by the Arians,
too, see *De Trin.* 4, 11: *memorant namque Dei Filium neque ex aliqua subiacente
materia genitum esse, quia per eum creata omnia sint.*

> "Not out of nothing, because He generated the Son from Himself."

This remark is stated against the Arians who say the opposite: the Son
must be out of nothing, since He cannot be from the Father, see *De Trin.*

4, 11: *neque ex Deo esse, quia decedere ex Deo nihil possit, sed esse ex his quae non erant, id est creaturam Dei perfectam*; on the Arian doctrine about Christ as the perfect creature see further *supra*, 56, *De Trin.* 1, 16 and *supra*, 72, *De Trin.* 2, 4.

"Not by way of childbirth, for in God there is neither change nor void."

The Arians reject the generation of the Son, since this, according to them, would imply changeability of God, see *De Trin.* 4, 4 and 6, 17 (these quotations are given *infra* in the commentary on this chapter). Therefore Hilary stresses that the generation does not imply any change in God, see *De Syn.* 33: *Non enim in eo nascente, ea de qua natus est, demutata natura est: sed indemutabilem essentiam natus obtinuit ex indemutabilis auctoritate naturae*, see further *De Trin.* 5, 37; 7, 2, 27, 28; 9, 36. The denial of any void in God in connection with the generation means that God does not lose anything in generating the Son, see *De Trin.* 7, 28 and *supra*, 84 ff, *De Trin.* 2, 8.

> "Not a part of Him either cut off or torn off or stretched out, for God is passionless and bodiless, but these things are characteristic of affections and of bodily existence, and, as the Apostle says, in Christ dwells all the fullness of the Godhead bodily."

For opposition to the concept of the Son as a part torn off from the Father see *supra*, 85, *De Trin.* 2, 8; for opposition to the Sabellian doctrine that the Son is an extension of the Father, see *supra*, 55, *De Trin.* 1, 16; for opposition to passibility of God in the act of generation see *supra*, 85, *De Trin.* 2, 8. One of the Arian objections against the *homoousion* is that this means that the Son is a portion cut off from the Father, but that the passion of such a division is impossible in the unchangeable God, see *De Trin.* 4, 4: ... *et ideo substantiae dicantur unius, quia portio desecta de toto in natura ea sit unde desecta est; nec posse in Deum cadere divisionis passionem, quia et demutabilis erit, si inminutioni per divisionem fiat obnoxius*, cf. *De Trin.* 6, 17 where the act of generation is said to imply a changeable and bodily nature of God: "*Si, inquit, ex Deo est Filius, demutabilis et corporeus Deus est, qui ex se protulerit vel extenderit quod sibi esset in filium.*" Against this Hilary states that the generation of the Son does not imply changeability, passibility or a bodily nature of God.

> "But incomprehensibly, ineffably, before all time and ages He begat the Only-begotten from what was unbegotten in Himself, bestowing through love and power His whole divinity on His birth."

On the incomprehensibility of the generation see *supra*, 87 ff, *De Trin.* 2, 9; on its eternity *supra*, 91 ff, *De Trin.* 2, 12 ff. In Hilary 'from God's nature' or similar expressions are meant to indicate the Son's ontological status, equal to the Father, – as clearly appears from this sentence. This may not, however, be the original meaning of this phrase, which was "that the Son derives from the Father by a process comparable to natural generation, as opposed to some process of 'making', like that of God's created works", see G. C. Stead, *Divine Substance*, p 233 (cf. 223-233). – The generation is described as an act of love, this is certainly caused by texts as *Matth* 3:17 (the 'beloved Son'), see *supra*, 85, and John 3:35 ('The Father loves the Son'), cf. Athanasius, *Contra Arianos* 3, 66: θελέσθω καὶ φιλείσθω τοίνυν ὁ Υἰὸς παρὰ τοῦ Πατρός ... ὁ Πατὴρ ἀγαπᾷ καὶ θέλει τὸν Υἱόν. On the generation as an act of God's power see *infra*, 138 f, *De Trin.* 3, 6.

> "And thus is from the unbegotten, perfect and eternal Father the only-begotten, perfect and eternal Son."

See on this statement *supra*, 86, 90, *De Trin.* 2, 8 and 2, 11. What has been said so far in *De Trin.* 3, 2-3 is a brief repetition of what was discussed extensively in the previous book. This repetition is necessary in order to explain the text 'The Father is in Me, and I am in the Father'. Before this text is discussed again a brief repetition is given of what was already said about the act of the incarnation.

> "But those properties which He has in accordance with the body which He took are caused by His goodness which wills our salvation."

Hilary wants to prepare his readers for a non-bodily interpretation of the text 'I am in the Father and the Father is in Me', therefore he now has to make it clear that the incarnation does not imply that the Son is confined to a human body. – On the act of the incarnation as a consequence of God's will to save see *supra*, 109 ff, ff, *De Trin.* 2, 24 ff.

> "For being invisible, bodiless and incomprehensible, because He was generated from God, He took upon Him matter and humility to such an extent as we had the power to understand, experience and behold Him. In doing this He rather adapted Himself to our feebleness than that He forsook His own being."

On the invisibility etc. of the Son see *supra*, 111, *De Trin.* 2, 25; on the insistence that Christ remained God in the act of the incarnation see *supra*, 46, 108 ff, *De Trin.* 1, 11 and 2, 24 ff. The assumption of flesh is an adaptation to our weakness, this means that we cannot perceive Him in His divine glory, this is repeated in *De Trin.* 3, 9, see *infra*, 142, cf. Irenaeus, *Adv. Haer.* 4, 62: *Et propter hoc Dominus noster in novissimis temporibus ... venit ad nos, non quomodo ipse poterat, sed quomodo illum nos videre poteramus. Ipse enim in sua inenarrabili gloria ad nos venire poterat: sed nos magnitudinem gloriae ipsius potare non poteramus*; Athanasius, *De Inc.* 8; 15; 16; 43.

Chapter 4

The eternal Son is the perfect Offspring of the Father and has the same nature as the Father.

Translation and Commentary:

(4) "So, being the perfect Son of the perfect Father, the only-begotten Offspring of the unbegotten God, who received all things from Him who has all things, God from God, Spirit from Spirit, Light from Light, He says with confidence: 'The Father is in Me and I am in the Father': Because as the Father is Spirit, so is the Son Spirit, too, as the Father is God, so is the Son God, too, as the Father is Light, so is the Son Light, too."

On the Son as the perfect Offspring of the Father and who has all the Father has, see *supra*, 85, *De Trin.* 2, 8. Of the titles 'God', 'Spirit' and 'Light' the title 'Spirit' is in this context the most important one, since this implies the omnipresence of both Father and Son and makes it possible that they are in each other (on the omnipresence of God as Spirit see *supra*, 118 ff, *De Trin.* 2, 31), see *De Trin.* 8, 24: *Namque idcirco dictum existimo in utroque Spiritus Dei, ne secundum corporales modos ita inesse Filium in Patre vel Patrem in Filio crederemus: scilicet ne loco Deus manens, nusquam alibi exstare videretur a sese*, cf. 7, 41, *In Ps.* CXXII 2; for opposition against a bodily interpretation of this text see also Athanasius *Contra Arianos* 3, 1: Πάσχουσι δὲ τοῦτο ἀκολούθως τῇ κακονοίᾳ ἑαυτῶν, σῶμα νομίζοντες εἶναι τὸν θεόν, καὶ μὴ νοοῦντες μήτε τί ἐστιν ἀληθινὸς Πατὴρ καὶ ἀληθινὸς Υἱὸς μήτε τί ἐστι φῶς ἀόρατον, καὶ ἀΐδιον ... καὶ χαρακτὴρ ἀσώματος, καὶ εἰκὼν ἀσώματος.

"So from that which is in the Father is that in which is the Son, that He is wholly Son generated out of Him who is wholly Father."

See on this statement *supra*, 90, *De Trin.* 2, 11.

"He does not receive His origin from something else, because nothing was before the Son."

This is opposition against the idea that the Son was created out of any already existing matter, see *supra*, 130, *De Trin.* 3, 3.

"He is not out of nothing, because the Son is from God."

This is opposition to the Arian doctrine that the Son is a creature, see *supra*, 56, *De Trin.* 1, 16.

"Not come into existence as part, because the fulness of Divinity is in the Son, not in some respects, since it is in all."

For opposition to the concept of the Son as a part of God see *supra*, 106, *De Trin.* 2, 22; for insistence on the full divinity of the Son see *supra*, 90, *De Trin.* 2, 11.

"According to the will of Him who had the power, according to the knowledge of Him who generated."

E. W. Watson, *op. cit.*, p LXV, rightly draws attention to the fact that Hilary differs from Athanasius, when he refers the generation of the Son to God's will. This deserves close examination (cf. for the following: E. Benz, *Marius Viktorin und die Entwicklung der abendländischen Willensmetaphysik*, Stuttgart 1932, C. van Essen-Zeeman, *De Plaats van de Wil in de Philosophie van Plotinus*, Arnhem 1946, K. Kremer, Das Warum der Schöpfung: "quia bonus" vel/et "quia voluit", *Parusia*, pp 241 ff, K. A. Neuhausen, *De voluntarii notione platonica et aristotelea*, Wiesbaden 1967, E. P. Meijering, *Orthodoxy and Platonism in Athanasius. Synthesis or Antithesis?* Leiden 1974², pp 70 ff, and the very important book of R. C. Gregg and D. E. Groh, *Early Arianism. A View of Salvation*, Philadelphia 1981, pp 170 ff.) Hilary says repeatedly that the Son is generated by the will of the Father, see *De Syn.* 37; 58; 59: *ante tempora omnia Pater ex naturae suae essentia, impassibiliter volens, Filio dedit naturalis nativitas essentiam, In Matth.* 16, 4. Hilary makes it clear that the generation out of the substance of God through the will of God is different from the creation out of nothing through the will of God. In referring the generation to God's will Hilary is in line with earlier Christian theologians, see *e.g.* Justin Martyr, *Dial.* 61, Novatian, *De Trin.* 31, 183: *Ex quo, quando ipse voluit sermo filius natus est*, 31, 186: *Hic ergo, quando pater voluit, processit ex patre* (more examples are given by H. A. Wolfson, *The Philosophy of the Church Fathers*, p 224). The way these theologians speak about the generation of the Son through the will of God could leave room for the Arian doctrine that the Son has a beginning in time. Therefore Athanasius denies that the Son is generated through the will of God and says that He is generated out of God's nature, see *Contra Arianos* 3, 59: Ταὐτὸν γὰρ σημαίνει ὁ λέγων, Βουλήσει γέγονεν ὁ Υἱός, καὶ ὁ λέγων, Ἦν ποτε ὅτε οὐκ ἦν, 3, 62: ὁ δὲ Υἱὸς ἴδιόν ἐστι τῆς οὐσίας τοῦ Πατρὸς γέννημα ... διὸ οὐδὲ βουλεύεται περὶ αὐτοῦ. The Son is Himself the Will of the Father and therefore cannot have been caused by God's will, see 3, 63-64. It can only be said that the Father wants the Son in so far as the Father wants His own being, see 3, 66 (quotations given *supra*, 132). Hilary does not share Athanasius' anxieties in this respect, since he believes that it was God's eternal will to generate the Son; here he is in line with the Cappadocians, see *e.g.* Gregory of Nazianze, *Oratio Theol.* 3, 6. – Another reason why Athanasius rejects the idea that the Son is generated through the will of the Father is that according to him free will is an indication of ambiguity, in one's free will one can want this today and the opposite tomorrow, see *Contra Arianos* 3, 62; 66; 1, 35-39; 52. Therefore he denies that the Father has in this sense a free will, like man. Hilary describes free will as a *motus mentis*, see *De Trin.* 9, 72: *Non est itaque diversus* (sc. *deus*) *compositae divinitatis partibus ... ut velle aliquid, nisi ad volendum motus sit, non putetur* (cf. *De Trin.* 12, 39 and *supra*, 102). But having made it clear that God is not moved in a temporal and human way to want certain things, Hilary emphasizes God's sovereign free will, see *e.g. De Syn.* 44: *Extra corporalis enim naturae necessitatem liber manens, quod vult, et cum vult, et ubi vult, id praestat ex sese, De Trin.* 12, 8 (on Christ's free will see *infra*, 142 f), here Hilary is entirely in line with *e.g.* Irenaeus, *Adv. Haer.* 2, 1, 1; 2, 1, 2, 3; 2, 9, 2; 2, 11, 1; 3, 8, 3; 4, 20, 1; 5, 18, 2; 2, 56, 1 and Tertullian, *Adv. Marc.* 2, 6. According to Hilary it is typical of God that in Him will and power are identical, see apart from this section in *De Trin.* 3, 4 the statement made in *De Trin.* 5, 5: *Deus est, creator est, Dei Filius est, potest omnia. Parum est ut quod vult possit, quia semper voluntas virtutis est,* – here he is in line with Irenaeus, *Adv. Haer.* 2, 44, 2, Tertullian, *Adv. Marc.* 1, 11, 6-7; 1, 17, 4; *De carne Chr.* 3, 1, *Adv. Prax.* 10, 9 (cf. R. Braun, *op. cit.*, p 111), Origen, *Contra Celsum* 3, 70; 5, 23, cf. Augustin *Conf.* 7, 4; Cyril of Alexandria, *Adv. Anthr.* 13. So according to Hilary the Son is caused by God's will, power, knowledge (wisdom) and generation; a similar equation is found in Athanasius, *Contra Arianos* 3, 63: ὡς γὰρ αὐτὸς ὢν ἡ φρόνησις ... καὶ αὐτὸς ὢν ἰσχὺς καὶ δύναμις ... οὕτω ... αὐτὸς ἂν εἴη τοῦ Πατρὸς ἡ ζῶσα βουλή (with this important difference that according to Hilary the Son *is caused* by the Father's will, power and wisdom, whilst according to Athanasius the Son *is* the Father's will, power and wisdom).

> "What is in the Father is in the Son, too, what is in the Unbegotten One is in the Only-begotten One, too. The One is from the Other and they two are a unity."

This a repetition of what was said *inter alia* in *De Trin.* 2, 11, see *supra*, 91.

> "The two are not One, but One is in the Other, for that which is in Both is the same."

The Father and the Son are *unum*, not *unus*, on this play of words see *supra*, 56 ff, *De Trin.* 1, 17. The Father and the Son have the same nature – this is said against the Arians; but they are not identical – this is said against the Sabellians.

> "The Father is in the Son, because the Son is from Him; the Son is in the Father, because the Father is His sole origin, the Only-begotten is in the Unbegotten, because He is the Only-begotten from the Unbegotten. So they are mutually in each other, for as all is perfect in the unbegotten Father, so all is perfect in the only-begotten Son."

Now that the perfectly divine nature of both Father and Son has been made clear, it is obvious that the text 'The Father is in Me and I am in the Father' cannot be interpreted in a bodily way.

"This is the unity in the Son and the Father, this the power, this the love, –
this is the hope, this is the faith, this the truth, way and life, not to detract
God's own powers, not to depreciate the Son, since He was mysteriously
and powerfully generated, to compare nothing with the unbegotten Father,
not to dissociate the only-begotten One from Him either in time or in
power, to confess the Son as God, because He is from God."

The unity of the Father and the Son is caused by the fact that the Son is
generated from the Father through power and love, see *supra*, 130 ff, *De
Trin.* 3, 3. It is strange that after "this is the love", which must mean
God's love in generating the Son, Hilary goes on without any interrup-
tion to speak about what is our hope and faith. The word 'love' (here
used for God's love) may remind him of 'hope' and 'faith' (love, hope
and faith belonging together, I *Cor.* 13), and these three concepts remind
him of three more concepts which belong together: truth, way, life (*John*
14:6). On this *asyndeton*, which is meant to express emotion and liveliness,
see M. F. Buttell, *op. cit.*, pp 76 ff. – The Arians dispute God's power in
the act of generation, see *infra*, 141 f, *De Trin.* 3, 8. They do not want to
compare anything with the Father, but they express this desire in a wrong
way, by depreciating the Son, see *De Trin.* 4, 8: *Conantur enim sola Dei
Patris divinitate celebrata Filio auferre quod Deus est.*

2.

The miracles of Christ as illustrations of the incomprehensibility of the
divine generation
(5-8)

The miracles are acts of God which man can admire without being able
to explain how they happened. Hilary lists as particular examples the
wedding at Cana and the multiplication of the loaves of bread. These are
not examples of how the generation takes place, the only point of analogy
being the swiftness of the divine action. – The miracles are not meant to
stun man, God does not need honour for His actions from men who are
sinners. These miracles must make men realize that they cannot pass
judgements on God's possibilities, *e.g.* His possibility to generate as the
One Father the One Son without a second generating principle.

CHAPTER 5

The wedding in Cana.

Translation and Commentary:

(5) "There are such powers in God, of which the way they operate is incomprehensible to our understanding, but credence in them is certain

because the truth manifests itself. We shall find this not only in the spiritual sphere, but also in the corporeal sphere: it is manifested not in order to serve as an example of the generation but in order to cause admiration of an intelligible act (to haven taken place)."

The mysterious divine powers operate in the act of the generation of the Son which transcends human understanding, but in which man can believe. The miracles wrought by Christ in the bodily sphere are not meant as an example of the divine generation (such an example will always be inadequate, see *supra*, 61, *De Trin.* 1, 19, even if it is an example of a miracle), but it is an analogy of the fact that one can admire an act of God without seeing the way it is wrought, and this is what man should do with respect to the generation of the Son (cf. *De Trin.* 3, 18, *infra*, 162 f). The generation of the Son is an example of God's power in the spiritual sphere, the miracles are examples of God's power in the bodily sphere, in both spheres it can be believed without man being able to understand how it operates. The 'intelligible act' which must be admired is the generation which transcends miracles wrought in the sensible world.

> "On a wedding-day in Galilee water was made wine. Certainly we cannot explain with words or understand with our senses the way in which the nature was changed, how the simplicity of water disappeared and was replaced by the full flavour of wine. It was not a mixing, but a creation, and a creation which did not have a beginning in itself, but came into existence by the transformation of one thing into another. It was not the decanting of a stronger liquid which resulted in a weaker one, but what was was abolished and what was not began to be."

It is understandable why Hilary does not want to interpret this as an example of the way the generation of the Son takes place: whilst a creation out of nothing is excluded, which means that the Arian doctrine about the Son as a creature is excluded as well, this example would nevertheless come dangerously close to the Sabellian doctrine (cf. *supra*, 55, *De Trin.* 1, 16). – In describing the miracle the notion of a *transfusio* (implying diminution) is rejected, this is in line with his doctrine of the generation, where emanation and transfusion are rejected as well. Emanation was rejected in *De Trin.* 2, 22 (*supra*, 106), transfusion is rejected in 5, 37: *Verum et absolutum et perfectum fidei nostrae sacramentum est, Deum ex Deo et Deum in Deo confiteri, non corporalibus modis sed divinis virtutibus, nec naturae in naturam transfusione sed mysterio et potestate naturae*, cf. 7, 31, 41 where *transfusio* is clearly distinguished from *nativitas* (see R. J. Kinnavey, *op. cit.*, p 174). – But it is, of course, impossible to say that in the act of generation the Father was abolished and the Son began to be, this again would come close to the Sabellian doctrine that the Father became His own Son.

"The bridegroom was in sadness, the family disturbed, the festival of the marriage-meal was in danger. Jesus is asked for help, He does not rise and come nearer, but this is a work He does in rest. Water is poured into the vessels, wine is served in cups. The perceiving knowledge of him who serves contradicts the perceiving knowledge of him who pours. They who poured believed water to be served, they who serve believe wine to have been poured in. The intervening time does not help to explain the beginning and abolition of a nature."

The only analogy with the generation of the Son is, that this event is beyond time as well (cf. *infra*, 101 ff, *De Trin.* 3, 6 and *supra*, 138, *De Trin.* 2, 20).

"The way in which the act was wrought eludes sight and mind, nevertheless God's power can be perceived in what has here been done."

This remark is made in order to show that the miracle at the wedding in Cana is a confirmation of what was said in the beginning of this chapter: On can see that something has happened without understanding how it happened.

CHAPTER 6

The multiplication of the loaves of bread.

Translation and Commentary:

(6)   "But also in the case of the five loaves there is the admiration of a similar fact. By their increase the hunger of five thousand men and countless women and children is stilled. We cannot understand this act with the perception of our eyes."

This miracle also confirms what was said in the beginning of the previous chapter: God's power operates in a way which man cannot understand, but man can perceive and admire the results of this operation.

"Five loaves are offered and broken, under the hands of those who break pieces off certain new fragments come into being. The loaf from which pieces are broken does not become smaller and yet the hand of him who breaks off is constantly full of pieces. The swiftness of the movements eludes sight. While you follow with your eyes the hand full of fragments, you see that the contents of the other hand are not diminished. In the meantime the pile of pieces grows. Those who break off the bread are serving, those who eat are busy, the hungry are satisfied, what remains fills two baskets."

Again the actual analogy with the generation of the Son would only be that there is no diminution, see *supra*, 106, *De Trin.* 2, 22, and that the generation is beyond time, see *supra*, 103 ff, *De Trin.* 2, 21.

"Neither mind nor vision can follow the actual process of so conspicable an operation. There is what was not, there is seen what is not understood, the only resource is to believe that God is omnipotent."

The result of the divine act can be seen, the process of its taking place cannot be perceived and therefore it cannot be explained. In all this God's omnipotence must be believed. This omnipotence appears in these miracles wrought in the bodily sphere, and equally appears in the great miracle wrought in the spiritual sphere: the generation of the Son. On God's omnipotence in the generation of the Son see *De Trin.* 6, 21: *Inpossibile enim tibi nihil est et genitum a te Filium omnipotentiae tuae virtute non ambigo.* (The Arians come forward with an argument against the generation of the Son which can only be countered with God's omnipotence, see *De Trin.* 3, 8, *infra*, 141 f).

CHAPTER 7

There is no need for God to reveal Himself in miracles.

Translation and Commentary:

> (7) "So there is no flattering in the divine actions, and there is no subtle pretence in God either to please or to deceive. These works of the Son of God were done for no desire for self-display: for He whom countless myriads of angels serve never flattered man."

Since God's omnipotence is beyond men's understanding God need not flatter men in order to receive honour from men. Furthermore this could be polemics against the Greek 'sons of God' who have to legitimate themselves with miraculous deeds, see Origen, *Contra Celsum* 1, 67; 3, 22 (C. Andresen, *Logos und Nomos. Die Polemik des Kelsos wider das Christentum*, Berlin 1955, pp 53 f). Hilary wants to show that to the Lord of heaven and earth such 'showing off' is not necessary, cf. Athanasius, *De Inc.* 43: ... γιγνωσκέτωσαν ὅτι οὐκ ἐπιδείξασθαι ἦλθεν ὁ κύριος, ἀλλὰ θεραπεῦσαι καὶ διδάξαι τοὺς πάσχοντας.

> "What was there of ours that He needed, through whom all that we have was created?"

On the theme that God does not need us (because God is self-sufficient) see further *De Trin.* 6, 19, *In Ps.* II 14, 15: *Hominem, non quod officio eius in aliquo eguerit, instituit, sed quia bonus est, participem beatitudinis suae condidit et rationale animal in usum largiendae suae aeternitatis vita sensuque perfecit*; this is a commonplace in early Christian theology, see *e.g.* Aristides, *Apologia* 1, 2; 10, 2; Justin Martyr, *Apologia* I 10, 1; 13, 1; Irenaeus, *Adv. Haer.* 4, 25, 3; 4, 29; 4, 31-32; 4, 49, 2; Tertullian, *Adv. Marc.* 2, 18, 3; *Ad Scap.* 2, 8, *Adv. Jud.* 5, 3 ff; on insistence on God's self-sufficiency in Pagan literature see E. Norden, *Agnostos Theos, Untersuchungen zur Formengeschichte religiöser Rede*, Stuttgart 1956⁴, pp 13 f, B. Gärtner, *The Areopagus Speech and Natural Revelation*, Uppsala 1955, pp 216 ff.

"Did He demand honour from us who are now still heavy with sleep, now
sated with nightly lust, now laden with feelings of guilt after quarrels and
bloodshed during the days, now drunken after banquets, – He whom archangels, dominions, principalities and powers, without sleep, without
disturbing activities, without sin, praise in heaven with eternal and
unwearied voices?"

God needs no honour from man, in the first place because man is a sin-
ner. Especially in his commentary on the Psalms Hilary frequently gives
examples of a "Lasterkatalog", see *In Ps.* I 4, II 39, CXXIII 7, CXXV
4 f, CXXIX 8, CXXXVI 3, 13, CXVIII, xix 10, cf. Athanasius, *Contra
Gentes* 5, *De Inc.* 5 (on literature about the subject of "Lasterkataloge" see
O. Michel, *Der Brief an die Römer*, Göttingen 1963[12], p 70 n. 1). – God
needs no honour from man, in the second place, because he permanently
receives honour from his Angels, cf. *In Ps.* CXVIII, xv 9: *Nihil enim illic
otiosum, nihil iners est: omnes virtutes coelestes in opere ministerii sui permanent.*

"They praise Him, because He, the Image of the Invisible God, created
them all in Himself, made the ages, established heaven, appointed the stars,
fixed the earth, laid the foundations of the deep; and because afterwards He
Himself was born as man, conquered death, broke the gates of hell, won for
Himself a people to be His fellow-heirs, lifted flesh from corruption up into
eternal glory."

This statement implies that God does not seek temporal glory from man
for the acts of creation and incarnation, He who accepts eternal glory for
these acts from the angels. – The praise for the acts in the incarnation is a
continuation of the praise for the acts in creation, both the creation and
the incarnation are caused by God's will. – On the consequences of the
incarnation (the destruction of death etc.) see *supra*, 49 ff, *De Trin.* 1, 13.
On the descent to hell cf. the interesting passage in *De Trin.* 10, 34 where
the Arians claim that the Son feared hell as much as death to which
Hilary counters that in the descent to hell Christ was not absent from
Paradise (which He promised to the robber).

"So He needed nothing from us, so that these works which transcend our
speech and understanding should extol Him with us, as if He needed praise.
But God foresaw the error of human wickedness and folly and knew that
disbelief would go so far as to presume to pass a judgement on the things of
God, and therefore vanquished our audacity with examples of those things
about which doubt could be expressed."

The Arians have the audacity to pass judgements on God, see *supra*, 53 f,
De Trin. 1, 15. As appears from *De Trin.* 3, 8 they claim that God cannot
generate a Son. The miracles wrought are tokens that God can, in a
mysterious way, generate a Son. Here the miracles are called examples of
the generation (as they are in *De Trin.* 3, 18); in 3, 5 it was denied that
they are examples, see *supra*, 136 ff. They are *inadequate examples* (cf. *supra*,

61, *De Trin.* 1, 19). This explains that it is said that they are examples and that they are not.

CHAPTER 8

The Arian objection that it is impossible for the Father to generate a Son.

Translation and Commentary:

> (8) "For there are many wise men of the world whose wisdom is folly with God, who, when they hear that God is generated from God, True from True, Perfect from Perfect, One from One, contradict us as though we taught impossible things, pinning their faith to certain axiomatic reasonings, when they say: 'Nothing could be born of one, because every birth requires two parents. If this Son is born of One, He has received a part of His Begetter. And if He is a part, then neither of the two is perfect, for something is missing in Him from whom the Son departed, and there cannot be fulness in Him who consists of a portion of the other. Thus neither is perfect, since the Begetter loses His fulness and the Begotten does not obtain it.' "

The wise men of the world whose wisdom is folly with God are the Arians who argue with the subtlety of Pagan philosophy, this appears clearly from *De Trin.* 8, 3: *Iam vero hic quanta saecularis ingenii subtilitate contendunt ... cum asserunt, ex uno nasci nihil posse, quia universarum rerum ex duorum coniunctione nativitas est*; 8, 52: *... hoc philosophia non sapit, unum ex uno ...* The Arians object to the orthodox doctrine that this implies that the Son is a part of the Father, an objection which is, of course, rejected by Hilary, see *supra*, 85, *De Trin.* 2, 8. Hilary stresses that the Father does not lose in giving to the Son, see *supra*, 86, *De Trin.* 2, 8.

> "God foresaw this wisdom of the world even in the prophet's days and therefore condemned it in the following way: 'I shall destroy the wisdom of the wise and reject the understanding of the prudent'."

It is a commonplace in early Christian theology to claim that heresies were already foreseen in the Bible, see *e.g.* Tertullian, *Adv. Marc.* 2, 2, 4, Athanasius, *Contra Arianos* 3, 8.

> "In the same way He says in the Apostle: 'Where is the wise? Where is the scribe? Where is the inquirer of this world? Has God not made foolish the wisdom of this world? For because in the wisdom of God the world through wisdom knew not God, it pleased God through the foolishness of preaching to serve them that believe. For the Jews seek signs, the Greeks seek wisdom, but we preach Christ crucified, to the Jews a stumbling-block and to the Gentiles foolishness, but unto them that are called, both Jews and Greeks, Christ the power of God and the wisdom of God. Because the foolishness of God is wiser than men and the weakness of God is stronger than men.' "

The philosophical reasonings of the Arians are here contrasted with the wisdom of God, about which Paul speaks in I *Cor.* 1:20 ff; similarly Tertullian attacks the *censores divinitatis* with these words from Paul, see *Adv. Marc.* 2, 2, 4 f. On I *Cor* 1:17 see further *infra*, 176 ff, ff, *De Trin.* 3, 24 ff.

3.

The glorification of the Son by the Father and of the Father by the Son
(9-17)

The first question treated is how the hour of passion can be the hour of glorification. The answer is that the miraculous events surrounding the crucifixion testify that it was the Son of God who died on the cross. – The second question is how the Father and the Son, who are both fully and perfectly divine, can be glorified by each other. The Father is glorified by the Son through the Son's obedience to the Father and through the fact that the Son reveals Him to men who knew about God's divinity but who were ignorant about God's (eternal) fatherhood. The glory the Son receives from the Father consists of the fact that He received from the Father the power to restore eternal life to mortal men. When the Son is glorified, His human nature is glorified and in this mankind is glorified and deified.

CHAPTER 9

Christ's prayer to be glorified by the Father.

Translation and Commentary:

> **(9)** "So the Son of God, caring about mankind, became man in the first place that man may give Him credence and that He may bear witness to things divine to us as one of us, and that He may, through the weakness of the flesh, preach God the Father to us who are weak and carnal."

The incarnation is *inter alia* an adaptation to human weakness, because man cannot perceive God in His glory, see on this theme *supra*, 131 f, *De Trin.* 3, 3.

> "In doing so He fulfilled the will of the Father, as He says: 'I did not come to do my own will, but the will of Him who sent Me.' Not that He Himself, too, did not want what He did, but He shows His obedience resulting from the Father's will, whereby He Himself wanted to fulfill His Father's will."

It is very important to Hilary that Christ was obedient to the Father out of free will, for he draws a clear distinction between obedience caused by necessity and acting out of free will, see *De Trin.* 9, 50: *Facere autem plus est quam voluntati oboedire: quia oboedire voluntati, habet exterioris necessitatem, facere voluntatem, proprium est unitati, cum factum sit voluntatis*; cf. *In Ps.* CXXXIX 12 and Irenaeus, *Adv. Haer.* 4, 24, 2: ... *maior et gloriosior operatio libertatis, quam ea quae est in servitute obsequentia.* Christ's obedience is an act of free will which He performed in the incarnation, *De Trin.* 11, 30: ... *qui fit oboediens suscipit ex voluntate quod oboedit, dum per id quod se humiliat, fit oboediens*, cf. 9, 39. The Son's free obedience to the Father is used as an argument against Sabellius' doctrine that the Father and the Son are not the same, see *De Syn.* 51: *Et vel in eo quidem maxime non comparatur nec coaequatur Filius Patri, dum subditus per oboedientiae obsequelam est, dum pluit Dominus a Domino, ne a se ipse secundum Photinum aut Sabellium pluerit ... dum in omnibus voluntati eius qui se misit obsequitur*, but in the same context he also stresses that this does not imply ontological subordination: *Sed pietatis subiectio non est essentiae diminutio, nec religionis officium degenerem efficit naturam.* Here Hilary is largely in line with Novatian, who also uses the obedience of the Son to the Father as a proof that the Father and the Son are not the same; there is, however, this difference that to Novatian this implies a kind of ontological subordination of the Son to the Father, see *De Trin.* 31, 190: *ita dum se patri in omnibus obtemperantem reddit, quamvis sit et Deus, unum tamen deum patrem de oboedientia sua ostendit, ex quo et originem traxit*, cf. 21, 122; 22, 128; 26, 147; 27, 153 (on the subordination of the Son see especially 27, 148).

> "This was that will to fulfill the (Father's) will of which He testifies in the words: 'Father, the hour has come, glorify Thy Son, that Thy Son may glorify Thee, as Thou hast given Him power over all flesh, that whatsoever Thou hast given Him, He should give it eternal life. And this is life eternal, that they should know Thee, the only true God and Him whom Thou didst send, Jesus Christ. I have glorified Thee upon earth, having accomplished the work which Thou gavest Me to do. And now, O Father, glorify Me with Thine own self with the glory which I had with Thee before the world was. I have manifested Thy name unto the men whom Thou hast given Me.' In words short and few He revealed the whole work He had to do in His task of granting salvation, yet with these words He safeguards the truth of faith against all tempting of the devil's cunning."

The meaning of these words from *John* 17:1-6 will be discussed in the next eight chapters. – It is interesting that Hilary suggests that Christ here reveals His whole task in the incarnation *despite* the brevity of the statement. On brevity Hilary makes statements which are not always consistent. Usually he says that brevity is desirable and that it is his intention to be brief in his expositions, see *e.g. De Trin.* 4, 25, *In Ps.* XIV 2; but here it should at once be noticed that Hilary sometimes calls 'short' what we would not regard as such: in *De Trin.* 7, 8 he says of the expositions given in 7, 3-7 on the heretics who fight each other and in doing so help the church (see *supra*, 72), that they were given in few words. Similarly the rather lengthy expositions on the two 'natures' of Christ in *De Trin.* 9, 3-14 are said to have been given in few words (*De Trin.* 9, 14: *Haec igitur demonstranda a me paucis fuerunt*). Brevity is a means to obtain clarity, see *De Trin.* 10, 70: *Non per difficiles nos Deus ad beatam vitam quaestiones vocat, nec multiplici eloquentis facundiae genere sollicitat. In absoluto nobis ac facili est aeternitas, Jesus et suscitatum a mortuis per Deum credere, et ipsum esse Dominum confiteri.* – But Hilary also says the opposite, *viz.*, that brevity is undesirable and can cause obscurity. (Quintilian says something similar, see *Inst.* 4, 2, 44-45: *Non minus autem cavenda erit, quae nimium corripientes omnia sequitur, obscuritas, satiusque est aliquid narrationi superesse quam deesse. Nam supervacua cum taedio dicuntur, necessaria cum periculo subtrahuntur. Quare vitanda est etiam illa Sallustiana ... brevitas ... media haec tenenda sit via dicendi quantum opus est et quantum satis est.*) This is the implication of what is said here in *De Trin.* 3, 9, that *despite* the brevity Christ can reveal the whole task in the incarnation (cf. *De Syn.* 35: *Brevibus expositio fidei huius, sed absolutissimis usa est definitionibus*), and this is said explicitly in connection with the *homoousion*, here brevity can be misleading, *De Syn.* 62: *Fallit enim plerumque et audientes et docentes brevitas verborum*, cf. 69, 77. (These contradictory statements can, of course, be harmonized to the view that expositions should be as lengthy as necessary and as brief as possible, which is a recommendation given by Quintilian, *Inst.* 4, 2, 45-46, of the quotation given *infra*). Similar contradictions can be detected in what Hilary says about repetitions. On the one hand he says that repetitions should be avoided, see *e.g. De Trin.* 4, 19; 9, 31: *eadem revolvere admodum otiosum est; In Ps.* CXXX 1, CXVIII ii 7; on the other hand he says that because of man's difficulties to understand divine things repetitions are necessary, *De Trin.* 6, 9: *Naturae humanae tarda ac difficilis ad res divinas intellegentia exigit, de his quae semel dicta a nobis sunt frequentius admoneri*; 9, 43: *tamen quia non modo non obest, sed etiam ad religionem proficit, fidem retractari, eundem ipsum* (sc. *locum qui in alio libello a nobis tractatus fuerit*), *quia causa postulat, revolvamus.* – It was a commonplace amongst early Christian theologians either to recommend brevity or to say that one tries to pursue it in one's writings, see *e.g.* Irenaeus, *Adv. Haer.* 3, 12, 12; Tertullian, *De anima* 2, 7; *Adv. Marc.* 2, 28, 3; *De or.* 1, 6 (but in *De pat.* 5, 1 he says: *loquacitas in aedificatione nulla turpis*); Lactance, *Inst.* 1, 1, 21; 4, 9, 4; Novatian, *De Trin.* 21, 121; 26, 146; 30, 173; Athanasius, *De Inc.* 1, 35, 54, 56 (in *Contra Arianos* 2, 72 he says of the long expositions on *Prov.* 8:22 in the chapters 44-71 that they were given in a few words, so he, just like Hilary, regarded as brief what we would not), *Contra Arianos* 3, 18; *Ad Ser.* 1, 33; 2, 1; 3, 1, 7 (but Athanasius also recommends repetition or admits that he repeats himself, *De Inc.* 20, 45, *Contra Arianos* 1, 29, 31, 48; 2, 22, 80; 3, 54.) – Pagan authors recommend brevity as well, see T. Janson, *op. cit.*, pp 96, 154 f;

of special interest is Quintilian who gives the following general rule on brevity, *Inst.* 4, 2, 43: *nos autem brevitatem in hoc ponimus, non ut minus sed ne plus dicatur quam oporteat* (cf. H. Lausberg, *op. cit.*, pp 169 ff, see further on the subject of brevity E. K. Curtius, *Europäische Literatur und lateinisches Mittelalter*, pp 479 ff).

"So let us run through the force of His own words."

This will be done in the chapters to come.

CHAPTER 10

The mutual glorification of the Father and the Son.

Translation and Commentary:

> **(10)** "He says: 'Father, the hour has come, glorify Thy Son, that the Son may glorify Thee.' He does not say that the day or the time, but that the hour has come. In the hour there is a fraction of the day. And which hour will this be? The hour, of course, of which He spoke strengthening His disciples at the time of His passion: 'Lo, the hour has come that the Son of man should be glorified'."

Hilary restricts the glorification to an hour, because he interprets the 'hour' as the time Christ was hanging on the cross and even specifically the hour of death. As to most ancients the hour was to Hilary the smallest time unit which could be defined precisely, after the hour he speaks vaguely of 'moments', see *In Ps.* II 23: *Tempora enim, in hunc suum motum atque cursum ab origine saeculi et constitutione dimensa sunt, cum per momenta et horas et menses et annum revolubili in se successione discreta sunt*, cf. on this subject E. P. Meijering, *Augustin über Schöpfung, Ewigkeit und Zeit. Das elfte Buch der Bekenntnisse*, Leiden 1979, p 64.

> "So this is the hour in which He prays to be glorified by the Father, that He Himself may glorify the Father. But what is this? Does He, about to glorify, expect to be glorified, does He, about to give honour, ask it for Himself and does He miss what He is about to confer?"

The question raised here will, of course, be answered with a clear: No;— see *De Trin.* 3, 12-13, *infra*, 150 ff.

> "Let here the sophists of the world and the wise men of Greece object and let them with their syllogisms try to ensnare the truth. Let them ask how, whence and why. And when they get stuck let them hear: 'God has chosen what is foolish in the world'. So let us understand through our foolishness these things which the wise men of the world cannot understand."

The philosophers do not understand how the Son can glorify and ask to be glorified at the same time, and how He can miss what He is about to confer, cf. *De Trin.* 8, 52 where Hilary says of the philosophers: *hoc filosofia non sapit: unum ex uno et totum a toto, Deum et Filium, neque per nativitatem Patri ademisse quod totum est, neque hoc ipsum totum non secum nascendo tenuisse.* But it seems more likely that he has the Arians in mind who use philosophical arguments againts the equality of Father and Son, see *De Trin.* 3, 8, *supra*, 141 f, where I *Cor* 1:19 ff is also quoted. In the explanation given to *John* 17:1 ff in *De Trin.* 9, 41 he addresses the Arians in the following way: *Adfers nunc, quisquis es heretice, flexuosae doctrinae tuae inevolubiles quaestiones! Quae cum se nodis suis inligent, in nullo tamen agmine haerendi molestiam continebunt.*

> "The Lord had said: 'Father, the hour has come.' He had revealed the hour of His passion, for He spoke these words at that moment. Then He added: 'Glorify Thy Son'. But how was the Son to be glorified? For born from the virgin He had, from cradle and childhood, become an adult man. Through sleep, thirst, weariness and tears He had lived human life, and now, in addition to that, He was to be spat on, scourged, crucified."

Christ's human life had already seemed a contradiction of His divinity, and certainly the crucifixion seemed to contradict it. So how can this be understood as the hour of glorification, when it appears to be the exact oppposite?

> "So what does this mean? This was only to testify to us to the manhood in Christ."

According to Hilary the thirst, hunger and tears of Christ are meant to indicate the mystery of the incarnation, but Hilary denies that Christ was really affected by all this: He did not cry for Himself and did not conquer thirst and hunger by eating and drinking, see *De Trin.* 10, 24: *Quodsi praeter fletus et sitis et esuritionis mysterium, adsumpta caro, id est homo totus, passionum est permissa naturis, nec tamen ita ut passionum conficeretur iniuriis: ut flens non sibi fleret, ut sitiens sitim non potatura depelleret, et esuriens non se cibo escae alicuius expleret*; cf. 10, 55 f; 10, 63: ... *Christum non sibi flere, sed nobis* ..., 10, 67, *In Ps.* LIII 7, cf. P. Smulders, *La doctrine trinitaire*, pp 203 ff. These aspects of Christ's life had long been used as proof that Christ was really man, but Hilary goes further than, *e.g.*, Irenaeus in declaring that Christ did feel hunger etc. but did not conquer it by eating etc., according to Irenaeus Christ did eat etc., see *Adv. Haer.* 3, 31, 2: *Aut si nihil sumsisset ex Maria, numquam eas quae a terra erant percepisset escas, per quas id quod a terra sumtum est nutritur corpus ... nec lacrymasset super Lazarum ... nec dixisset quod 'Tristis est anima mea'.* Tertullian quotes in *Adv. Prax.* 16 heretics who regard Christ's hunger etc. as unworthy of the Son of God (meant are the Marcionites), Tertullian stresses that these acts were done on man's behalf, *Adv. Marc.* 2, 27, 7 (see E. Evans, *Tertullian's Treatise against Praxeas*, pp 284 f); Athanasius interprets Christ's hunger etc. as an indication of his true humanity, see *De Inc.* 18, this is what He decided to do as man, not as the Divine Word, see *Contra Arianos* 3, 31, 34, 54. Athanasius and Hilary agree with the Marcionites that hunger, tears etc. are unworthy of God, but not unworthy of the human nature which Christ assumed on man's behalf. On Hilary's denial that Christ tried to conquer His hunger etc. see further *infra*, 166, *De Trin.* 3, 20, on Christ's body.

> "But we are not put to shame by the cross, we are not first sentenced to lashing, we are not defiled by spitting."

Whilst passions like hunger etc. are ordinary human experiences, and can as such be interpreted as indications of Christ's true humanity, the crucifixion and the surrounding events are according to Hilary no ordinary events. So this is something special and can therefore be interpreted as a glorification of a special kind.

> "The Father glorifies the Son. How? Finally He was nailed to the cross. Then what follows? The sun did not set, but fled. Why do I say 'fled'? It was not overshadowed by a cloud, but failed to give its normal light. And together with the sun the other elements of the universe sensed their destruction, and lest any heavenly operations took part in this crime they escaped inevitable witnessing by a certain self-abolition."

The heavenly bodies did not want to witness the crime of Christ's death; on this sense of *intercessio* see *In Ps.* CXVIII i 8 and CXVIII ii 9. The darkness which covered the earth is explained, not by clouds, but by the fact that the sun failed to give its normal light, this must underline the miraculous character of the event. In the New Testament (*Luke* 23:44-45) it only says that the sun was eclipsed. Hilary extends this eclipse to the heavenly bodies in general and qualifies it as *quaedam sui abolitio* by which the heavenly bodies escaped the necessity of beholding the scene. This, too, underlines the miraculous character of the event, since Hilary stresses the fact that the heavenly bodies move according to fixed laws, see *e.g. In Ps.* CXVIII xii 2, CXXXIV 11, CXLIII 18, cf. Lactance, *Epit.* 21, Athanasius, *Contra Gentes* 35, where this fact is used – just as it is in Stoicism – as a proof of the existence of God (see Cicero, *De nat. deor.* 2, 2, 4; 2, 5, 15; 2, 38, 96 ff.) These 'heavenly bodies' are, of course, the stars, (cf. *Col.* 2:8, *supra*, 48, *De Trin.* 1, 13). The reason why he adds that the stars refused to shine as well is that he explicitly denies that the darkness was caused by clouds. Then the stars and the moon cannot have given light either. How this happened is not explained by Hilary, who simply says that the stars somehow abolished themselves.

> "But what did the earth do? It trembled at the sight of the Lord hanging on the cross, testifying that it could not comprise Him who was going to die. And did not rock and stone refuse to play their part either? They split,

having been rent, they lose their nature and thereby confess that the rock-
hewn coffin of sepulchre cannot contain the body which will be buried.''

The miraculous events in heaven and on earth which happened around
Christ's crucifixion and resurrection are frequently interpreted by Hilary
as a proof of Christ's triumph and divinity, see *De Trin.* 10, 48; *In Ps.*
LVIII 10; CXXXIV 19, CXXXVIII 27; in *In Matth.* 33, 7 the trembling
of the earth is explained by the fact that it could not contain Christ's
body, the splitting of the rocks is explained by the fact that the powerful
Word of God could penetrate even solid things (cf. *supra*, 165 ff, *De Trin.*
3, 20). Similarly Irenaeus stresses that none of the prophets suffered and
died under such circumstances, see *Adv. Haer.* 4, 56, 2; according to
Athanasius in these events creation witnessed the divinity of the Son, see
De Inc. 19, with these events the Father showed that even in the crucifixion He was in the Son, *Contra Arianos* 3, 56.

CHAPTER 11

The miraculous events during Christ's crucifixion prove His glorification as Son of God.

Translation and Commentary:

> **(11)** "And next? The centurion of the cohort, the guardian of the cross,
> also proclaims: 'Truly this is the Son of God'. Creation is set free by the
> mediation of this sin-offering, the rocks do not retain their solidity and
> strength. Those who had nailed Him to the cross confess that he is truly the
> Son of God. The outcome agrees with the prayer."

The confession of the centurio is caused by the miraculous events around
the crucifixion, cf. *De Trin.* 6, 52, *In Ps.* LVIII 10, Athanasius, *Contra
Arianos* 3, 56. In the previous chapter it was said that the elements of the
world wanted to escape inevitable witnessing of the crime of Christ's
death (see *supra*, 147). Now it is said that this death was in fact the *media-
tion* of His sin-offering through which the whole of creation is set free.
Both times the word *intercessio* is used, but with different meanings. – On
the rocks which lose their solidity see *supra*, 148, *De Trin.* 3, 10 where it
says that they lose their nature (which is that they cannot split).

> "The Lord had said: 'Glorify Thy Son'. He testified to being the Son of
> God not only in name but also in that peculiar nature because of which He
> is called 'Thy'."

See on this *supra*, 85, *De Trin.* 2, 8 (in connection with 'My Son, the
beloved'), and *De Trin.* 8, 25; 12, 13 ff.

> "For we are sons of God in multitudes, but He is not such a son of God."

In *De Trin*. 1, 11 Hilary had said that there are only very few who become through faith sons of God, here in *De Trin*. 3, 11 he says that there are many, a statement which is repeated in *De Trin*. 6, 23 (*donavi adoptionis plurimis nomen*). This contradiction is solved by a remark made in *In Ps*. LVIII 9: From all the nations there are a few believers from each, these few from each are together counted as many.

> "For He is the (Father's) own and true Son, by origin, not by adoption, in reality and not by name only, by generation, not by creation."

These words are meant to stress the eternal and essential divinity of the Son. The Father is the eternal origin of the Son, see *e.g. De Trin*. 4, 6: *Confitetur* (sc. *ecclesia*) *Patrem aeternum et ab origine liberum. Confitetur et Filii originem ab aeterno: non ipsum ab initio, sed ab ininitiabili*; 12, 54: ... *post te ita confitendus* (sc. *Filius*) *ut tecum: quia aeternae originis suae auctor aeternus es.* Adoption implies a beginning of the sonship, see *De Trin*. 12, 13: ... *nos cum filii non fuissemus, ad id quod sumus efficimur. Ante enim filii non eramus, sed postquam meruimus hoc sumus.* – On the difference between 'in reality' and 'by name' see *supra*, 97 f, *De Trin*. 2, 15. The Arians claim that the Son has been created (in time), not (eternally) generated, see *supra*, 56, *De Trin*. 1, 16.

> "So after His glorification the confession followed reality. For the centurio confessed Him as the true Son of God, lest any of the believers may doubt what one of the prosecutors had not denied."

This remark is, of course, made against the Arians: they deny what one of the Pagan prosecutors of Christ had confessed (cf. *supra*, 148). In addition Hilary wants with this remark to underline the truth of the faith in Christ as the true Son of God: even a Pagan confesses it to be true, see *De Trin*. 6, 52: *Tanta ratio veritatis et tanta vis fidei est, ut vincat voluntatem veri necessitas, et Christum Dominum gloriae aeternae vere Dei Filium esse nec qui crucifixerat denegaret* (cf. *De Trin*. 6, 22, *In Ps*. LVIII 10). Hilary believes to have explained hereby why the hour of passion was the hour of glorification: in the hour of passion Christ was by the surrounding miraculous events revealed as the Son of God and even by the Pagan cohort confessed as such. But the question still remains whether Christ lacked the glory which He received in the hour of passion. If He did lack it, then He cannot have been the *eternal* Son of God. This problem will be discussed in the next chapters.

CHAPTER 12

The Father and the Son glorify each other without needing to be glorified by each other.

Translation and Commentary:

> **(12)** "But perhaps the Son is believed to have been destitute of that glorification for which He prayed and will be found weak, since He expects the glorification by a Greater One."

This objection against Christ's perfect sonship was already made in *De Trin.* 3, 10, see *supra*, 145.

> "And who will not confess the Father as greater, distinguishing Him as the Unbegotten in relation to the Begotten, as the Father in relation to the Son, as He who sent in relation to Him who was sent, as He who wills in relation to Him who obeys. And He Himself will be the witness to us: 'The Father is greater than I.'"

On the Father as the Unbegotten and the Son as the Begotten, see *supra*, 99 ff, *De Trin.* 2, 18 ff; on the obedience of the Son, see *supra*, 142 ff, *De Trin.* 3, 9, where it is stressed that the Son's obedience is an act of the Son in the state of the incarnation. Hilary's interpretation of *John* 14:28 is in line with this: this text proves that the church does not confess two Unbegotten Ones, see *De Trin.* 9, 51: *Exciditne tibi ecclesiam duos innascibiles nescire et duos Patres non confiteri?* The Father is more than the Son who is in the state of the incarnation when He empties Himself; see *ibid.*: ... *ignorandum existimas, hanc dispensationem salutis tuae exinanitionem formae Dei esse?* The Father is as the Father and Origin of the Son more than the Son, but the Son not less than the Father, see *De Trin.* 9, 56: *Maior itaque Pater est, dum Pater est, sed Filius, dum Filius est, minor non est. Nativitas Filii Patrem constituit maiorem. Minorem vero Filium esse nativitatis natura non patitur. De Syn.* 64, *In Ps.* CXXXVIII 17, cf. C. F. A. Borchardt, *op. cit.*, p 111, n. 255, and P. Smulders, *La doctrine trinitaire*, pp 182 ff.

> "These words have to be understood as they are."

This remark is made against the Arians who do not understand the texts as they are, but twist texts with arbitrary interpretations, see *supra*, 60, 68 f.

> "But we must take heed lest with ignorant people the honour of the Father lessens the glory of the Son."

The Arians honour the Father (as the sole God) in order to lessen the glory of the Son (by declaring Him to be God's perfect creature), see *De Trin.* 4, 9 ff and 11, 4 ff.

> "This very glorification for which the Son prays does not tolerate such a lessening either. For the words 'Father, glorify Thy Son' are followed by these words: 'so that the Son may glorify Thee.' So the Son is not weak, because He Himself, whilst having to be glorified, will return glorification."

The fact that the Son returns glory is a proof that He is not weak, *i.e.* without glory, cf. *De Trin.* 9, 31, 35. But this does not solve the problem, since there still remains the question:

> "But if He is not weak, why did He pray? Everybody only asks for what he does not have."

This objection will receive its definite answer in *De Trin.* 3, 16, *infra*, 157 ff. In the present chapter Hilary does hardly more than *claim* that this prayer does not imply weakness in the Son.

> "Or is the Father weak, too?"

This is, of course, impossible, cf. *De Trin.* 9, 39: *Pater namque non eget gloria, nec se exinanierat de forma gloriae suae.*

> "Or did He so lavishly give away what He has, that glorification has to be given back to Him through the Son?"

This would imply that the Father would lose what He has in giving to the Son, an idea which was already rejected by Hilary, see *supra*, 86, 106, *De Trin.* 2, 8, 22.

> "But neither was the latter in need nor does the former desire. And yet One will give to the Other. So the prayer for glory to be given and to be paid back in turn neither takes away anything from the Father nor weakens the Son.

If the Father had given away something to the Son which then the Son returned to the Father, this would imply that the Father lost something and that the Son first did not have something, then had it and then gave it back again. This would be a temporal process of diminution and growth to which Hilary is completely opposed.

> "But it shows the same power of divinity in Both of Them, since the Son prays to be glorified by the Father, and the Father does not scorn the glorification given to Him by the Son. But these acts of reciprocally giving and receiving glory show the unity of the power in the Father and the Son."

These words can only be understood against the background of Hilary's view that the Son in the state of incarnation did not cease to be fully God, see *supra*, 46, *De Trin.* 1, 11 and *infra*, 157 ff, *De Trin.* 3, 16.

CHAPTER 13

The Father's and the Son's glory is that the Son received from the Father the power over all flesh.

Translation and Commentary:

> **(13)** "But we must gain the knowledge of what this glorification is and where it finds its origin."

This remark indicates that he still has not found the answer to the question how the Son can pray for glorification without needing it, see *supra*, 145 ff, 150 f, *De Trin.* 3, 10, 12.

> "God is, I believe, not changeable and eternity is not subject to defect or emendation, progress or loss. But He always is what He is, for this is a characteristic of God. What always is cannot in its nature be liable to not being."

On the unchangeability of God see *supra*, 130 ff, *De Trin.* 3, 3; on the denial of loss or progress in God see *supra*, 102, 129, *De Trin.* 2, 8, 19; on the idea that God is what He is eternally, see *supra*, 30 ff, *De Trin.* 1, 5. All this applies as much to the Son as it does to the Father, so the question remains:

> "So how can be glorified what does not lack what is its own and what does not defect from itself, and there is nothing that He can receive in Himself and can have lost in order to recover it?"

> "We get stuck and linger. But the evangelist does not forsake the weakness of our understanding, he explains which kind of glorification the Son returns to the Father with the words: 'As Thou hast given Him power over all flesh, that all Thou hast given Him, He may give it eternal life. And this is eternal life, that they should know Thee, the only true God, and Jesus Christ whom Thou hast sent.' So the Father is glorified through the Son by the fact He can be known by us. And the glorification was this, that the Son had received power over all flesh from Him, and that He, having become flesh Himself, would restore eternal life to ephemeral, bodily and mortal beings."

When the believer gets stuck in logical reasonings, he should look to Scripture for help, see *supra*, 75 ff, 84 ff, *De Trin.* 2, 5, 8-19. In *De Trin.* 9, 35 he says, after quoting *John* 17:3: *Quid haeres, quid moraris?* Now it is no longer necessary to do what one did before reading this text. The glorification of the Father through the Son is His revelation to men through the Son, see *infra*. The glorification of the Son is to have received power over all flesh: on the meaning of this see *infra*. In the incarnation the Son restores eternal life to ephemeral, bodily and mortal men. The brevity and fragility of human life is a commonplace in early Christian and ancient literature, see *e.g.* Irenaeus, *Adv. Haer.* 2, 5, 1, Theophilus, *Ad Aut.* 2, 3, Lactance, *Inst.* 3, 12, 4, 13, Athanasius, *Contra Gentes* 32, 41, *Contra Arianos* 2, 76, Cicero, *Tusc. Disp.* 1, 38, 91; 1, 39, 94 (see further *Ciceronis Tusculanarum disputationum libri V ... erklärt von* M. Pohlenz, Stuttgart 1957 (I-II), pp 111 f.)

> "But our eternal life was not the result of the creation of a new entity but of bestowing a power, since not a new creature would receive eternal glory, but simply the knowledge of God."

The Son does not create new creatures when He grants eternal life, but the creatures which already existed received eternal life through the knowledge of God. The meaning of this statement must be that recreation cannot be an entirely new creation, since in that case a better creation would be created than the first one, in which case there would be a kind of progress in God. Similarly Athanasius argues, *De Inc.* 44, that it was the task of the Saviour to heal what already existed, not what was non-existent. It needed the divine will to create what did not exist, it needed the incarnation to heal what was created.

> "So no glory was added to God, for it had not departed from Him so that there could be an addition. But He is glorified through the Son with us who are ignorant, exiled, defiled, dead without hope in darkness without law. And He is glorified by the fact that the Son has received from Him power over all flesh in order to give eternal life to it. So by these works of the Son the Father is glorified. So when the Son received all things, He was glorified by the Father. And on the other hand the Father is glorified (through the Son) when all things are fulfilled through the Son. And the glory received is returned in such a way that the glory which is in the Son, is in its totality the glory of the Father, since He received all from the Father. For the honour of the servant redounds to the glory of Him who sent Him, and the glory of the Begetter is in the glory of the Begotten."

No glory is added to the Father, since His glorification consists of the fact that men who had been estranged from Him received knowledge of Him. The change takes place in men, not in God. This is furthermore stressed by the fact that the power to restore eternal life to men is given by the Father to the Son in the act of generation, as Hilary says explicitly in *De Trin.* 9, 31: ... *acceptio potestatis sola est significatio nativitatis in qua accepit id quod est.* Since the generation is eternal, it is God's eternal glory to have given this power to the Son. When this power is actually executed, men who are sinners are changed, not God. The Son is glorified in receiving this power from the Father before the world was made through Him. The Son's glory is to have received power over all flesh from the Father before the world came into being (that this took place before the world came into being is indicated in this chapter by the fact that one aspect of this power was that all things were made through the Son, it is indicated in *De Trin.* 9, 31 by the fact that the granting of the power is identified with the generation which is eternal); the glory of the Father is to have given this power to the Son, and therefore the glory of the Son is referred to the glory of the Father, and the glory of the Father consists of the glory of the Son.

CHAPTER 14

Knowledge of God, the Begetter and the Begotten, grants eternal life.

Translation and Commentary:

> **(14)** "But in what then does the eternity of life exist? He says Himself: 'That they know Thee, the only true God, and Jesus Christ whom Thou hast sent'. Why make difficulties here, why dispute about words?"

Hilary repeatedly opposes Christian faith, based on the revelation given in Scripture, to the subtle philosophical reasoning (*quaestiones*), see *De Trin.* 1, 13; 2, 12 (*supra*, 48, 92); 10, 67, 70; 12, 19; – here he is in line with Tertullian (with, of course, this difference that according to Tertullian Christian faith is primarily based on the *regula fidei*), *De praescr.* 7, 6-7, see J. Doignon, *op. cit.*, pp 147 and 333 (on the subject of the *quaestiones* more in general see J. Doignon, *op. cit.*, pp 332-340) and with Irenaeus, *Adv. Haer.* 2, 18, 4: *Et minutiloquium, et subtilitatem circa quaestiones, cum sit Aristotelicum, inferre fidei conantur*; it is interesting to see that at least in one instance Hilary dismisses as a useless question what Irenaeus and Tertullian do not regard as such, *viz.*, the question whether the world was created because of man or man because of the world see *In Ps.* I 2: *Cum enim quaeras ... utrum mundus homini aut homo mundo ... circa haec impietatis suae consilia agitur semper*; Irenaeus and Tertullian choose sides in this question and say (like most other early Christian theologians) that the world was created because of man, see Irenaeus, *Adv. Haer.* 2, 41, 1; 4, 14; 5, 29, 1; 4, 8; Tertullian, *Adv. Marc.* 1, 13, 2; 2, 4, 3; 2, 4, 5; *De spect.* 2, 4; *De pat.* 5, 5 (cf. further Theophilus 2, 10, *Epist. ad Diogn.* 10, Lactance, *De ira* 13; 14, *Epit.* 24, 63 f, *Inst.* 7, 4; this question was debated by Stoics and Academics, the former holding the view that the world was created because of man, the latter that man was created because of the world, see H. Chadwick, *Origen contra Celsum*, pp X f). – The quarrel about words is the same as the difficult (philosophical) questions and is also put in contrast to faith, cf. *De Trin.* 12, 56: *Neque sit mihi inutilis pugna verborum, sed incunctantis fidei constans professio, Ad Const.* II 5: *Dum in verbis pugna est, dum de novitatibus quaestio est ... prope iam nemo Christi est.*

> "Life is to know the true God, but the bare knowledge of Him does not give it. So what is added? 'And Jesus Christ whom Thou hast sent'."

The Arians use the expression 'the only true God' as a proof that the Son is not truly God, see *De Trin.* 4, 8; 9, 28. Therefore Hilary stresses that Christ immediately adds that the believer also has to know Jesus Christ. Similarly he uses I *Cor.* 8:6 as a proof that the bare belief in the one God and Father is not enough but must be combined with the belief in the one Lord Jesus Christ, see *De Trin.* 8, 34.

"Due honour is returned to the Father by the Son when He says: 'Thee, the only true God'. Nevertheless the Son does not separate Himself from the true being of God, because He adds: 'And Jesus Christ whom Thou hast sent'."

The Arians claim that the Son does want to separate Himself from the true being of God, see *De Trin.* 9, 28: *In eo namque quod ait 'te solum verum Deum', separare se a veritate Dei per exceptionem solitarii existimatur.* Here in *De Trin.* 3, 14 Hilary briefly dismisses this Arian exegesis, but in *De Trin.* 9, 33 ff he refutes them in a more detailed way (the discussion of this text starts in 9, 28 ff). There Hilary picks up the attack on difficult questions and says that he knows that the readers do not like laboured solutions of difficult questions (in fact, he recommends such a dislike here in *De Trin* 3, 14), but says that a discussion of the heretical interpretation of this text can be advantageous to faith. This is typical of a broad stream in early Christian theology: it opposes philosophy and heresy inspired by philosophy because of their subtle syllogisms, but in refuting them it has to come forward with such syllogisms itself (cf. *supra*, 92 f).

"There is no separation between the Two in the confession of the believers, because in Both rests the hope of life. And the true God is not less in Him who is named in immediate succession. So when it says: 'that they may know Thee, the only true God, and Jesus Christ whom Thou has sent', under these terms of Sender and Sent, the true divinity of Father and Son is not separated by variance in denoting or by splitting, but our devout faith is instructed towards confessing the Begetter and the Begotten."

Christ is truly God, because man's hope of eternal life rests on Him as well, cf. *De Trin.* 9, 32: *non intellego quomodo nobis a Deo vero separandus ad fidem sit, qui non sit separabilis ad salutem.* Christ's words in *John* 17:3 do not allow to split the confession of the Father and the Son, cf. *De Trin.* 9, 36: *Neque verum Christum Deum confitendo, non et solum verum Deum Patrem confitetur* (sc. *ecclesiae fides*). *Neque rursum solum verum Deum Patrem confessa, non confitetur et Christum.* It is not allowed to separate the true divinity of the Father and the Son, *i.e.* by declaring the Father to be truly God and the Son to be a creature (as the Arians do). Father and Son are inseparable and both truly God because of the generation of the Son by the Father, cf. *De Trin.* 9, 36: *Nec qui ex subsistente Deo secundum divinae generationis naturam Deus substitit, ab eo qui solus verus Deus est, separabilis est veritate naturae.*

CHAPTER 15

How the Son's glory is the Father's glory and the Father's glory is the Son's glory.

Translation and Commentary:

> **(15)** "So the Son fully and finally glorifies the Father in the words which
> follow: 'I have glorified Thee on earth, having accomplished the work which
> Thou hast given Me to do'. All the Father's praise is from the Son, because
> in which the Son will be praised, the Father will be praised, for He ac-
> complishes all the things which the Father (has) willed."

The glorification of the Father by the Son also consists of the obedience of
the Son, cf. *De Trin* 9, 39: ... *cum dixisset 'haec est autem vita aeterna ...'*
*subiecit secundum dispensationis suae oboedientiam: 'Ego te clarificavi super terram
...'*. The Father receives glory from the Son and in that which glorifies
the Son the Father is glorified, too, because the Father is active in the
Son's life. This is illustrated in the following way:

> "The Son of God is born as man, but the power of God is in the virgin
> birth."

See on this *supra*, 112 ff, ff, *De Trin.* 2, 26-27.

> "The Son of God is seen as man, but God appears in the works of this
> man."

See on this *supra*, 115 ff, *De Trin.* 2, 28-29.

> "The Son of God is crucified, but in the cross God conquers man's death.
> Christ, the Son of God, dies, but all flesh is made alive in Christ."

See on this *supra*, 49 ff, *De Trin.* 1, 13.

> "The Son of God is in hell, but man is brought back to heaven."

On Christ's descent into the underworld cf. *supra*, 140, *De Trin.* 3, 7.

> "To the extent to which these things are praised in Christ, to an even
> greater extent will He receive praise from whom Christ is God."

One would expect that the Father and the Son receive praise to the same
extent, but in a strange way Hilary says in this sentence that they receive
it to the same extent (*in quantum*) and that the Father receives it even more
(*tanto plus*), since He is the origin of the Son. For this mildly subordinationist doctrine cf. *supra*, 134 f, *De Trin.* 3, 4 (on the Father's will to
generate the Son) and Hilary's interpretation of *John* 14:28 ('The Father
is greater that I') that this implies that as the Father the Father is greater
than the Son, but as the Son the Son is not less than the Father (*supra*,
150, *De Trin.* 3, 12). In *In Ps.* CXLIV 3 Hilary says that, since the Father
is in the Son and the Son is in the Father, the Father is praised in the Son
and the Son in the Father, so that it makes no difference which of the
Two is praised, – so there the subtle distinction that the Father's praise is
the same as the Son's and greater than the Son's at the same time, is not
made.

"So in these ways the Father glorifies the Son on earth and in His turn the Son glorifies, to the ignorance of the heathen and the stupidity of the world, through His powerful works Him, from whom He is Himself."

The Son is glorified by the Father through His works and through these works He Himself glorifies the Father by revealing Him to men of this world who do not know Him, cf. *supra*, 151 ff, *De Trin.* 3, 13 and *infra*, 160 f, 3, 17.

> "And this exchange of glory has nothing to do with progress of the Godhead, but it implies that honour which arose from the knowledge of those who were ignorant. For in what was the Father not abundant, out of whom are all things? Or what was lacking in the Son in whom it pleased all fulness of the Godhead to dwell? So the Father is glorified on earth, because His work, which He commanded, is done."

On the rejection of progress in God see *supra*, 102, 152, *De Trin.* 2, 20; 3, 13. One question still remains: why does the Son ask for glorification if He is fully and truly God? This will be answered in the following chapter.

CHAPTER 16

The glorification of the Son is the glorification of His human body.

Translation and Commentary:

> **(16)** "Let us see what kind of glory the Son expects from the Father. And indeed, it is certain. For it is said in what follows: 'I have glorified Thee on earth, I have completed the work which Thou hast given Me to do. And now, O Father, glorify Thou Me with Thine own self with the Glory which I had with Thee before the world was. I have manifested Thy name unto men'."

The one question remained: how can the Son, if He is perfect God, still expect glorification from the Father? A renewed interpretation of *John* 17:4-6 must give the final answer.

> "So the Father is glorified by the works of the Son, in that He is recognized to be God, in that He is revealed as the Father of the Only-begotten, in that He even willed the Son to be born man from the virgin for our salvation, in whose passion is completed all that began in the virgin birth."

Christ's miracles are a proof of His divinity, see *supra*, 93, 139, and especially of the fact that the Father works in Him, cf. *De Trin.* 9, 44; in these works the Father is revealed as the Father of the Only-begotten, cf. *De Trin.* 11, 12 where Hilary explains *John* 5:19 (*Non potest Filius facere ab se quicquam*) as meaning that of the things which He does according to His generation, the Father is the Author: *Dum non ab se facit, ad id quod agit secundum nativitatem sibi Pater auctor est.* – The will of the Father is the cause of the incarnation, see *supra*, 109, *De Trin.* 2, 24; in the virgin birth God's glory began to be revealed in humility, see *supra*, 109 ff, *De Trin.* 2, 24 ff, and this was completed in the passion. With this remark Hilary wants to show that in the hour of passion Christ did not enter an entirely new stage of His life.

> "So because the Son of God, in all aspects of His being perfect and generated in the fulness of divinity before all time, was now, being man since His incarnation, finally taken to death, He asked to be glorified with God, as He Himself glorified the Father on earth, for then God's powers were glorified in the flesh before an ignorant world."

The perfect and eternal divinity of Christ is stressed again, undoubtedly in order to exclude the error that the prayer for glory is in fact a prayer for deification. Christ is glorified as man (and mankind in Him, see *infra*). Nothing can have been added to Christ's divine nature, since when the Son glorified the Father nothing was added to the Father's divine nature either: the Father's powers are, of course, eternal, but they were revealed by the Son to an ignorant world; see on this further *De Trin.* 3, 17, *infra*, 160 f.

> "But now, what kind of glorification does He expect with the Father? That, of course, which He had with Him before the world was."

According to Hilary there is a difference between 'to be with God' and 'to have with God', 'to be with God' refers to the Son's eternal coexistence with the Father; 'to have with God' refers to the mystery of His divine nature, see *De Trin.* 9, 39: *Esse enim apud te, consistentem significat; habere autem apud te, naturae sacramentum docet.* Through the incarnation He was separated from the complete unity of glory with God, and He asks to be reinstated in the divine nature which He had before the incarnation. This does not mean that Christ ceased to be God in the incarnation, Hilary is absolutely opposed to that idea (see *supra*, 46), but Christ prayed that the assumption of flesh may not alienate Him from His divine nature; see *De Trin.* 9, 39: *Ut enim in unitate sua maneret ut manserat, glorificaturus eum apud se Pater erat, quia gloriae suae unitas per oboedientiam dispensationis excesserat; scilicet ut in ea natura per glorificationem rursus esset, in qua sacramento erat divinae nativitatis unitus, essetque Patri apud semetipsum glorificatus, ut quod apud eum ante habebat, maneret, neque alienaret ab eo formae Dei naturam formae servilis adsumptio.* The same idea appears here in *De Trin.* 3, 16: Christ asks to be glorified as man in the stage of the incarnation:

> "He had the fulness of divinity and still has it, for He is the Son of God. But He who was the Son of God also began to be the son of man, for He was the Word made flesh. He had not lost what He was, but He had begun to be what He was not. He had not forsaken what was His own, but He had

assumed what was ours. He prayed that what He assumed might be promoted to that glory which He had not forsaken.''

So Christ asks that His human nature may be glorified, since He remained fully God in the incarnation, His divinity needed no glorification
(cf. *supra*, 142 ff). In the incarnation He did not cease to be God but
began to be man, cf. the famous lines in the "*Mirabile Mysterium*": *id quod
fuit permansit, et quod non erat assumpsit*, which can perhaps be traced back
to Gregory Nazianzen, *Or.* XXXIX 13: ὅπερ ἦν μεμένηχε καὶ ὃ οὐκ ἦν
προσέλαβε, cf. Dom Louis Bron, Saint Grégoire de Nazianze et l'antienne
"Mirabile Mysterium" des landes de la circoncision, *Ephemerides
Liturgicae* (58) 1944, pp 17 f.

> "So since the Son is the Word, and the Word is made flesh, and the Word is
> God, and this was in the beginning with God, and since the Word which
> was before the creation of the world is the Son, the Son now made flesh ask-
> ed that the flesh might begin to be to the Father what the Word is, that what
> was temporal might receive the glory of that glorification which is beyond
> time, so that the corruption of the flesh might be swallowed up by being
> transformed into the power of God, the incorruption of the Spirit (read: *in-
> corruptionem*).''

The Son of God is God's eternal Word, the eternal Word assumed a temporal body, now the Son asks that His temporal body may share the eternal glory of the Word. In this transformation of Christ's body mankind is
transformed, see *supra*, 49 ff, *De Trin.* 1, 13 and *supra*, 109 ff, 2, 24. A
similar explanation of *John* 17:4-6 is found in Athanasius, *Contra Arianos*
1, 38: οὐκοῦν εἰ καὶ πρὸ τοῦ τὸν κόσμον γενέσθαι τὴν δόξαν εἶχεν ὁ Υἱός ... οὐκ
ἄρα καταβὰς ἐβελτιώθη ἀλλὰ μᾶλλον ἐβελτίωσεν αὐτὸς τὰ δεόμενα
βελτιώσεως, cf. Novatian, *De Trin.* 13, 68.

> "So this is the prayer to God, this is the confession of the Son to the Father,
> this is the prayer of (Christ's) flesh. In this flesh all men will see Him on the
> day of judgement, pierced and bearing the marks of the cross, in this flesh
> His glory was foreshown on the mountain, in this flesh He ascended to
> heaven, in this He sat down at the right hand of God, in this He was seen by
> Paul, in this He was worshipped by Stephen.''

With this Hilary wants to stress the identicalness of the risen body of
Christ and Christ's body which He assumed in the incarnation (cf. on
this *infra*, 165 ff, *De Trin.* 3, 20). On the day of judgement Christ's body
will bear the marks of the crucifixion; (this statement is undoubtedly
caused by the story of Christ's appearance to Thomas, *John* 20:25 ff, cf.
20:20, and by those texts which predict Christ's appearance on the day of
judgement), and already in His earthly life, *viz.*, during the transfiguration on the mountain, the eternal glory of Christ's body was seen. This
shows that the temporal body which Christ assumed, became indeed participant in eternal glory.

CHAPTER 17

The progress in revelation of God, the Father.

Translation and Commentary:

> **(17)** "So having the name of the Father manifested to men He uttered this
> prayer. But which name? Surely the name of God was not unknown? Moses
> heard it from the bush, Genesis announced it at the beginning of the history
> of creation, the Law proclaimed it and the prophets extolled it, men have
> sensed it in these works of His world, the heathen have worshipped it even
> with their lies. So the name of God was not unknown. And yet it was clearly
> unknown, for nobody will know God, unless he confesses Him both as the
> Father, the Father of the only-begotten Son, and as the Son, not by parti-
> tion or extension or emanation, but generated out of the Father in a way
> which transcends speech and understanding, as the Son from the Father,
> possessing the fulness of divinity out of which and in which He has been
> generated, the true, infinite and perfect God."

God was already known through the revelation given in the Old Testament, through the revelation in the harmony of the world (see on this
infra, 178 ff, *De Trin.* 3, 25) and even in the falsehood of Pagan worship of
God (see on this his remarks on the science of the magi, *De Trin.* 4, 38,
quoted *supra*, 114). So God was not unknown, but this is not a perfect
knowledge of God, since perfect knowledge of God consists of knowing
Him as the Father of the Son. The underlying idea of this is that there is a
progress in revelation, in which God is first known as God the Creator
and then as the Father of the Son (cf. *supra*, 42 ff, *De Trin*, 1, 10, and *infra*,
170 ff, 3, 22). Hilary's views on this are not always entirely consistent.
The progress in revelation which is briefly expressed here is discussed
more extensively elsewhere: the theophanies in the Old Testament are a
prefiguration of the incarnation, with this difference that in the
theophanies God was only *seen* in man, in the incarnation God is *born* in
man: *De Trin.* 5, 17: *Sacramenta enim legis mysterium dispensationis evangelicae
praefigurant ... Visus est autem tum tantum Deus in homine, non natus est; mox
etiam hoc quod est visus, et natus est*, cf. Tertullian, *Adv. Marc.* 2, 27, 3; *Adv.
Prax.* 16, 3, for further examples of this common interpretation of the
theophanies testified in the Old Testament see *e.g.* P. Smulders, *La doctrine trinitaire de S. Hilaire*, pp 129 ff, E. Evans, *Tertullian, Adversus Marcionem, Edited and Translated* (O.E.C.T.). Oxford 1972, p 161, n. 1 and G.
Quispel, *De Bronnen van Tertullianus' Adversus Marcionem*, p 44. Hilary's
statement, made here in *De Trin.* 3, 17 and in 5, 27 (see the quotation
given *infra*, 171) that to the Jews God was not yet known as the Father (of
the Son) is in line with this. Entirely in line with Irenaeus and Tertullian,
who stress against Marcion and the Gnostics the identicality of the God of
the Old Testament and of the New Testament, Hilary does likewise, see

e.g. In Ps LXVII 9: *Verum haec qui in nobis Deus ... per virtutem resurrectionis operatus est, idem omnia ad huius spei nostrae praeparationem adumbrata gessit in lege: ut non alius prophetarum, alius Evangeliorum Deus possit intellegi,* and 15. But on the other hand Hilary also says that the Old Testament reveals the Trinity, which is incompatible with his statement that the Jews did not know God as the Father of the Son, see *De Trin.* 4, 16 ff; 4, 22; 34; 5, 23. – What is said about the Son is a summary of his doctrine of Son, – on the rejection of partition see *supra*, 85, *De Trin.* 2, 8; of extension, *supra*, 55, *De Trin.* 1, 16; on the ineffability and incomprehensibility of the generation, *supra*, 87 ff, *De Trin.* 2, 9-10; on the fulness of Christ's true and perfect divinity, *supra*, 90 f, *De Trin.* 2, 11.

> "For this is the fulness of God. For if anything of this is lacking, then it will no longer be the divine fulness which pleased to dwell in Him. This name is proclaimed by the Son, this is manifested to the ignorant. In this way the Father is glorified by the Son, when He is acknowledged as the Father of such a Son."

On the fulness in which nothing can be lacking see *supra*, 152, *De Trin.* 3, 13. This is the fulness of the divinity of the Father and the Son, in the revelation of this fulness to ignorant men the Father is glorified through the Son and the Son through the Father.

4.

Renewed discussion of the incomprehensibility of the generation
of the Son
(18-21)

The miraculous nature of the generation of the Son out of the Father is again discussed. It had been made clear that the mutual glorification of the Father and the Son does not imply that either Father or Son is in Himself imperfect. Now it is stressed, against Arian objections, that the generation of the Son out of the Father does not imply any loss by the Father. This cannot be understood, but must be believed. Two miraculous deeds of God are produced as analogies of something which cannot be doubted although it surpasses comprehension: the virgin birth is briefly discussed and the Lord's appearance to Thomas is discussed extensively. Then God's works in the creation are referred to: they testify to us that God's powers should not be doubted. To want to destroy God's creation has been made impossible to man, since he has been confined to a bodily existence, to doubt God's truth is a possibility of which man (especially the Arians) makes use.

CHAPTER 18

Attack on Arian doubts about the generation of the Son.

Translation and Commentary:

> **(18)** "So the Son, wanting to give an assurance of this generation of His,
> gave us the example of His works, so that we may, through the ineffable
> working of His ineffable deeds, be instructed about the power of His inef-
> fable generation: when water changed into wine, when five loaves filled
> twelve baskets with their fragments after five thousand men – women and
> children not counted – had been satisfied. The matter is seen and not
> known, it happens and is not understood, the way it happens cannot be
> grasped, the result is obvious."

After the expositions on the mutual glorification of the Father and the
Son, Hilary returns to the theme of the ineffability of the divine generation. In *De Trin*. 3, 5-6 (*supra*, 136 ff) he had used the miracle at the wedding in Cana and the miracle of the multiplication of the loaves of bread
as analogies for the generation: as the miracles are inexplicable but real,
so is the generation inexplicable but real. In *De Trin*. 3, 5 he had denied
that these are *examples*, bearing in mind that examples taken from the
created sphere are inadequate to describe the Divine. Here in *De Trin*. 3,
18 he does call these miracles examples. Apart from this small difference
what is said here is a summary of *De Trin*. 3, 5-6.

> "But it is stupid to extend an enquiry, which is in fact a detraction, into
> some matter, when because of its nature that matter about which the ques-
> tion will be put is incomprehensible."

According to Hilary the Arians do not agree with this, since they are
quoted by him as saying that faith is useless if nothing can be understood,
see *De Trin*, 2, 11, *supra*, 90 f. Furthermore they reject what is impossible,
see *De Trin*. 3, 8, *supra*, 141 f. So he accuses the Arians of doing what he is
rejecting here.

> "For as the Father is ineffable in that He is unbegotten, so the Son is inef-
> fable in that He is only-begotten, because He who is begotten is the image of
> Him who is unbegotten."

If the Father is ineffable (see *supra*, 81 ff, *De Trin*. 2, 7), the Son as His
image must be ineffable as well, which implies that the Father cannot be
confined to a circumscribed image which is the man Jesus, see on this
supra, 28, *De Trin*. 1, 4.

> "For we must in thoughts and words understand the image when we
> perceive Him whose image it is."

If the Father could be conceived, *i.e.* if He were not infinite and beyond human understanding, then the Son as His image could be conceived in thought and speech as well. But this is not the case:

> "But we are pursuing invisible things and dealing with things which are beyond understanding, we whose understanding is confined to visible and corporeal things."

If man realizes that what he is dealing with is in fact beyond understanding, then Hilary is not opposed to making modest efforts to *understand* something of what one *believes*, see *supra*, 40, 83, 91.

> "We are not ashamed of our stupidity, we do not accuse ourselves of irreverence detracting from the mysteries of God and the powers of God."

Here Hilary ironically speaks as if he were an Arian. He himself refuses to do what is said here and he accuses the Arians of stupidity, see *supra*, 141 f, *De Trin.* 3, 8; of irreverence, cf. *supra*, 53 f, *De Trin.* 1, 15, of being detractors, see *e.g. De Trin.* 2, 23; according to him the Arians are not ashamed of their stupidity, *De Trin.* 7, 26, but they should be ashamed (see *De Trin.* 4, 41, where he tells his Arian opponent: *confundere et erubesce*); cf. Athanasius, *Contra Arianos* 3, 1.

> "How is the Son, and whence is the Son, what did the Father lose by His birth, or out of which portion of the Father was He born? That is what we ask."

Hilary still speaks ironically like an Arian. The Arians do ask questions about the way of the generation, see *De Trin.* 2, 9-10, *supra*, 87 f, they answer the question whence the Son is by saying that He is out of nothing, see *supra*, 56, they claim that the Father lost by the Son's birth, since He is out of a portion of the Father, see *supra*, 141, *De Trin.* 3, 8.

> "But in the example of His miraculous deeds you had an assurance that you can believe that God is able to do things of which you do not understand how they are being done."

The generation of the Son is possible because of God's incomprehensible omnipotence manifesting itself in the miracles, cf. *supra*, 138 f, *De Trin.* 3, 6.

CHAPTER 19

The virgin birth as an analogy for the fact that the eternal generation of the Son implies no loss by the Father.

Translation and Commentary:

> (19) "You ask how the Son's spiritual generation took place. I put to you a question about corporeal things. I do not ask how He was born from the

virgin nor whether her flesh suffered any loss in generating His perfect flesh. And certainly she did not conceive what she gave birth to, but flesh brought forth flesh without the shame of our beginnings, and she bore Him perfect without any loss of her own. And it would certainly be right to believe that it is not impossible with God what we know to have been possible through His power in a human being.''

The eternal generation is called 'spiritual' in order to distinguish it clearly from a bodily birth, see *De Trin.* 12, 8. Already in *De Trin.* 3, 5 Hilary had said that not only in spiritual matters but also in corporeal matters things can happen which surpass our understanding, see *supra*, 136 ff. The Arians had objected to the generation of the Son that this would imply a loss in the Father, see *De Trin.* 3, 8 and 18, *supra*, 141 f, 162 f. The virgin birth is only briefly adduced as an analogy to the idea that a birth is possible without any loss to the person who gives birth. It is strange that Hilary says that he does not want to confront the Arians with questions about the virgin birth, and that he therefore deals with this only in passing, since the virgin birth indeed provides a clear analogy for a birth without any loss to the parent. The reason could be that Hilary, although he here stresses the miraculous and extraordinary character of the virgin birth, may in fact have doubts about this *extraordinary* character, since elsewhere he says that if he wanted to, he could produce from certain natures examples of births which take place without loss to the parents and without sexual intercourse, see *De Trin.* 6, 17: *Adferrem tibi ... etiam ex rebus mundi quarundam naturarum quae gignuntur exemplum ... ne nascentium naturas detrimenta crederes esse gignentium, ut etiam multa sine corporali admixtione ex viventibus in viventes animas gignerentur.* – The denial that the virgin conceived Him, is in fact the denial that Christ's existence began with the conception, Christ existed before the conception, see *De Trin.* 10, 47: *Nam cum natus sit lege hominum, non tamen hominum lege conceptus est: habens in se et constitutionem humanae condicionis in partu, et ipse extra constitutionem humanae condicionis in origine*; 10, 17: *Non enim corpori Maria originem dedit*, cf. 10, 18. The Son creates His own body through the virgin Mary, see *supra*, 110 ff. – That the virgin gave birth to Christ without the shame of the human beginning means without the shame of sexual intercourse, this is the cause of Christ's sinlessness, see e.g. *De Trin.* 10, 25: ... *homo natus non vitiis humanae conceptionis est natus*, cf. *De Trin.* 2, 26 (*supra*, 113) and *De Trin.* 1, 13 (*supra*, 49 ff), *In Ps.* LXVII 25: ... *quia ipsae illae corporum atque elementorum nostrorum origines sint pudendae*, further Athanasius, *De Inc.* 8: ... ἀλλὰ λαμβάνει τὸ ἡμέτερον καὶ τοῦτο οὐχ ἁπλῶς, ἀλλ' ἐξ ἀχράντου καὶ ἀμιάντου ἀνδρὸς ἀπείρου παρθένου καθαρόν ... and 17: ... οὐδὲ ἐν σώματι ὢν ἐμολύνετο ἀλλὰ μᾶλλον καὶ τὸ σῶμα ἡγίαζεν.

CHAPTER 20

The miraculous appearance of the risen Lord in a closed house as an illustration of the generation of the Son out of the Father.

Translation and Commentary:

> (20) "But you, whoever you are, pursuing the unsearchable and severe judge of divine mysteries and powers, I turn to you for counsel, that you may explain to me, an unskilled and simple believer of God in all He has said, at least this fact."

The Arians make the mistake that they pass with their finite minds judgements on the infinite God, see *supra*, 54 f, *De Trin*. 1, 15. So this sentence is obviously meant ironically. On the authority of the words spoken by God see *supra*, 128 f, *De Trin*. 3, 1. There he had said that the authority of God, *i.e.* the fact that God has spoken words, does not in itself excuse the believer from the task of searching reverently for the meaning of these words. So here in *De Trin*. 3, 20 he ironically asks the Arians to explain to him what he believes. But since the Arians are not reverent searchers after the truth, they are, of course, not at all qualified to provide an explanation of what Hilary believes to be true.

> "I hear – and since I believe what has been written I know – that the Lord after His resurrection frequently offered Himself with His body to the sight of many unbelievers, certainly to Thomas, who would not believe unless he had touched His wounds, as he says: 'Unless I see in His hands the print of the nails and put my finger into the place of the nails, and thrust my hand into His side, I shall not believe'."

On the authority of Scripture, here expressed in the statement that credence in divine words is in fact knowledge, see *supra*, 128 f, *De Trin*. 3, 1. The reality of Christ's appearance after His resurrection is not doubted by Hilary and will certainly not have been doubted by the Arians either. Just as in the case of the miracle at the wedding in Cana and that of the multiplication of the loaves of bread, the Arians are challenged to explain the miracle, and if they cannot do so, they are asked to stop asking for an explanation of the generation of the Son out of the Father.

> "The Lord adapts Himself to every weakness of our understanding, in order to satisfy the doubts of unbelievers He works a mysterious miracle of His invisible power."

As the incarnation is an act of adaptation to human weakness, see *supra*, 130 ff, 142 ff, *De Trin*. 3, 3 and 9, God's whole revelation is in fact such an adaptation, see *supra*, 61, *De Trin*. 1, 19.

"Explain how this happened, whoever you are who pry into heavenly
things. The disciples were in a closed room, and having assembled secretly
after the passion of the Lord were sitting together. The Lord shows Himself
to Thomas in order to assure his faith on the terms laid down. He offers the
possibility to feel His body and to touch His wound. And certainly, since He
was to be recognized by His wounds, He must have produced the body in
which He was wounded."

Here the identicality of the risen body with the earthly body is stressed. It
is interesting to see that according to Hilary also the other way round the
earthly body could be identified with the risen body, so that, according to
him, there is no difference at all between Christ's body before His death
and after His resurrection. Hilary explains the events taking place before
Christ's death and after His resurrection by the extraordinary nature of
Christ's body: in *De Trin.* 10, 23 he says that one could wound Christ's
body without inflicting any pain, so in His passion Christ did not suffer
pain. This is explained by the fact that Christ's body did not have the
same nature as our bodies, but that it could walk on water and penetrate
walls, cf. *In Ps.* LV 5 where he says that while He was in the human body
Christ was in full command of His divine power, which leads to the consequence: *non enim carne est degravatus, ne super undas ambularet ... neque ut non
solida parietum, corpore interlabente, penetraret.* Here Hilary differs from, *e.g.*,
Origen, who in referring to Christ's walking through closed doors says
that at the time of His resurrection Christ was in a sort of intermediate
state between the solidity of the body as it was before His passion and the
condition of a soul not covered by any body, *Contra Celsum* 2, 62.

"So I ask through which parts of the closed house He entered with His
body. For in his narration the evangelist has carefully chosen his words:
'Jesus came when the doors were shut and stood in their midst'. Or did He
penetrate the bricks and mortar of the walls and the solidity of wood and
thereby pass through a nature which cannot be penetrated? For He stood
there in His body, not feigned or in deceit. So let the eyes of your mind
follow His entrance through penetration, and let your intellectual vision ac-
company Him as He enters the closed house. Nowhere there is a breach and
all has been barred; yet lo, He stands in the midst, to whom all things are
pervious through His power."

Here Hilary 'visualizes' how the passing through closed doors was possible: since all things are pervious to God, Christ can pass through closed
doors. But this is not a rational explanation, since Hilary stresses that the
fact that God is inside and outside all things surpasses human understanding, see *supra*, 33 ff, 78 ff, *De Trin.* 1, 6 and 2, 6. With the help of
this tenet Hilary had explained the difficult text that the Father is in the
Son and the Son in the Father, see *supra*, 127 ff, 133, *De Trin.* 3, 1 and 4,
and now he uses it as an analogy for the miraculous eternal generation of
the Son.

"You are a detractor of invisible things, I challenge you to explain visible things."

This is the argument *a minore ad maius* (cf. *supra*, 88): if certain visible things cannot be explained, then it is certainly not surprising if invisible things remain inexplicable as well.

"Everything remains firm as it was and by their nature neither wood nor stones let anything invisibly glide through it."

It is Hilary's view that Christ glided with His body through the walls, see *In Ps*. LV 5 (quotation given *supra*).

"The body of the Lord does not dissolve in order to come together again out of nothing. And whence is He who stands in the midst?"

The idea that the Lord appeared suddenly in the closed house out of nothing (first having reduced Himself to nothing outside the house) is rejected. Since Christ's miraculous appearance is used as an illustration of His miraculous generation out of the Father, this remark could also be directed against the Arian view that Christ was created by the Father out of nothing (cf. *supra*, 56). Furthermore Hilary may want to stress the difference with the miracle at the wedding in Cana, which he had produced as an analogy for the divine generation (see *De Trin*. 3, 5, *supra*, 136 f), there he had said that water was abolished and wine began to be. The walking through a closed door should not be understood in a similar way, in the sense that the body was first abolished and then again created out of nothing.

"Understanding and speech fail here and the reality of the fact is beyond human reason."

Since reason is beyond sense and speech (see *supra*, 37 ff, *De Trin*. 1, 7), it has to be added that this miraculous appearance is not only beyond sense and speech, but also beyond reason.

"So therefore, as we deceive about the generation, let us in the same way also lie about the Lord's entrance. Let us say that it did not happen, since we can come to no understanding of this fact, and let the reality of the fact itself disappear because our sense fails."

These words are, of course, meant ironically. The Arians doubt the generation of the Son out of the Father, because it is impossible, and they accuse the orthodox of coming forward with a false doctrine. Hilary confronts them with the consequence that they would have to doubt Christ's appearance as well and mark the story about it as a lie, if what is beyond sense and understanding cannot happen. The force of this argument is that the Arians do not deny such miracles as the appearance of the risen Christ (cf. *supra*, 93 f, *De Trin*. 2, 12).

"But the evidence of the fact overcomes our lies. The Lord stood in the closed house in the midst of the disciples, and the Son is born from the Father."

Christ's miraculous appearance is a fact, because it is written in the Bible, see *supra*, 65 ff. Therefore it can be an illustration of something which can happen although it cannot be understood:

"Do not deny that He stood there, because the weakness of your understanding makes it impossible to you to follow the entrance of Him who stood there. Do not be ignorant of the fact that God the only-begotten perfect Son was generated by God the unbegotten and perfect Father, because the power of the generation transcends understanding and speech of the human nature."

CHAPTER 21

Creation testifies to God's power and is an illustration of God's power to generate, whatever man does or would like to do.

Translation and Commentary:

(21) "Moreover, all God's works in the world could testify to us not to believe it to be allowed to express doubts about the things and powers of God. But we in our unbelief attack truth itself, and we make violent efforts to overthrow God's power. If possible, we would raise our bodies and hands to heaven, we would confuse the fixed annual courses of the sun and other stars, disarrange the low and high tide of the ocean, also frustrate the streams of the fountains and make the rivers flow backwards, we would shake the foundations of the earth and would go completely mad in this destruction of these works of God our Father."

The miracles are an illustration of God's power, but the whole of the wonderful creation reveals God's power as well. So, having used miracles as examples of the divine generation, Hilary uses the harmony of the creation as such an example. As we have seen when dealing with Hilary's views on *curiosity* (*supra*, 74 ff, *De Trin.* 2, 5), it is his conviction that man should reverently bow before the works of God in the world when he does not understand the causes of things. It is useless to scrutinize causes which cannot be found. What is described here in *De Trin.* 3, 21 is even worse than such a futile curiosity: here man not only searches the unsearchable, but tries to destroy what he cannot understand. That is what the Arians do with respect to the generation of the Son; when they cannot understand it, they become so furious that they attack it (cf. also *De Trin.* 1, 15, *supra*, 53 ff). They in fact behave like children who want to kill their father (This *parricidium* is what he repeatedly accuses the Jews of having done, see *De Trin.* 10, 55, *In Ps.* II 26, CXVIII 4, CXXXIV 24). (On the fixed courses of the heavenly bodies see *supra*, 147, *De Trin.* 3, 10). The same attitude is attacked in *De Trin.* 9, 40: *Quid limosi corporis graves animae et sordente peccatis conscientia foetidae caenosaeque mentes usque ad iudicium divinae de se professionis inflamur, et arbitros nos naturae caelestis deputantes, inpiis ad Deum calumniae nostrae disputationibus rebellamus?*

> "But fortunately the nature of our bodies confines us to this necessary modesty."

The nature of our bodies is such that we cannot ascend to heaven and destroy God's creation, this fact forces us to be modest, *i.e.* to do no more than we have the possibility of doing.

> "Certainly we leave no doubts about what we would do if we had the chance to do it. For since we have the possibility of doing it, we distort with the blasphemous insolence of our will the nature of the truth and wage ware against the words of God."

Man does have the possibility of rejecting and attacking God's truth in his mind, this is a proof that man (*i.e.* the Arians) would not hesitate to attack God's creation physically if he had the possibility of doing it, that man does not do it is caused by *force majeure*. The power behind this *force majeure* is, of course, God. So when God confined man to his body, He in a way protected man against the sin of attacking God. Similarly Irenaeus explains the fact that Adam became mortal after his first sin by saying that in this way God protected him against an infinite and incurable sin, see *Adv. Haer.* 3, 35, 2: ... *miserans eius, ut non perseveraret semper transgressor, neque immortale esset quod esset circa eum peccatum, et malum interminabile et insanabile. Prohibuit autem eius transgressionem, interponens mortem, et cessare faciens peccatum;* cf. Theophilus, *Ad Aut.* 2, 26 Καὶ τοῦτο δὲ ὁ θεὸς μεγάλην εὐεργεσίαν παρέσχεν τῷ ἀνθρώπῳ, τὸ μὴ διαμεῖναι αὐτὸν εἰς τὸν αἰῶνα ἐν ἁμαρτίᾳ ὄντα. Here in Hilary God protects man against sin by confining him to a certain space, in Irenaeus God does so by confining him to a certain time.

5.

The revelation of the Father through the Son
(22-23)

After the digression on the incomprehensibility of the divine generation Hilary returns to the theme of the Father's revelation through the Son. Christ does not reveal God as the Creator, but as the Father. If Christ were God's first creature, he would only reveal God as the Creator, but since He is the Son he reveals God as Father, and the knowledge of God as Father transcends the knowledge of God as Creator.

If the Son really reveals the Father, then the Son may not be ontologically inferior to the Father and must have been with the Father from all eternity.

CHAPTER 22

Christ does not reveal God as His Creator, but as His eternal Father.

Translation and Commentary:

> **(22)** "The Son said: 'Father, I have manifested Thy name to men'. What reason is there for detraction and fury here? Do you deny the Father? But this was the primary task of the Son, that we may know the Father. Clearly you deny Him, when according to you the Son is not born out of Him."

The Arians do not deny that God is the Father of the Son, but they deny that He is the eternal Father of the eternal Son. According to Hilary this means that the Father is not the Father by nature and therefore not really the Father, see *De Trin.* 2, 3, *supra*, 68 ff, and 2, 4, *supra*, 70 ff.

> "And why should He be called the Son if He is, like other things, created according to God's will?"

The Arians say that the Son as a creature is *created* by God's will and therefore has a beginning in time and is a contingent being, Hilary says that the Son is eternally *generated* by God's will, see *supra*, 134 f, *De Trin.* 3, 4, and excludes the possibility that He could be contingent.

> "I can admire God, because He creates Christ, the Creator of the world, and it is a power worthy of God, to have made the maker of the archangels and angels, the visible and invisible things, heaven and earth and the whole of this creation."

This is a well-known Arian doctrine: Christ is God's first creature and as such the mediator of the rest of the creation, see *De Trin.* 4, 13 and 6, 6; Athanasius, *Contra Arianos* 2, 24. The expression of admiration of God as the Creator of Christ could be ironical (in which case one ought to translate 'I could admire God ...'), for elsewhere Hilary criticizes this doctrine as a belittling of the Son: if the Son was created because of the creation of the world through Him, then the Son is a servant of the world, see *De Trin.* 12, 43: *Aut forte velis ... ut Christus causa efficiendorum operum sit creatus, ut ipse servus potius et operator mundi maneret, non Dominus gloriae natus esset, et ad ministerium efficiendi saeculi crearetur, non etiam semper esset Filius dilectionis et rex saeculorum*, cf. Athanasius, *Contra Arianos* 2, 30, who says that in that case men were not created because of the Son, but the Son because of men: ... φαίνεται μᾶλλον αὐτὸς ὁ Υἱὸς δι᾽ ἡμᾶς γεγονὼς καὶ οὐχ ἡμεῖς δι᾽ αὐτόν· οὐ γὰρ δι᾽ αὐτὸν ἐκτίσθημεν ἀλλ᾽ αὐτὸς δι᾽ ἡμᾶς πεποίηται (a

similar argument occurs in Irenaeus, *Adv. Haer.* 2, 19, 1-2 with reference
to the world and the divine *pleroma* of *aeones*). According to Athanasius
this doctrine is in fact also a belittling of the Father, since it implies
weakness of the Father: He can only make the Son, for the rest of the
creation He needs help, see *Contra Arianos* 2, 24, 25, 29, *De Decr.* 7; and it
implies jealousy in the Father: He taught only one mediator how to
create, *Contra Arianos* 2, 29.

> "But this is not the primary concern of the Lord that you may understand
> that God is almighty in the act of creating, but that you may know that God
> is the Father of that Son who speaks."

If Christ revealed God as the almighty Creator, then there would be no
progress in revelation, since the Jews already knew God to be God, not
that He is the Father of the Son, *De Trin.* 5, 27: *Iudaei namque sacramentum
mysterii Dei nescientes et per hoc Dei Filium ignorantes, Deum tantum, non et
Patrem venerabantur.* This thought is also important to Athanasius: the
knowledge of God as the Father of the Son transcends the knowledge of
God as the unoriginated Creator of the world. The Arians only know
God as the unoriginated Creator and therefore have the same knowledge
of God as the Greeks, cf. *Contra Arianos* 1, 33: Λέγοντες μὲν γὰρ ἐκεῖνοι τὸν
θεὸν ἀγένητον, ἐκ τῶν γενομένων ἔργων αὐτὸν ... ποιητὴν μόνον καὶ
δημιουργὸν λέγουσι, νομίζοντες ὅτι καὶ τὸν Λόγον ποίημα ἐκ τούτου σημαίνειν
δύνανται κατὰ τὴν ἰδίαν ἡδονήν· ὁ δὲ τὸν θεὸν Πατέρα λέγων ἐκ τοῦ Υἱοῦ τοῦτον
σημαίνει, οὐκ ἀγνοῶν ὅτι Υἱοῦ ὄντος ἐξ ἀνάγκης διὰ τοῦ Υἱοῦ τὰ γενητὰ πάντα
ἐκτίσθη, καὶ οὗτοι μὲν ἀγένητον λέγοντες μόνον ἐκ τῶν ἔργων σημαίνουσιν
αὐτὸν καὶ οὐκ ἴσασι καὶ αὐτοὶ τὸν Υἱὸν ὥσπερ Ἕλληνες, see further 1, 34; 2,
42; 2, 59; *De Decr.* 31.

> "In heaven there are more active and eternal powers, but there is only one
> only-begotten Son, not merely differing from the others in power – for
> through Him all things are."

The active and eternal powers in heaven are undoubtedly the angels.
Their activity is primarily the protection of men, see *In Ps.* CXXIX 7
and CXXXIV 17. As the Creator of the angels (see *De Trin.* 10, 41)
Christ does not surpass them quantitatively in power, but He surpasses
them in being. According to the Arians Christ, as the most perfect
creature, surpasses all other creatures quantitatively, see *supra*, 56, 72.

> "But since He is the true and only Son, let Him not become a bastard, born
> out of nothing."

This remark is, of course, directed against the well-known Arian doctrine
that the Son is as a creature created or generated out of nothing, see
supra, 56.

"Your hear 'Son', believe that He is the Son. Your hear 'Father', keep in mind that He is the Father. Why do you sow into the names doubt, ill-will and audacity? The divine things received names according to the insight in their nature."

This means that the names given to God conform to the realities to which these names refer, cf. further *supra*, 69 ff. The Arians force the names by letting them refer to things different from what they indicate:

"Why do you strain the truth of the words? You hear the names Father and Son. Do not doubt that They are what They are called."

On the arbitrary exegesis of the Arians see *supra*, 118, *De Trin.* 2, 31. The Arians claim that the Son is merely *called* Son, but *is* not really the Son, see *supra*, 69 ff, *De Trin.* 2, 3.

"The end and aim of the earthly life of the Son is that you may know the Father. Why do you frustrate the labour of the prophets, the incarnation of the Word, the virgin birth, the operating of miracles, the cross of Christ? This was all spent upon you, performed on your behalf so that through this the Father and the Son may be revealed to you."

The Arians make the mistake that they refer to Christ's nature what Christ in the incarnation took upon Himself on man's behalf, see *De Trin.* 5, 18, cf. 2, 24, *supra*, 109 ff.

"You now substitute the notions 'will', 'creation', 'adoption'."

The Arians substitute the will of God, see *supra*, 133 ff, *De Trin.* 3, 4; on Christ as a creature and as a merely adopted Son see *supra*, 56, 72.

"Look at Christ's struggle and at what He earns. For He proclaims: 'Father, I have revealed Thy name to men'. You do not hear Him say: 'You have created the Creator of heavenly things', not: 'You have made the Maker of earthly things', but: 'Father, I have revealed Thy name to men'. Use this gift of your Saviour."

The Arians do not pay attention to Christ's work, *viz.*, to reveal God as the Father, but they regard Christ merely as a tool in God's work as Creator. This means that to them Christ is not the Saviour who took human existence upon Himself. – Christ's struggle (*militia*) is that He wants to reveal the Father, as was stated in the beginning of this chapter. For this struggle He receives a reward (*stipendium*) for the believers to whom God is revealed as the Father.

"Know that there is a Father who generated, a Son who was generated, generated out of that Father who *is*, in reality, truth and nature."

Since the Father really *is* (see *De Trin.* 1, 4, cf. *Exodus* 3:14), the Son also really *is*, see *De Trin.* 2, 11, *supra*, 89 f.

"Keep in mind that it has not been revealed to you that the Father is God, but that it has been revealed that God is the Father."

God was already known as God by the Jews (and to a certain degree by the Pagans, see *supra*, 171), Christ reveals that God is also the Father, see *De Trin.* 5, 27 (quotation given *supra*).

CHAPTER 23

Father and Son must be distinguished, but should not be separated.

Translation and Commentary:

(23) "You hear: 'I and the Father are one'. Why do you rend and tear the Son away from the Father? They are one, *viz.*, He who is and He who is from Him, the latter having nothing that is not also in Him from whom He is."

This is a brief repetition of what was said in the *De Trin.* 1, 11, *supra*, 44 ff.

"When you hear the Son say: 'I and the Father are one', adjust reality to the persons. Grant to Him who generates and to Him who is generated the true meaning of what they declare about themselves. Let them be one, as are He who has generated and He who has been generated. Why do you exclude the nature and why do you take away true reality?"

This is again an attack on the Arian view that the words 'Father' and 'Son' are merely names, to these names they give arbitrary interpretations and thereby try to rob the Son of His truly divine nature, see *supra*, 69 ff, *De Trin.* 2, 3. On Hilary's interpretation of *John.* 10:30: *Ego et Pater unum sumus*, see further *supra*, 58, *De Trin.* 1, 17.

"You hear: 'The Father is in Me and I am in the Father'. Also the Son's works testify to this about the Father and the Son. We do not in our thoughts put one body into another, neither do we pour one into the other as water into wine, but we confess in both not only the equivalence in power but also the fulness of divinity."

The works of the Son bear witness to the Father and the Son being in each other, because these works reveal that God's power is at work in the Son, cf. *supra*, 93 f. Man can, of course, conceive that one body is put into another, but this is no explanation of the mutual indwelling of the Father and the Son, since man cannot conceive that one body is at the same time inside and outside another body, see *supra*, 33 ff. This mutual indwelling ought not to be interpreted in a corporeal, but in a spiritual way, see *De Trin.* 3, 4, *supra*, 133; on the same power and divinity of Father and Son see also *De Trin.* 3, 4, *supra*, 133, and *De Trin.* 2, 11 ff, *supra*, 89 ff.

"For the Son received all things from the Father, and He is the Form of God and the 'Image of His substance' (*Heb.* 1:3)."

On the Son receiving all He is from the Father see *supra*, 86, 156, *De Trin.* 2, 8 and 3, 15.

> "The apostle distinguishes Him who *is* from Him who is the Image of His substance, only in order to make us believe in His distinct existence, not in order to make us speculate about any difference in nature."

On the Son, who *is* and receives His being from the Father who *is*, see *supra*, 89 f, *De Trin.* 2, 11, cf. *supra*, 26 ff, 1, 4. So when Christ is called the Image of God's substance, this indicates against the Sabellians His distinctive being (see *supra*, 55), but this does not support the Arian view that the Son is different in being and nature from the Father, cf. *supra*, 68 ff, 74 ff, *De Trin.* 2, 3 and 2, 5. – On the difference between faith and speculation see *supra*, 40, *De Trin.* 1, 8 and *supra*, 74, *De Trin.* 2, 5 (on the *libertas intellegentiae*).

> "But that the Father is in the Son and the Son is in the Father, that is the perfect fulness of divinity in Both of Them."

See on this *supra*, 90, 2, 11 and 133 ff, 3, 4.

> "For the Son is not a diminution of the Father, nor is the Son an imperfect offspring from the Father."

On the rejection of any diminution in the divine generation see *supra*, 106, 2, 22. The Son is not an imperfect offspring from the Father, but fully shares the Father's perfection, see *supra*, 90, *De Trin.* 2, 11. The Son would be an imperfect offspring, if He were a part of the Father, see *supra*, 85, *De Trin.* 2, 8 and 135, 3, 4.

> "An image is not on its own, a likeness is not with itself."

That the Son is not on His own and not only with Himself was already stated in *De Trin.* 2, 14, *supra*, 95 f, with a reference to the fact that He is eternally with the Father. Now it is added that as an Image (of somebody else) He cannot be alone.

> "But nothing can be like God unless it is out of Him. For what is in all things similar to Him is not from elsewhere, neither does likeness of the one with the other permit the addition of a difference to the Two."

If, as the Arians say (see *supra*, 56, 72), the Son were created out of nothing, then He would not be in all things like the Father who is uncreated. – Where there is likeness, there cannot be difference, – on this rhetorical argument from opposites see *supra*, 56, and G. C. Stead, Rhetorical Method in Athanasius, p 126.

> "Do not disturb this likeness and do not separate what is truly inseparable, because He who said 'Let us make man in our image and likeness' shows by speaking about 'our likeness' that they are mutually similar."

The Arians make the mistake that they disturb the likeness of Father and Son and separate them as different Beings. The plural in *Gen.* 1:26 indicates that Father and Son have their own existence, but are similar in being, cf. *De Trin.* 4, 17 ff where this text is quoted as a proof that God is neither *solitarius* nor *diversus* (see also 5, 7 ff).

> "Keep your hands off, do not touch, do not corrupt this."

Man should realize that he cannot comprehend the relation between Father and Son, if he nevertheless tries to define this he corrupts the divine mystery, see *supra*, 84 ff, 89 f, *De Trin.* 2, 8 and 2, 10.

> "Hold on to the names which express the nature, hold on to the Son's declaration."

The Arians make the mistake that they do not regard the names as expressions of the nature, see *supra*, 69 f.

> "I would not have you flatter the Son, so that you praise Him with what is of your own: it is as well that you are content with what is written."

The Son needs no praise from sinners, see *supra*, 139 ff, *De Trin.* 3, 7. The Arians praise Him with what is of their own by saying that He is an outstanding creature, in this they compare Him with themselves, since they are creatures as well (be it not: outstanding creatures!), see *supra*, 56, 72; with these statements about the Son they go beyond the revelation given in Scripture, see *supra*, 74 ff, *De Trin.* 2, 5.

6.

Human wisdom and divine wisdom
(24-26)

Hilary returns to what he said in the beginning of this book: God's power transcends human understanding. It is typical of human folly to believe that God can only do what man can understand. Man must forsake this kind of folly (which, however, is still typical of the Jews, the Greeks and the Arians) and must believe in God's 'folly', which is in fact God's real and incomprehensible wisdom. If man submits to this divine wisdom then he sets no bounds to God's infinite power, which wants to save men through the incarnation of the Son.

CHAPTER 24

As a finite being man has a finite knowledge and should realize this.

Translation and Commentary:

> **(24)** "But one should not have confidence in human wisdom to such a degree that one believes one has a perfect knowledge of what one knows, and that one thinks that the complete and certain understanding lies in that which one believes to be certain on account of an in all respects balanced opinion about truth, which one has reached through reasoning."

If man can establish a clear knowledge of truth through his own reasoning, then man himself determines what can be true and what cannot be true. This leads to the consequence that man prescribes laws to God about what God can and cannot do, and it is this consequence to which Hilary is opposed, see *infra*, 181 f, *De Trin.* 3, 26.

> "For things which are imperfect do not conceive what is perfect, and what receives its existence from somebody else cannot obtain a complete knowledge either of its author or of itself: it perceives itself only in so far as it is, and it cannot extend its perception further than the nature which has been given to it."

Man receives his existence from God, who is infinite (see *supra*, 33 ff, 78 ff, *De Trin.* 1, 6 and 2, 6), therefore man is a finite being with a finite knowledge (based on a finite perception). As this finite being man cannot obtain a clear knowledge of God, see *De Trin.* 1, 12, *supra*, 46 ff; 1, 15, *supra*, 53 ff; 4, 14: *Neque enim scientiam caelestium per semet humana imbecillitas consequetur, 5, 21: neque enim nobis ea natura est, ut se in caelestem cognitionem suis viribus ecferat; 9, 72: ... natura moderata et infirmis naturae infinitae et potentis sacramentum intellegentiae opinione non occupet.* But as a finite being man also has only a finite knowledge of himself (and the created world in general), man can only perceive what is before his senses, see *De Trin.* 11, 46: *Communis autem haec naturalium causarum intellegentia est, nihil in sensum cadere nisi quod sensui subiacet,* and human reason can only judge that to which it is prior in time: ... *Non nisi earum rerum tantum opinio ei* (sc. *rationi*) *quarum ipsa sit senior relinquatur.* This limitation of perception to what is within reach of human senses makes it impossible to have a perfect knowledge of oneself, – see Hilary's scepticism about knowledge about one's growth as an embryo, *De Trin.* 2, 9, *supra*, 87 ff.

> "For it owes its movement not to itself, but to its author. And therefore that which receives its existence from an author, is imperfect unto itself, since it exists from elsewhere."

'Imperfect' is here the same as 'finite': what receives its existence from elsewhere has a beginning in time and is finite (Hilary identifies 'infinite' with 'total', see *De Trin.* 2, 6, and 'total' with 'perfect', see *De Trin.* 2, 11).

> "And necessarily it must be unwise in that it believes it has perfect

knowledge, because, not observing the necessary limitations of its own nature and believing that all is contained within the bounds of its own weakness, it boasts with what is wrongly called knowledge.''

As a finite being man can only have a finite knowledge; if he thinks that he has a perfect knowledge, this very illusion proves that he is unwise. Man has no power over the law of his nature – this means that he has no power to exceed his finite nature, cf. *De Trin.* 3, 21, *supra*, 168 f. In *De Trin.* 1, 18 Hilary says that man should guide his sense to God's substance in an infinity of knowledge; on the surface the opposite is said there of what is said here, but there Hilary speaks of the regenerated mind of the believer (see *supra*, 58 ff), cf. *De Trin.* 1, 12, where the *fidei infinitas* is put in contrast with the *sensus* (supra, 47). If man believes that within the bounds of his finite nature a knowledge of all things is possible, then he takes pride in the wrong wisdom; this is undoubtedly an attack on Pagan philosophy, an attack that was common amongst early Christian writers, see *supra*, 20, *De Trin.* 1, 2.

> ''Because it cannot have wisdom beyond the power of its understanding and because it is as weak in its understanding as it is in its power to exist on its own.''

Since man's whole existence is weak and finite, man's understanding and knowledge must be weak and finite as well.

> ''And therefore, when a creature of an imperfect nature boasts to have the wisdom of a perfect understanding, it is ridiculed with the reproach of stupid wisdom, in the words of the apostle.''

Man becomes a fool, when he wants to exceed the bounds set to him by his Creator, cf. *De Trin.* 3, 21, *supra*, 168 f.

> ''For Christ sent me not to baptize, but to preach the Gospel, not in the language of wisdom, lest the cross of Christ should be made void. For the word of the cross is foolishness to them that are perishing, but unto them that are being saved it is the power of God. For it is written, 'I will destroy the wisdom of the wise and the understanding of the prudent I will reject'. Where is the wise? Where is the scribe? Where is the enquirer of this world? Has not God made foolish the wisdom of this world? For seeing that in the wisdom of God the world through its wisdom knew not God, God decreed through the foolishness of preaching to save them that believe. For the Jews ask for signs and the Greeks seek after wisdom, but we preach Christ crucified, unto Jews indeed a stumbling-block, and to the Gentiles foolishness, but to them that are called, both Jews and Greeks, Christ the power of God and the wisdom of God. Because the wisdom of God is stronger than men and the foolishness of God wiser than men.''

The words from I *Cor.* 1:17 ff are quoted against the heretics and philosophers (the heretics being followers of the philosophers, see *supra*,

92), cf. *De Trin.* 3, 8; 2, 12; 5, 1. The next chapter, *De Trin.* 3, 25, provides a detailed discussion of this section from the first letter to the Corinthians.

> "So all unbelief is foolishness, because using the wisdom of its own imperfect understanding and measuring all things with the view formed by its own weakness, it believes that what it does not understand cannot be done. For the cause of unbelief stems from the view formed by weakness, in that somebody thinks that what he determines to be impossible cannot have happened."

The greatest mistake man can make is to determine with his finite perception and finite knowledge what is possible and what is impossible, for then he sets a bound to God's power which is omnipotent, see *infra*, 181 f, *De Trin.* 3, 26. On man's tendency to regard only as possible what can be perceived and understood by finite mind and finite sense see also *De Trin.* 8, 53: *Humana mens hoc solum sapit quod intellegit, et mundus hoc tantum quod potest credit, secundum elementorum naturas id tantum possibile existimans, quod aut videret aut gereret,* and 3, 25, *infra*, 180 f.

CHAPTER 25

Human foolishness and God's wisdom.

Translation and Commentary:

> **(25)** "And therefore the apostle, knowing that the imperfect thought of human nature thinks that only this can be true what it understands, says that he does not preach in the language of wisdom, lest the assertion of his preaching be void."

The verses from I *Cor.* 1:17-25, quoted in the previous chapter (*supra*, 177), are now discussed in detail. Paul's statement that he did not preach in the language of wisdom is interpreted as meaning that Paul did not want to preach in that false wisdom, which believes only to be true and possible what man can see and understand, see *De Trin.* 3, 24, *supra*, 178.

> "And lest he be reckoned to be a preacher of foolishness, he added that the word of the cross is foolishness to those who are perishing, because the unbelievers believed only that to be wisdom what they could understand, and, since they only understood what is within the limits of their weak nature, regarded as foolishness that which is the only perfect wisdom of God, this being the cause of their foolishness, revealing itself in a view based on their weak wisdom."

Since Hilary himself is an advocate of such crude rhetorical alternatives as "If he did not preach wisdom, then he must have preached foolishness" (see *supra*, 56), he points out what the true wisdom of God is and what the real human foolishness is, *viz.*, not to know the true wisdom of God which transcends the limits of human sense and knowledge.

"So what is foolishness to those who are perishing, is the power of God to those who are being saved, because they measure nothing (that God does) with the weak understanding of their nature, but weigh the working of the divine power according to the infinity of the heavenly majesty."

Elsewhere Hilary says that the foolishness of God which appears in the cross of Christ is the revelation of God's *power* through the resurrection of Christ, see *In Ps.* LXVII 21: *Ipsum enim nobis, quod Judaeis scandalum, gentibus vero stultitia est, id est, Dei ... crux ... per resurrectionis potestatem virtutis aeternitas.*

"And that is why God rejects the wisdom of the wise and the understanding of the prudent, because salvation is given to the believers through a recognition of human foolishness, for the unbelievers determine as foolish what is outside their understanding, and the believers leave to God's power and majesty all the mysterious ways of granting them their salvation."

Both the acceptance of salvation by the believers and its rejection by the unbelievers is a recognition of human foolishness: the believers ascribe to the power of God what they cannot understand in their natural foolishness, the unbelievers describe as foolish what is beyond their understanding and in doing so reveal their own foolishness.

"So there is no foolishness in the things of God, but it is the unwise wisdom of human nature which goes so far as to demand from its God either signs of wisdom as the condition of belief. And it is typical of the Jews to demand signs, because they have a certain knowledge of the name of God through the acquaintance with the law, but are confused by the offence of the cross. And it is typical of the Greeks to demand wisdom, because with Pagan folly and human wisdom they seek a rational reason why God was crucified."

The Jews were, through their acquaintance with the law, not ignorant of the fact that God appears in man, see *e.g. In Ps.* LIV 13; what they did not expect was that Christ would be crucified. They want other signs of His divinity than the cross which confuses them. – The Greeks want a rational explication of the crucifixion of a man who is also God. Elsewhere Hilary says that it seems foolish to the Pagans that Christ should in this way take upon himself the sins of men, see *In Ps.* LXVIII 8. The Greeks regard it as folly that the Christians give the second rank, after the eternal and unchangeable God, to a man who was crucified, see Justin, *Apol.* I, 13, 4. Celsus opposes (with the help of a Jew) the idea that Christ suffered for the benefit of mankind, see Origen, *Contra Celsum* 2, 38; according to Origen he mocks the Christians as people who worship somebody who has been crucified, *Contra Celsum* 2, 47; according to Athanasius the Greeks ridicule the cross of Christ, *Contra Gentes* 1, *De Inc.* 33, cf. further Lactance, *Epit.* 46 ff, who discusses the objection that Christ, if He had to die, should have died a more honourable death, see also *Inst.* 4, 26. It is interesting to see that Hilary refuses to give another reason for the crucifixion than that God willed it and in this revealed His wisdom, see *In Ps.* LXVII 21: ... *Dei* ... *crux* ... *per rationem divinae voluntatis perfecta coelestisque sapientia est*, – similarly he gives no other reason for the moment of the incarnation than God's will (see *supra*, 109).

> "Since this reason remains hidden in a mystery if it is measured by the understanding of the weak human nature, human foolishness turns to unbelief, since the imperfect mind decrees that what it cannot naturally conceive is outside the field of wisdom."

Finite mind cannot understand the reason why Christ died on the cross, therefore it rejects this idea, since it does not fit into the field of the competence of the human mind. Here belief is made dependent upon understanding, whilst according to Hilary man should first believe and then try to understand, see *supra*, 40. On the same grounds the Pagans reject Scripture, according to Hilary, see *In Ps.* CXVIII vi 8: *Et quia pro impietate ingenii sui divinorum dictorum capaces esse non possunt, ad contumeliam caelestium verborum pro excusatione hebetudinis suae prorumpunt, dicentes nihil in his rationabile, nihil esse perfectum.* The reproach against Christian faith that it is unreasonable was a common one, see *e.g.* Origen, *Contra Celsum* 1, 9, Athanasius, *Contra Gentes* 1, cf. J. C. M. van Winden, Notes on Origen, Contra Celsum, *Vig. Christ.* (20), 1966, pp 207 ff and G. Ruhbuch, *Apologetik und Geschichte, Untersuchungen zur Theologie Eusebs von Caesarea*, Heidelberg 1962, pp 42 and 69.

> "But because of this unwise wisdom of the world, which previously did not know God through the wisdom of God, *i.e.* has not venerated the wisdom of its Creator through this magnificence of the world and the splendour of this so wisely made handiwork, it pleased God to save the believers through the preaching of foolishness, *i.e.* that faith in the cross grants eternal life to mortal men."

This is an interpretation of I *Cor* 1:21 (quoted in the previous chapter: *in sapientia Dei non cognovit mundus per sapientiam Deum*) the original sense of which can only be: God in His wisdom caused man in his earthly wisdom not to know God –, but Hilary gives a different interpretation: Man failed to know God through the revelation of God's wisdom in creation. He is forced to this interpretation since he had stated that man had some knowledge of God through the creation, see *De Trin.* 1, 7 and 3, 17, *supra*, 37 ff, 160 f. On this revelation through the splendour of the creation see further *De Trin*. 6, 21: *Sapientem te mihi etiam ipsa mundi creatio prodidit; In Ps*. LII 2: *Quis enim mundum contuens, Deum esse non sentiat? In Ps*. LXV 10: *nemo coelum contuens Deum esse non sentiat*, this is a well-known commonplace in early Christian literature, see *e.g.* Athenagoras, *Suppl*. 16, Theophilus, *Ad Aut*. 1, 7, Irenaeus, *Adv. Haer*. 2, 8, 1, Tertullian, *Adv. Marc*. 1, 13, Novatian, *De Trin*. 3, 20, Lactance, *Inst*. 1, 2, Athanasius, *Contra Gentes* 35, *De Inc*. 12; 32; 54, cf. M. Spanneut, *Le Stoicisme des Pères de l'Eglise*, Paris 1957, pp 372 ff.

> "So that, the view of human understanding having been put to shame, salvation might be found there, where one believes foolishness to be. For Christ, who is foolishness to the Gentiles and a stumbling-block to the Jews, is God's Power and God's Wisdom, because that which is in the things of God regarded as weak and foolish by human understanding, that prevails over earthly wisdom and power by its Wisdom and Power."

Man regards as foolish what he cannot understand, but since what man here rejects is truly wise and powerful, man's wisdom is put to shame and belief starts there where wisdom cannot begin: with God's wisdom and power which transcend the human mind.

CHAPTER 26

Man as a creature should not prescribe laws to God and thereby limit God's power.

Translation and Commentary:

> (26)   "So none of God's actions ought to be dealt with with the opinion of human mind, neither should the product of His handiwork pass decrees on its Creator."

Man, as God's creature, should not lay down rules for God's actions, cf. *De Trin*. 1, 15 (*supra*, 54, where the Arians are accused of doing this); 8, 3.

> "But we should adopt foolishness in order to obtain wisdom, not with the understanding of our unwisdom, but in consciousness of our nature, so that the reason of the divine power may intimate to us what the reason of our earthly thought does not understand."

The choice of what is foolish is the choice of what transcends our earthly mind and what is wrongly regarded by us as foolishness, but is in reality God's incomprehensible wisdom.

> "For when we have recognized how far the understanding of our foolishness reaches and thus have understood the ignorance of our natural wisdom, then we will be instructed towards God's wisdom through the sagacity of divine wisdom."

When man has seen that he cannot know God with his own finite mind, then he can expect revelation from God, see supra, 37 ff.

> "When we measure the powers and strength of God without any limitation, when we do not confine the Lord of nature within the laws of nature, when we understand that only this is the right belief about God about which He Himself is to us Witness and Author."

As finite beings we make a mistake if we limit God's power to what we can understand, as the Author of nature God is not subject to the laws of nature, *In Ps.* LI 18: ... *decernenti legem, lex non affert necessitatem; De Trin.* 9, 72: *Non subiacet naturae legibus, a quo legem omnis natura sortitur*; 10, 70: *Pietas est ... neque modo circumscribere potestatem (Dei),* cf. Tertullian. *De anima* 2, 2, who objects to Pagan philosophy: *omnia praescribit ... nihil divinae licentiae servat*; for Irenaeus' insistence on God's freedom see E. P. Meijering, *God Being History*, pp 19 ff.

As the last chapter of the previous book resumed the beginning of that book (see *De Trin.* 2, 35, *supra*, 124), and as the end of the first book resumes the theme of the beginning of that book (see *De Trin.* 1, 37 where he speaks about the *praecipuum officium* of his life, with the search of which that book began, *De Trin.* 1, 1, *supra*, 16), so this last chapter of the third book resumes a theme of the beginning of this book: God's power transcends human understanding (see *De Trin.* 3, 1, *supra*, 127). This, too, is an indication that the end of this book was not originally meant as a peroration of the first three books (cf. *supra*, 2 ff).

SOME FINAL OBSERVATIONS

At first sight Hilary is an unattractive theologian, and his verbosity does not invite a close examination. But the better one gets to know him, the more one likes him. To a certain degree we find in him a combination of the best of Athanasius and the best of Tertullian. In his polemics against the Arians Athanasius has only one theme: the Son is ontologically equal to the Father, practically all he says centres around this. Tertullian fights on many fronts and therefore has many themes, in his polemics he makes statements which often contradict each other and cannot be combined into a theological system. Tertullian is the advocate of more or less isolated positions. On the surface it looks as if we find *multa* in Tertullian and *multum* in Athanasius. But it appears that Tertullian has the gift to advocate his *multa* with admirable sagacity. He who has only one theme, like Athanasius in his fight against the Arians, cannot be called a systematic theologian; he who advocates many more or less isolated positions, like Tertullian, cannot be called a systematic theologian either. In the case of Athanasius this statement has to be modified in so far as his apologetic treatise *Contra Gentes – De Incarnatione Verbi* betrays a highly systematic mind. But those two pieces of writing were directed against an enemy outside the church who had already lost the war: Pagan religion and Pagan philosophy; in his fight against the Arians, *i.e.* an enemy inside the church who could certainly not be regarded as already beaten, he abandoned the systematic approach. – Hilary can in this be regarded as a combination of Athanasius and Tertullian, for he attacks the Arians as a systematician, *i.e.* as a writer who combines many themes under one *Leitmotiv*. This *Leitmotiv* is not the ontological equality of Father and Son, but the infinity of God. It seems strange that the ontological equality of God (to which Hilary adheres with one restriction) should not be the *Leitmotiv* of his polemics against the Arians (as it was in Athanasius' polemics against them), since that is what the battle was about. That Hilary chooses the *Leitmotiv* of the infinity of God shows that even at the height of the battle he could remain the somewhat detached systematician who did not allow his enemies to dictate his themes.

The infinity of God led him away from Pagan idolatry which confines God to finite and created beings. The infinity of God's being and power also appeared to be the conclusive argument against the Arian objections against the equality of Father and Son: the Arians speak in a human way about a Father and a Son and do not realize that both the Father and the

Son are as God infinite and therefore can have a relation which transcends human understanding. In itself it was not uncommon to accuse the Arians of a relapse into Paganism (Athanasius does so repeatedly); but Hilary uses this accusation in a systematic way, and it is the link between the Prologue and the bulk of the *De Trinitate*. On the surface this Prologue has little to do with what will follow, but the idea of the infinity of God makes it clear: once he had been convinced that God is not a finite being and that therefore the Pagan worship of gods is rejectable idolatry, he could not succumb to the temptations of Arianism, since the Arians make God a finite being as well and in doing so return to Paganism. Athanasius constantly hammers his one theme, the ontological equality of Father and Son, into his readers' minds; Hilary does not do the same with the idea of the infinity of God, but this idea is the background of all he says in extensive expositions, whether it is the nature of the Father, the nature of the Son, the eternal generation, the incarnation of the Word in a finite body, the nature of the Holy Spirit, the mutual indwelling of Father and Son, their mutual glorification, the incomprehensible power of God. In his polemics against the Arians he covers a fairly wide field with an admirable sagacity that is not second to Tertullian, but unlike Tertullian he proves to be a systematician who wants to remain consistent and who is guided by a *Leitmotiv*. Tertullian has many themes without a *Leitmotiv*, Athanasius has one theme (at least in his polemics against the Arians) and therefore needs no *Leitmotiv*, Hilary has many themes with a clear *Leitmotiv*. Although ancient rhetoric with its attractive and unattractive elements is clearly present in the *De Trinitate*, Hilary even in his attack on his enemies remains more a systematician than a polemist. We believe Harnack to be right when he says that Hilary as a theologian surpasses Athanasius (*Lehrbuch der Dogmengeschichte* II, p 252).

We do not, of course, suggest that Hilary consciously wanted to combine Athanasius and Tertullian. Such a conscious combination cannot even be proved in the actual contents of his doctrine of the Trinity, which on the one hand emphasizes the Nicene faith that Father and Son are ontologically equal and on the other hand stresses (much more than Athanasius did) that the Father as the Origin of the Son is more than the Son, and in doing so appears in line with the subordinationist views of Tertullian. Here Hilary shows a striking similarity with the Cappadocians, who combine Athanasian orthodoxy with the subordinationist views of Origen.

Just like the Cappadocians Hilary was a broad and profound theologian whose writings deserve close examination and still prove to be theologically fruitful.

INDICES

I. INDEX OF QUOTATIONS FROM ANCIENT AUTHORS

II. INDEX OF SUBJECTS

III. INDEX OF MODERN AUTHORS

PHILOSOPHIA PATRUM

INTERPRETATIONS OF PATRISTIC TEXTS

Edited by

J. H. Waszink and J. C. M. van Winden

1982. Prices may be changed without notice.

E. J. Brill — P.O.B. 9000 — 2300 PA Leiden — The Netherlands

MEDE VERKRIJGBAAR DOOR BEMIDDELING VAN DE BOEKHANDEL